PRAISE FOR *AMERICAN ISLAMOPHOBIA*

"Deftly pairing his deep legal expertise with a searching moral dialogue, Khaled A. Beydoun breaks down U.S. Islamophobia as the full-fledged system that it is—one with a very specific history, but tightly linked to other forms of white supremacy. This book meets the moment, but it is also packed with staying power."

Naomi Klein, author of *No Is Not Enough* and *This Changes Everything*

"A triumphant act of moral restitution. Written with bravura flair, academic authority, and panoramic scholarly panache, it declares the birth of an American Muslim intellectual who wholly claims the land and envisions a bold future for it."

Hamid Dabashi, author of *Iran Without Borders: Towards a Critique of the Postcolonial Nation*

"This is an urgent book for anyone seeking a comprehensive understanding of Islamophobia today."

Evelyn Alsultany, author of *Arabs and Muslims in the Media: Race and Representation after 9/11*

"A highly readable, deeply personal, and fiercely intellectual, lucid, and penetrating analysis of endemic social and structural Islamophobia throughout American history. This book is required reading for any thinking human being."

Khaled Abou El Fadl, Omar and Azmeralda Alfi Professor of Law, UCLA School of Law

"Political commentary, intellectual history, legal exegesis, and autobiography, this book is a powerful and moving articulation of how Islamophobia has shaped and been shaped by U.S. democracy."

Devon W. Carbado, coauthor of *Acting White? Rethinking Race in "Post-Racial" America* and Harry Pregerson Professor of Law, UCLA School of Law

Named in remembrance of

the onetime *Antioch Review* editor

and longtime Bay Area resident,

the Lawrence Grauman, Jr. Fund

supports books that address

a wide range of human rights,

free speech, and social justice issues.

The publisher and the University of California Press Foundation gratefully acknowledge the generous support of the Lawrence Grauman, Jr. Fund.

American Islamophobia

American Islamophobia

*Understanding the Roots
and Rise of Fear*

KHALED A. BEYDOUN

UNIVERSITY OF CALIFORNIA PRESS

University of California Press, one of the most distinguished university presses in the United States, enriches lives around the world by advancing scholarship in the humanities, social sciences, and natural sciences. Its activities are supported by the UC Press Foundation and by philanthropic contributions from individuals and institutions. For more information, visit www.ucpress.edu.

University of California Press
Oakland, California

Library of Congress Cataloging-in-Publication Data

Names: Beydoun, Khaled A., 1978– author.
Title: American Islamophobia : understanding the roots and rise of fear / Khaled A. Beydoun.
Description: Oakland, California : University of California Press, [2018] | Includes bibliographical references and index. |
Identifiers: LCCN 2017049894 (print) | LCCN 2017054557 (ebook) | ISBN 9780520970007 (Epub) | ISBN 9780520297791 (cloth : alk. paper)
Subjects: LCSH: Islamophobia—United States. | Islam and politics—United States.
Classification: LCC BP67 (ebook) | LCC BP67 .B49 2018 (print) | DDC 305.6/970973—dc23
LC record available at https://lccn.loc.gov/2017049894

Manufactured in the United States of America

26 25 24 23 22 21 20 19 18
10 9 8 7 6 5 4 3 2

This book is dedicated to the following:

*My sister, Khalida, and Muslim
sisters everywhere*

*My brother, Mohammed, and Muslim
brothers everywhere*

*My father, Ali, buried in a country that lured him
far away from his own*

*And most of all, my mother, Fikrieh, to whom I owe
everything*

I am an Oriental writing back at the Orientalists, who for so long have thrived upon our silence.

Edward Said

Contents

Acknowledgments

I learned virtually everything from two women: my mother, Fikrieh Beydoun, and my law professor and mentor, Kimberlé Crenshaw. Through my mother, a single parent who struggled through countless odds jobs to provide for my two siblings and me and shuttled us through eleven houses from Dearborn to Detroit in pursuit of a suitable home, I became a man. Through Kim Crenshaw, whom I studied under and worked alongside, I learned what I wanted to do with my life. A giant as a scholar and a dynamo as an activist, Professor Crenshaw demonstrated that innovative scholarship did not, and should not, have to be confined to the world of ivory towers and complex ideas, but instead should be activated to bring about change, on the ground, during times of great crisis and mass action. These two women gave me life, changed my life, and saved my life.

Special gratitude is owed to Devon Carbado, Ediberto Roman, Hisham Aidi, and Luke Harris for invaluable mentorship but more importantly, for believing and having confidence in me. I have also learned immensely from Cheryl Harris,

Khaled Abou El Fadl, Laura Gomez, and other members of the UCLA Critical Race Studies Department, in which I had the privilege of serving as a visiting assistant professor from 2012 through 2014. I am also grateful for the intellectual community and cutting-edge work provided by the University of California Islamophobia Research & Documentation Project (IRDP), and most notably, its founder, Hatem Bazian. Furthermore, I owe thanks to my colleagues at the University of Detroit Mercy School of Law, particularly Dean Phyllis Crocker, Richard Broughton, Erin Archerd, Kyle Langvart, Catherine Archibald, and Karen Henning, who have consistently supported my scholarship, advocacy, and public intellectual work.

I am blessed to have the support of a brilliant and generous community of colleagues and friends within the legal academy, including Cyra Choudhury, Ediberto Roman, Ericka Wilson, Priscilla Ocen, Addie Rolnick, Nancy Leong, Sumi Cho, Adrien Wing, Luke Harris, SpearIt, Brant Lee, Nareissa Smith, Vinay Harpalani, Sahar Aziz, Amna Akbar, Justin Hansford, Bernadette Atuahene, Atiba Ellis, Alvin Starks, Michael Morley, and Ben Edwards. I also owe gratitude to Erik Love, Dalia Mogahed, Namira Islam, Margari Hill, Kumar Rao, Hattem Beydoun, Michael Song, Joann Moolsintong, Richard Alvarez, Donna Auston, Killoud Dabaja, Desiree Ferguson, Kameelah Rashad, Veryl Pow, Maia Anthony, Steve Jenkins, Nura Sedique, Ahmed Abouznaid, Laith Saud, Daanish Faruqi, Jameel Harb, Nabil Silmi, Abbas Barzegar, Layla Abdulah-Poulos, Ifrah Magan, Aminah Bakeer Abdul-Jabbaar, Mariam Masri, Linda Sarsour, Dawud Walid, Omid Safi, and many others that I advocate alongside and from whom I draw energy, intellectual community, and most importantly, optimism.

Most notably, I owe immense gratitude to Asha Noor, Nadim Hallal, Nadia Salibi, Hamada Zahawi, Mohammed Maraqa, George Naggiar, Ahmed Al-Rumaihi, Jason Oh, and Abed Ayoub for immeasurable support, and for reminding me that family is not always a relationship bound by blood. I cannot adequately express my appreciation for Naomi Schneider and the University of California Press, for valuing my voice and trusting that I could deliver on a project that met the magnitude of the moment and the urgency faced by Muslims, people of color, and marginalized peoples in the United States and beyond.

I cannot thank my mother, siblings, nieces and nephew enough for believing in me and my work; Erin Durrah for supporting and loving me through the most turbulent times; Michelle Long, her mother, for being a model for both of us to follow. Finally, I thank my home city, Detroit, which has nourished me with the grit, tenacity, and self-belief to overcome the odds I have faced and those I will confront moving forward. For that, I will always remain loyal to my soil, a proud Detroiter wherever I go and wherever I reside.

The past several years have afforded me with the opportunity, which I took on as an obligation, to share my research on national security policing, civil liberties, and the focus of this book, Islamophobia, on college campuses, at law schools, and in communities across and outside of the United States. While I have been closely examining these topics for some time, even before beginning my legal academic career, the 2016 presidential election brought an immediate urgency to and proliferated interest in my work. I spent much of 2015, 2016, and early 2017 on the road, speaking to undergraduates and graduate students, faculties and community members, educating them about the meaning, parameters, and threat of Islamophobia, and in the process, hearing their personal stories, building friendships, and expanding my community during a time of national crisis.

I have interwoven several of these stories into this book, which presented an opportunity to memorialize the rich tapestry of experiences, memories, and people with whom I crossed paths. But most importantly, this book presented a lasting opportunity to extend my mission to educate people about Islam, Muslim Americans, and the deeply rooted and rising system—Islamophobia—that distorts, demonizes, and drives state and private violence against the faith and its adherents.

Introduction

Crossroads and Intersections

> Nobody's going to save you. No one's going to cut you
> down, cut the thorns thick around you.... There is no
> one who will feed the yearning. Face it. You will have
> to do, do it yourself.
>
> Gloria Anzaldúa, *Borderlands/La Frontera*

> If you know who you are, nobody can tell you what
> you are or what you are not.
>
> My momma, Fikrieh Beydoun

I took my seat in the back of the Uber car, plugged in my phone
and reclined my head to recharge on the way to the hotel. *The
road ahead is going to be a long one,* I thought as I sank into the back-
seat, settling in for a temporary respite from the oncoming
storm.

"As-salamu 'alaikum," the young driver greeted me in
Spanish-inflected Arabic, abruptly ending my break.

"Wa 'alaikum al-salam," I responded, thoroughly surprised
that these familiar words came out of the mouth of my tattooed
Latino Uber driver, Juan.[1] *Was he Muslim?* I pondered, wondering

whether his neat beard signified more than a recent fad or fashionable grooming.

"It's an honor to meet you, Professor," he said, and continued, "I'm very familiar with your writing and work, and I'm happy you're here speaking at Cal State LA. I wish I could've been there to hear your talk." Another sign that Juan might in fact be Muslim, given that my work centers on Muslim American identity and, increasingly, Islamophobia.

"Thank you so much," I responded, taken aback by the fact that he knew who I was, and still contemplating whether he was a recent Muslim convert or born into a Muslim family. As a longtime resident of Los Angeles and a scholar familiar with Muslim American demographics, I was well aware that Latinx Muslims were the fastest-growing segment of the Muslim American population. I had attended Friday prayers with sermons delivered *en español* in California and in Florida, where I lived and taught law for two years, and prayed alongside brothers from Puerto Rico, the Dominican Republic, and Mexico as often as I did next to Muslims from Egypt, Syria, or Pakistan.[2] However, I was still unsure about Juan's religious identity, and to which destination he might steer this conversation.

I learned, en route from the East Los Angeles campus to my downtown hotel, that Juan was neither born to a Muslim family nor a convert. He was, rather, a man on the cusp of embracing Islam at a moment of unprecedented Islamophobia and rabid xenophobia, of imminent Muslim bans and Mexican walls.

"I have been studying Islam closely for some time now, and try to go to the mosque on some Fridays," he shared. "I am considering making my *shahada*," Juan continued, referencing the oath of induction whereby a new Muslim proclaims that "there is only one God, and Mohammed is his final messenger."

"Everybody assumes that I am a Muslim already," he said, with a cautious laugh that revealed discomfort with his liminal status. Juan turned down the radio, and the voice of Compton native Kendrick Lamar rapping, "We gon' be alright," to engage in a more fluid conversation. And, it appeared, to seek a response from me about his spiritual direction.

"That's wonderful," I responded to Juan, who was likely no more than twenty-three or twenty-four years old, trying to balance my concern for the challenges his new religious affiliation would present with the answer that I thought he wanted to hear, and perhaps expected, from a Muslim American scholar and activist whose name and work he recognized.

As he drove, we discussed the political challenges posed by the Trump administration, and specifically, the policies that would directly or disproportionately target Muslim and Latinx communities. Indeed, Trump capitalized heavily on demonizing these vulnerable groups, as evidenced most clearly by the two proposals—the Muslim ban and the Mexico wall—that became the rallying cries of his campaign. We also discussed how our kindred struggles with poverty complicated our pursuit of education, and how Trump's economic vision exacerbated conditions for indigent Americans, including the 45 percent of Muslim Americans living below, at, or dangerously close to the federal poverty line.[3] The city's infamous, slow-moving traffic enabled a fast-paced conversation between my new friend and me and gave rise to an LA story seldom featured in newspapers or on television.

Juan's responses focused on his everyday struggles living in LA and the stories of family and friends from his Pico Union neighborhood. He pointed out that the onslaughts on Muslims and Latinx communities were hardly separate and independent, or parallel and segregated. Rather, they were, and are, overlapping, intersecting, and, for him, very intimate.

"As an undocumented Latino from El Salvador living in Pico Union"—a heavily concentrated Latinx community on the margins of downtown Los Angeles—"I am most fearful about the pop-up checkpoints and the immigration raids," he told me. These fears were more than imminent under the administration of President Obama, dubbed the "Deporter in Chief" by critics who opposed the accelerated mass deportations carried out during the final stages of his second term. But without question, Juan's fears have become more visceral, more palpable during the Trump administration.[4]

"I think about this every time I drive to school, work, or visit a family member," Juan recounted, reminding me of the debilitating fear that comes over me after any terror attack. Yet his fear was far more immediate and frequent than mine, and loomed over him at every moment, including this one—while he and I weaved through Los Angeles traffic, talking animatedly about politics, faith, and fear. He could be stopped at any time, whether alone or while whizzing customers through the city he knew better than the life lines on his palms.

I thought about the very imminent dangers these xenophobic policies and programs posed for Juan and people in similar situations in Los Angeles and throughout the country. I knew this city well and understood that the armed and irrational fear directed at nonwhite, non-Christian people was intense in LA, descending (among other places) on the city's galaxy of dense and large Latinx neighborhoods. This armed xenophobia was aimed particularly at those communities gripped by poverty, where Spanish was spoken primarily, and was concentrated on people and families lacking legal documentation—indeed, the very intersection where Juan began and ended each day, and lived most of his hours in between.

.   .   .

Years before I rode with Juan, Los Angeles was my home away from my hometown of Detroit, the city where I began my career as a law professor, earned my law degree, and only two weeks into my first year of law school at UCLA, the setting from which I witnessed the 9/11 terror attacks. I remember the events of that day more clearly than I do any other day, largely because every terror attack that unfolds in the United States or abroad compels me to revisit the motions and emotions of that day. For Muslim Americans, 9/11 is not just a day that will live in infamy or an unprecedented tragedy buried in the past; it is a stalking reminder that the safeguards of citizenship are tenuous and the prospect of suspicion and the presumption of guilt are immediate.

My phone kept ringing that morning, interrupting my attempt to sleep in after a long night of studying. As I turned to set the phone to vibrate, I noticed that my mother had called me six times in a span of fifteen minutes. My eyes widened. *Was something wrong at home?* Three hours behind in California, I called her back to make sure everything at home in Detroit was alright, still in the dark about the tragedy that would mark a crossroads for the country, my community, and indeed, my life.

"Turn on the TV," she instructed, in her flat but authoritative Arabic that signaled that something serious was unfolding: "Go to your TV right now." I had an eerie sense of what she was alluding to before I clicked the television on and turned to the news, but I could not have imagined the scale of the terror that unfolded that early Tuesday morning. My eyes were glued to the screen as I awoke fully to what it would mean for me, my family, and Muslim Americans at large if the perpetrators of the attacks looked like us or believed like us.

I recall the surreal images and events of that day as if they happened yesterday. And just as intimately, I remember the four words that repeatedly scrolled across my mind after the first plane crashed into the World Trade Center. "Please don't be Muslims, please don't be Muslims," I quietly whispered to myself over and again, standing inside my small apartment, surrounded by bags and boxes not yet unpacked, a family portrait of my mother, sister, and brother hanging on an otherwise barren white wall. I was alone in the apartment, far from home, but knew in that very moment that the same fear that left me frozen and afraid gripped every Muslim in the country.

The four words I whispered to myself on 9/11 reverberated through the mind of every Muslim American that day and every day after, forming a unifying prayer for Muslim Americans after every attack.[5] Our fear, and the collective breath or brace for the hateful backlash that ensued, symbolize the existential tightrope that defines Muslim American identity today.[6] It has become a definitive part of what it means to be Muslim American when an act of terror unfolds and the finger-pointing begins.

Indeed, this *united state of fear* converges with a competing fear stoked by the state to galvanize hatemongers and mobilize damaging policies targeting Islam and Muslims. That state-stoked fear has a name: Islamophobia. This system of inculcating fear and calculated bigotry was not entirely spawned in the wake of the 9/11 terror attacks, I have gradually learned, but is a modern extension of a deeply embedded and centuries-old form of American hate. Following 9/11 it was adorned with a new name, institutionalized within new government structures and strident new policies, and legitimized under the auspices of a "war on terror" that assigned the immediate presumption of terrorism to Islam and the immediate presumption of guilt to Muslim citizens and immigrants.

Thousands of miles away from home and loved ones, my world unraveled. Islamophobia and what would become a lifelong commitment to combating it were thrust to the fore. Although raised in Detroit, home to the most concentrated, celebrated, and scrutinized Muslim American population in the country, my activism, advocacy, and intellectual mission to investigate the roots of American Islamophobia and its proliferation after the 9/11 terror attacks were first marshaled on the other side of the country. For me, 9/11 was both a beginning and an end, putting to rest my romantic designs on an international human rights law career for the more immediate challenges unfolding at home.

I left for Los Angeles a wide-eyed twenty-two-year-old in the late summer of 2001. I was the first in my family to attend university and graduate school, the first to pack his bags for another city, not knowing what direction his career or life would take. After three years and three wars—those in Afghanistan and Iraq, and the amorphous, fluidly expanding war on terror on the homefront—I was fully resolved to take on the rising tide of Islamophobia ravaging the country and ripping through concentrated Muslim American communities like the one I called home. I learned about the law at a time when laws were being crafted to punish, persecute, and prosecute Muslim citizens and immigrants under the thinnest excuses, at an intersection when my law professors, including Kimberlé Crenshaw, Cheryl Harris, and Devon Carbado, were equipping me with the spirit and skill to fight Islamophobia in the middle grounds it rose from, and even more importantly, at the margins.

On February 22, 2017, more than a decade and a half after 9/11, I found myself back in Los Angeles. I was now a law professor and a scholar researching national security, Muslim identity, and constitutional law. I was to give a series of lectures on Islamophobia at several colleges and community centers in the LA area. My expertise was in high demand as a result of the 2016 presidential election and the intense Islamophobia that followed. I delivered the lectures roughly one month after newly elected President Donald Trump signed the executive order widely known as the "Muslim ban."[7]

Seven days into his presidency, Trump delivered on the promise he first made on the campaign trail on December 7, 2015, enacting a travel ban that restricted the entry of nationals from seven Muslim-majority nations: Libya, Iraq, Iran, Somalia, Sudan, Syria, and Yemen. To me, the Muslim ban was not merely a distant policy signed into law in a distant city; it was personal in a myriad of ways. First, I am a Muslim American, and second, I had close friends from several of the restricted nations and had visited several of those nations. Moreover, since the war on terror had been rolled out in 2001, all of the countries on the list had been either sites of full-scale American military aggression or strategic bombings.

"The bombs always precede the bans," my mother said out loud as she watched the news one day, observing a truism that ties American foreign policy to immigration policy, particularly in relation to Muslim-majority countries.

The Muslim ban was the first policy targeting Muslims enacted by the man I formally dubbed the "Islamophobia president."[8] It certainly would not be the last law, policy, or program implemented by the man who capitalized on Islamophobia as a "full-fledged campaign strategy" to become the forty-fifth president of the United States.[9] President Trump promised a more hardline domestic surveillance program, which he called Countering Islamic Violence; a registry to keep track of Muslim immigrants within the United States; legislation that would bludgeon the civic and advocacy programs of Muslim American organizations; and other measures that would threaten Muslim immigrants, citizens, and institutions. He was poised to integrate Islamophobia fully into the government he would preside over and to convert his bellicose rhetoric into state-sanctioned policy.

If Trump demonstrated anything during his first week in office, it was an ability to follow through on the hateful promises most pundits had dismissed as "mere campaign rhetoric" months earlier. He kept his promises. Islamophobia was not merely an appeal for votes, but a resonant message that would drive policy and inform immigration and national security policing. His electioneering was not mere bluster, but in fact a covenant built on Islamophobia—an Islamophobia that motivated large swaths of Americans to vote for him. In exchange, he delivered on his explicit and "dog whistle" campaign messaging by generating real Islamophobic policies, programs, and action.[10] Trump, like many candidates before him and others who will follow, traded a grand narrative of nativism and hate for votes—which registered to great success at the ballot box.

Memories of the trials and wounds Muslim Americans endured in the wake of 9/11, which I witnessed firsthand and examined closely as a scholar, and those unfolding in this era of trumped-up, unhinged Islamophobia raced through my head as I walked to the Uber waiting for me outside the California State University–Los Angeles campus. Scores of mosques vandalized, immigrants scapegoated and surveilled, citizens falsely profiled and prosecuted, the private confines of Muslim American households violated in furtherance of baseless witch hunts, immigration restrictions and registries imposed, and innocent mothers and children killed. Yesterday, and with this intensified third phase of the war on terror, again today.

I set my bag down in the car, thinking about the turbulent road ahead. I thought about how the challenges ahead compared and contrasted with those that ravaged Muslim Americans following 9/11. More than fifteen years had passed, and the face of the country, the composition of the Muslim American population, and I myself had all undergone radical, transformative change. I had recently bid farewell to and buried my father, Ali, who in 1981 brought his three children and wife to the United States in search of all the things Donald Trump stood against, values his campaign slogan, "Make America Great Again," sought to erode. Life after loss is never the same, and my season of mourning was punctuated by the fear and hysteria that followed Donald Trump all the way to the White House.

The world and the country were spinning faster and more furiously than ever before, it seemed. Locked in between the two, my life raced forward at a rate I had never experienced. The Black Lives Matter movement unveiled institutional racism that was as robust and violent as ever, as evidenced by the killing of Trayvon Martin, Rekia Boyd, Mike Brown, Tamir Rice, Philando Castille, Sandra Bland, and a rapidly growing list of unarmed black children, men, and women gunned down by police, all of them memorialized and uplifted as martyrs by youth and adult, black and non-black activists marching up and down city blocks or taking protests to the virtual sphere on Twitter, Facebook, and other social media platforms.[11] Black Lives Matter inspired mass actions across the country and an ongoing march of social media protests that spawned new generations of activists and trenchant thought leaders. I saw this unfold, in dynamic fashion, on city blocks, in neighborhoods, on college campuses, and on social media feeds. It left an indelible impression on my activism, writing, and worldview.

In the face of a political world seemingly spinning out of control, I decided to write this book. I hope to provide general readers, students, and activists an intimate and accessible introduction to Islamophobia—what it is, how it evolved, how we can combat it in Trump's America, and most importantly, how to fight it beyond the current administration. As a Muslim American law professor and civil rights activist, I hope to help readers view Islamophobia through a unique lens. I draw on a range of sources—from court cases, media headlines, and scholarship to my own experiences in walking the walk every day. Along the way, I make links and assertions that might be new to many readers: pointing out how Islamophobia has a long, notorious history in the United States, for example, and showing how the Black Lives Matter movement intersects with, and inspires, activism against Islamophobia. My aim is to offer a succinct, informed handbook for anyone interested in Islamophobia and its prolific growth at this definitive juncture in our country's history.

I wrote this book at a time when American Islamophobia was intensifying at a horrific clip, giving immediate importance to my research and expertise and simultaneously endangering the people I love most. In addition to examining the roots and rise of American Islamophobia, this book also looks to humanize the individuals and communities impacted by it, so they can be seen beyond the frame of statistics. Many stories are interwoven—some are well known and others are not—to facilitate an understanding of Islamophobia that treats Muslim Americans not as distant subjects of study or analysis, but as everyday citizens. Citizens who, like members of other faith groups, are not only integral and contributing members of society, but are also part of a group that will define the future of the United States moving forward.

The United States is indeed at a crossroads. The rise of mass social protest movements fueled by calls for dignity, justice, and an end to structural racism have been met by an opposing front galvanized by demographic shifts toward a majority-minority population and eight years of scapegoating and systematic obstruction of the first black president. Echoing through it all is the dread of an "end of white America," a fear that politicians on the right readily stoked and fervently fed to the masses.[12] Much of this opposing front is fully wed to racism and xenophobia, and it backed a businessman who peddled a promise to "Make American Great Again"—a promise that was not just a campaign slogan, but was also a racial plea evoked at a time when whiteness was the formal touchstone of American citizenship and white supremacy was endorsed and enabled by law. Trump dangled before the electorate studies that project that people of color will outnumber whites by 2044[13] and that over half (50.2 percent) of the babies born in the United States today are minorities,[14] and he inflamed the ever-present fear that foreigners are stealing *our jobs*. As a cure for these supposed ills, Trump's campaign offered to a primed and ready audience a cocktail of nativism, scapegoating, and racism; his campaign met with resounding success and helped polarize the nation along the very lines that colored his stump speeches.

Much of Trump's fearmongering centered again on Islam and the suspicion, fear, and backlash directed at its more than eight million adherents living in Los Angeles, Detroit, and big and small American towns beyond and in between. Islamophobia was intensifying throughout the country, relentlessly fueled on the presidential campaign trail, and after the inauguration of President Trump on January 20, 2017, it was unleashed from the highest office in the land. Now more than ever, Islamophobia was not limited to the irrational views or hateful slurs of individuals, but was an ideology that drove the president's political worldview and motivated the laws, policies, and programs he would seek to push forward. This had also been the case during the Bush and Obama administrations, but the Trump moment marked a new phase of transparency in which explicit rhetorical Islamophobia aligned, in language and spirit, with the programs the new president was poised to implement.

I found myself wedged between the hate and its intended victims. Muslim Americans like myself were presumptive terrorists, not citizens; unassimilable aliens, not Americans; and the speeches I delivered on campuses and in community centers, to Muslims and non-Muslims, cautioned that the dangers Islamophobia posed yesterday were poised to become even more perilous today. The road ahead was daunting, I warned audiences after each lecture, hoping to furnish them with the awareness to be vigilant, and the pale consolation that today's Islamophobia is not entirely new.

· · ·

I was feeling alarmed for Juan, my Uber driver, even as I felt I should celebrate his being drawn toward Islam. I could not help but fear the distinct and convergent threats he would face if he embraced Islam. As an undocumented Latino Muslim in Los Angeles, Juan would be caught in the crosshairs of "terrorism" and "illegality." Los Angeles was not only ground zero for a range of xenophobic policies targeting undocumented (and documented) Latinx communities, but also a pilot city where, in 2014, the Department of Homeland Security launched its counter-radicalization program, Countering Violent Extremism, in partnership with the Los Angeles Police Department.[15] This new counterterror program, which effectively supplanted the federal surveillance model ushered in by the USA PATRIOT Act, deputized LAPD members to function as national security officers tasked with identifying, detaining, prosecuting, and even deporting "homegrown radicals." Suspicion was disproportionately assigned to recent Muslim converts, particularly young men like Juan, keen on expressing their newfound Muslim identity by wearing a beard, attending Friday prayers, and demonstrating fluency in Arabic—the language tied to Islam, and in line with Islamophobia, terrorism.

I feared for Juan's well-being, whether Muslim or not. I knew that the dangers he dodged every day would be far greater in number and more ominous in nature if he embraced Islam. The president, from inside the White House, was marshaling Islamophobia and mobilizing xenophobia to inflict irreparable injury on Muslims, Latinx communities, and the growing population of Latinx Muslims that Juan would be part of if he walked into a mosque and declared that "there is only one God, and Mohammed is his final messenger." He would be vulnerable to the covert counter-radicalization policing that was descending on Los Angeles mosques and Muslim student associations and simultaneously exposed to the ubiquitous threat of immigration checkpoints and deportation raids. He would also be a prime target for Victims of Immigration Crime Engagement, or VOICE, the new catch-an–"illegal-alien" hotline installed by President Trump.[16] This seemed far too much for any one person to endure all at once, and the boundary Juan contemplated crossing by becoming a Muslim, during the height of American Islamophobia, might very well be one that he should drive far away from.

All of this rushed through my head as Juan drove me to my hotel, sharing with me his concerns and fears about the country's current condition. I remained silent, gripped by the desire—if not the responsibility—to advise Juan to reconsider embracing Islam *at this time.* I tried to muster up the courage to tell him to postpone his conversion for a later time, when Islamophobic attitudes and policies were abating—when, and if, that time should come. I feared that if he did convert, the ever-expanding and extending arms of the state would find him at once, brand him a radical, and toss him from the country, sending him far from the only home he has ever known, and the second home that summoned me back during a fateful moment in his life and mine.

Before my conversation with Juan, I'd been gripped by memories of the post-9/11 period. But for those moments in the car, I felt overwhelmed by the dangers that would encircle Juan if he took his *shahada.* Islam in America has never been simply a religion one chooses. From the gaze of the state and society, Islam was and still is an indelible marker of otherness, and in war-on-terror America, it is a political identity that instantly triggers the suspicion of acts of terror and subversion. The urge to advise Juan against converting reached its climax when the car came to an abrupt stop near Grand Avenue and 11th Street, in the heart of downtown Los Angeles, not far from Pico Union.

Juan stepped out to greet me on the right side of the car. "It was an honor to meet and speak to you, Brother Khaled," he said, extending his hand to bid me farewell.

"Likewise Juan, I wish you the best," I told him, extending my hand to meet his. I then turned away from the stranger who, after a thirty-minute drive through grueling city traffic, had pushed me to grapple with my most pressing fears and had given me an intimate introduction to new fears that I could not turn away from.

I stopped, turned back toward Juan, and mustered up the strength to implore him, "But I ask you to think about whether now is the right time to become a Muslim," attempting to cloak a desperate plea with the tone and language of evenhanded guidance. This was more difficult than any lecture or presentation I had given during the past several months, and the many more I would give later. "Your status already puts you in a difficult position, and falling victim to Islamophobia would put you in a more dangerous place," I pled.

Voicing the words released a great weight off my shoulders. At the same time, they felt unnatural because they clashed with the spiritual aim of encouraging interest in Islam. The paradox mirrored the political confusion that gripped the nation. But the challenges and perils I lectured about in university classrooms, community centers, and mosques had to be extended to the street, and to the most vulnerable. My words were met with a look of utter surprise by Juan, who stood there and said nothing.

"Either way, you are my brother," I closed, before we walked off in opposite directions. He thanked me, circled back to the driver's seat, and turned right on 12th Street, in the direction of Pico Union, perhaps feeling disappointed in or spurned by the individual whose activism he admired.

I often wondered what decision Juan made, and whether he made his *shahada*. I also feared the worst, wondering whether he was still in the country. Was he profiled on the grounds of his Latino identity and detained because he was undocumented? Did he embrace Islam and fall victim to the counter-radicalization policing unfolding in Los Angeles? Or had he become a victim of the intersecting xenophobic backlash and Islamophobic violence authorized by Trump's rhetoric and policies, inflicted by a bigot on or off campus?

My fears were stoked daily by bleak headlines and backward actions taken by the Trump administration, but I tried to remain optimistic. I hoped that Juan was still enrolled in classes, zigzagging his car through the maze of Los Angeles traffic to help his mother make rent, to pay his college tuition, and to drive toward his goal of becoming the first member of his family to earn a college degree. And most importantly, I prayed that he was safe and sound while working toward realizing this and other aspirations—academic, professional, and spiritual—in a country where informants and officers, bans and walls threaten to crush these very dreams and the people precariously holding onto them.

I did not hear from Juan again. But his story hasn't left me, and the intersection he occupies is at the heart of this book. I share his story when speaking at colleges and universities, as well as intimately, among friends and activists, to signal that victims of Islamophobia are not merely Arab or Middle Eastern—sometimes they are not even Muslim!—and to signal that this rising system of hate is more frequently inflicted by the state than it is by individuals. Most importantly, I share it to show that Islamophobia often converges with other forms of hate, such as racism, xenophobia, sexism, and homophobia, morphing into a form of hatred custom-made for this specific target.

Juan has come to symbolize for me the new era of Islamophobia that is gripping the country. He also serves as an archetype for the stories of Muslims and non-Muslims pushed to the margins of the emerging narratives of victimhood featured in mainstream or social media. He represents people and communities excluded from portrayals of those impacted by Islamophobia—those living in the shadows of acknowledgement and advocacy and yet in dire need of that advocacy, in dire need of the protection that acknowledgment brings. Sixteen years after 9/11, "Islamophobia" is a widely known and uttered term. Yet the depth of its sources and the breadth of its victims are hardly understood, particularly where poverty, gender, legal status (or lack of it), and race intersect.

. . .

This book seeks to connect this history of anti-Muslim hostility and policy with the modern Islamophobia proliferating throughout the country today. By drawing these connections, this book reveals that Islamophobia, although a relatively new term, is anything but a new form of hate. While "Islamophobia" claimed popular purchase before the rise of Trump and gained widespread resonance during the campaign as he called for "a total and complete shutdown of Muslims entering the United States," Islamophobia long preceded the man who would become the face of it. It is a system that redeploys stereotypes of Muslims deeply rooted in the collective American imagination and endorsed by formative case law, foundational policy on immigration and citizenship, and the writings and rhetoric of this nation's founding fathers.

Islamophobia is a modern extension and articulation of an old system that branded Muslims as inherently suspicious and unassimilable and cast Islam as a rival ideology at odds with American values, society, and national identity. Centuries before the current era of Islamophobia, and "long before 9/11 and the war on terrorism, U.S. courts painted Islam as more than merely a foreign religion, but rather as a rival ideology and 'enemy race.' "[17] The term we are familiar with today rises from a hate America has always known, a hate that helped delineate who fits within the contours of American identity and who deserves to be excluded from those contours.

This book focuses closely on the roots and rise of American Islamophobia. Although Islamophobia is a global phenomenon, American Islamophobia is fluidly shaped and impacted by uniquely American stimuli, including our legal and political systems, history, racial and religious demographics, and private interests and actors. Certainly, events that unfold beyond the United States, particularly terror incidents and narratives emanating from Europe (especially states like France, where Islamophobia is rife and, with the recent emergence of Marine Le Pen, still rising), influence Islamophobia on the domestic front. Therefore I investigate foreign incidents that inform and fuel American Islamophobia, such as Brexit in Britain and the Paris attacks of November 13, 2015, but in general I am fundamentally concerned with the origins, expansion, and enforcement of Islamophobia in the United States.

Although the term "Islamophobia" has garnered widespread popularity and usage, prevailing understandings of it are narrow, vague, and oftentimes disconnected from the law and actions taken by the state. Failing to frame Islamophobia as a system of bigotry not only endorsed and emboldened by law, but also carried out by government actors, severely underestimates the scale of its menace and the process by which it inflicts injury and authorizes popular behavior. Failing to account for the law's role in authorizing and executing Islamophobia overlooks the relationship state actors have to the hateful violence of individual bigots, and it ignores the reality that the state enlists private citizens to partake in the national project of identifying and punishing individuals stereotyped as presumptive terrorists.

This ongoing dialogue between the state and its polity regarding Muslims by way of law, official rhetoric, and war-on-terror policy is central to this book's framing of Islamophobia.

Beyond defining Islamophobia as merely irrational fear or hatred held by a caricatured bloc or demographic,[18] or as deviant violence committed by individual actors, this book's definition is complex, multidimensional, and anchored in law and government policy.

Finally, by examining the earliest chapters of anti-Muslim discrimination and dehumanization (the experience of enslaved African Muslims in the antebellum South and the laws that for a century and a half prohibited Muslim immigrants from becoming citizens), as well as the myriad trials Muslim Americans face in the Trump era, this book seeks to offer a robust and genuine portrait of Muslim America. By honing in on histories, populations, and narratives that are often pushed to the margins or excluded, this book highlights the rich diversity that is Muslim America. As my legal research reveals, Muslim identity is regularly conflated with Arab (or "Middle Eastern") identity, a trope rooted in what the Palestinian American intellectual Edward Said theorized as "Orientalism"[19] and what Erik Love explains as the "racialization of Muslim identity" in his important book *Islamophobia and Racism.*[20]

Although conflated with Arab identity, the grand Muslim American narrative is actually rooted in blackness. And today, Muslim America is a richly diverse population that ranks as the most racially diverse and fastest-growing faith group in the country. African American Muslims comprise 24 percent of the Muslim American population, followed by South Asian and Arab American Muslims, at 23 and 22 percent respectively. The Latinx American Muslim community is estimated to comprise 6 percent and tally a total of 200,000, and in line with broader national demographic projections is the fastest-growing subset of the Muslim American population.[21] As Abdullahi Ahmed

An-Na'im writes in *What Is an American Muslim?* "There is simply no coherent way of regarding all American Muslims as a single monolithic community, or of speaking about them as such."[22] A glance at the racial demographics of Muslim America reveals that An-Na'im's words speak directly to the racial, socio-economic, and spiritual heterogeneity of Muslim Americans.

In addition to being racially diverse, Muslim Americans hail from "nearly 80 nationalities and cultural backgrounds,"[23] moving some to brand the Muslim American population a "microcosm of the Muslim world."[24] Thus, Islamophobia is rising at a time when Islam ranks as America's fastest-growing religion and the one with the most diverse following, which illustrates that many people are curious about the faith and are being drawn to it during this difficult time.

Disentangling Muslim from Arab identity requires more than simply sharing statistical portraits of Muslim American racial and ethnic diversity. It demands candid illustrations and analysis of how Islamophobia impacts black, Latinx, white, and other Muslim groups occupying intersections erased from mainstream media coverage or pushed to the fringes. This intersectional analysis[25] examines how Islamophobia—unleashed by the state and private individuals—impacts poor and working-class Muslims, Muslim women, LGBTQ Muslims, converts, those contemplating or on the cusp of conversion (like Juan), and other segments of the Muslim American milieu.

As Kimberlé Crenshaw, who coined the term "intersectionality," argues, "Intersectionality alone cannot bring invisible bodies into view. Mere words won't change the way that some people—the less-visible members of political constituencies—must continue to wait for leaders, decision-makers and others to see their struggle."[26] This book is driven by advocacy; my hope is that it inspires future interventions in Muslim American communities victimized by erasure and hostility from within and Islamophobia unleashed from without.

This book does not aim to provide a chronological and comprehensive history of Muslim Americans, or of Islamophobia, for that matter. Its aim is to trace the roots of the system of animus we now call Islamophobia, and to provide a lasting narrative that highlights what it actually is, what and where it stems from, and most importantly, who it impacts.

I am a legal scholar, and writing this book has provided me with an ideal opportunity to extend my legal research and writing to a broader audience. It has also enabled me, as an activist and grassroots educator, to highlight the stories and experiences I have been fortunate to collect, stories that have immensely enriched my work and, during my most trying moments, inspired me to march forward.

Above all, this book aims to honor those who have taught me so much. Only by understanding the expanse and identity of its victims, especially those most vulnerable and least visible, can we even begin to approach a genuine understanding of Islamophobia and the evils it summons. Giving face to the myriad victims, particularly those nameless Muslims at the furthest margins, the communities of Muslims erased from the pages of mainstream narratives, and those overlooked by prevailing discourses about Islamophobia, ranks as this book's highest concern.

CHAPTER ONE

What Is Islamophobia?

Through its policies of racial profiling and racially
targeted immigration enforcement, the state has
adjudged all "Muslim looking people" to be terrorists.
    Muneer I. Ahmad, "A Rage Shared by Law"

I think it is because of the way we look and the way
we dress.
    Yusor Abu-Salha

Yusor Abu-Salha was far more than the headscarf she carefully
wrapped around her head every morning and removed every
night. The twenty-one-year-old was a fresh college graduate,
having just earned a degree in biology from North Carolina
State University.[1] She had plans to attend the University of North
Carolina School of Dentistry—her top-choice program—in the
fall of 2015 and had begun prepping for it months before she
would formally set foot in a dental school class. She wore a wide
smile on her face nearly every day after ripping open the enve-
lope that contained her letter of acceptance, and she felt absolutely fortunate about the opportunities her country granted her.
She wrote, "Growing up in America has been such a blessing.

And although in some ways I do stand out, such as the hijab I wear on my head, the head covering, there are still so many ways that I feel so embedded in the fabric that is ... our culture."[2]

Yusor was also a newlywed. She had just married her college sweetheart, twenty-two-year-old Deah, who, like her, loved hip-hop music and community service, and who was working toward a career in dentistry. The two were tied at the hip, pushing their close friend Omar Alnatour to call them "the most perfect couple I have ever seen."[3] Deah himself was a second-year student at the UNC School of Dentistry and had helped his wife piece together a compelling application so that she could follow in his footsteps. In fact, the young couple frequently talked about establishing their own dental clinic and one day lending their skills to help poor patients in the Middle East, as well as serving neglected patient communities at home in North Carolina.

These are dreams that young people in their early twenties often have. But anybody who knew Yusor and Deah also knew that these two possessed the drive and work ethic to convert these dreams into reality. Yusor's younger sister, nineteen-year-old Razan, who roomed with the young couple in their Chapel Hill apartment, certainly believed that her older sister and brother-in-law would one day make good on their dreams. Razan, who had an infectious sense of humor and loved watching *Animal Planet,* had dreams of her own, which included becoming an architect, something she began to work toward as a freshman at the NC State School of Design.[4] Yusor, Deah, and Razan were three young Muslim Americans with their entire lives ahead of them, with dreams not unlike those held by other young people their age.

On February 10, 2015, the dreams of these three Muslim American students were permanently deferred and violently put to rest. Sometime before 5:00 p.m. on that day, a forty-four-year-old neighbor, Craig Hicks, executed Yusor, Razan, and Deah. The two girls were shot in the head and Deah was sprayed with bullets by Hicks after an alleged "dispute over a parking spot," several news outlets reported.[5] Yet the execution-style murder of the three students, and the blood that poured from their heads and stained their apartment carpet, evidenced that this was no parking dispute, but a hate crime—a hate crime aimed squarely at the faith of the three. "Parking disputes don't end in triple murders," my mother later told me, dismissing the weak motive that could hardly conceal the unhinged Islamophobia that triggered Hicks's actions that February afternoon. The gruesome facts, and the history of tension between Hicks and the three students, revealed that hate was at the heart of this murder. One didn't need a law degree to draw this conclusion.

Hicks's violent murder of Yusor, Razan, and Deah shook Muslim America. It spurred vigils on college campuses and at community centers, prayers at mosques nationwide, and heartfelt displays of mourning by friends, family, and complete strangers on social media. "It could've been my friends, or maybe even me," said my eighteen-year-old niece, Du'aa Hachem, then an incoming freshman at the University of Michigan–Dearborn who, like Yusor and Razan, wore the *hijab*—the headscarf many Muslim women choose to wear to express their spiritual devotion. This sentiment was hardly hers alone, but was shared by Muslim Americans across the country, particularly students and young women.

The murder of the three Muslim American students also signaled that Islamophobia was racing at a frightening new clip. The sisters' *hijab* often invited strange looks and stares from strangers. After all, North Carolina is in the heart of the South, which becomes more "southern" when one travels beyond the relatively tolerant confines of Chapel Hill, Durham, and the broader Research Triangle area. For Hicks, Yusor's and Razan's headscarves signaled that they were Muslims—a faith routinely vilified on Fox News, one singled out as the source of "home-grown radicalization" by the Obama administration's national security program, and one brazenly slandered by the entire field of Republican presidential hopefuls vying for their party's nomination. As Yusor said to her father before she was killed, "I think it is because of the way we look and the way we dress.'"[6] In the United States today, this hatred is especially potent given the heightening degree of Islamophobia coming from the media, the state, and other sources.

Although they lived next door to him, Hicks did not regard Yusor, Razan, and Deah as neighbors. In fact, he did not even perceive them primarily as college students. He perceived them, rather, as outsiders, interlopers, and foreigners—above all, as enemies of the state who warranted the suspicion and scowls he routinely darted their way when they crossed paths in the hallway, the common areas, or in the parking lot—and on that Tuesday afternoon inside the Finley Forest Condominiums in Chapel Hill, he believed they deserved extra-judicial punishment in the name of patriotism. Hicks decided to take the law, and the anti-terror objectives of the state, into his hands by executing them. While the students grew accustomed to Hicks's stares and scowls, they likely could have never imagined that their hate-filled neighbor would become their reaper. However, the ideas and images Hicks consumed about Islam, terrorism, and the *hijab* on television would mobilize his hate into unspeakable violence.

But what role did war-on-terror law and policy, founded on the narrative that Muslim identity correlates with terror suspicion, have on the murder of these three Muslim American students? Was Hicks's fear and hatred of Islam irrational, or was it fueled by the stereotypes of the faith and its followers he regularly heard on the radio and watched on television, and, therefore, rational? Furthermore, was he a deviant actor whose horrific acts were the result of his own motives alone? Or was Hicks collaborating in the broader national project of policing, prosecuting, and punishing Muslims—the formal mission of the war on terror, that ambiguous and unconventional war authorized by counterterror laws like the USA PATRIOT Act, Countering Violent Extremism, and, two years after the triple murder, the Muslim ban enacted by President Trump?[7]

Could Hicks's murder of the three students, fondly remembered as "our three winners" by their family members and Muslim American activists, be tied to formal state policy? To what degree does a broadening and deepening body of national security, immigration, and local law enforcement policy—policy that holds Muslim identity as presumptive of terror suspicion—encourage Hicks and other hatemongers to express their *private* Islamophobia through words or slurs, violence, or votes? What are the connections between the state policies and structures tasked with policing Muslim citizens and immigrants and the acts of individuals who target, victimize, and in the case of Yusor, Razan, and Deah, murder Muslims? By advancing a new and comprehensive definition of Islamophobia, this chapter uncovers this nexus and the other salient connections that tie the official pronouncements and programs of the state to the behavior of individuals.

The media coverage following the murders at Chapel Hill profiled Hicks as an irrational actor who was not influenced by the legal structures that aimed to cast Muslims as presumptive terrorists, a characterization that aligns with the prevailing understanding of Islamophobia as a "dislike of or prejudice against Muslims" generally exhibited by individuals.[8] However, this narrow framing not only overlooks the state's role in authorizing and emboldening the unfathomable acts (of private Islamophobia) undertaken by individuals like Craig Hicks, but it also overlooks the mutually reinforcing relationship between the state and media institutions like Fox News.

Furthermore, understandings of Islamophobia that tie it exclusively to private actors also fail to acknowledge that Islamophobia is structural. It is propagated by law and perpetuated by policy, policy that fluidly communicates damaging stereotypes and misrepresentations about Muslims to the broader polity, which has the effect of endorsing popular views and misconceptions, and at the extreme, emboldening hate and violence directed at Muslims and individuals incorrectly perceived as Muslims. Framing Islamophobia as more than merely hate held or violence inflicted by private individuals, and tying it to government structures and legal pronouncements and policies, is vital for uncovering and understanding each of its three principal dimensions. I will start with a foundational definition of Islamophobia, followed by a careful examination of these three dimensions.

A DEFINITION

This book offers a new understanding of Islamophobia, defining it as the presumption that Islam is inherently violent, alien, and unassimilable, a presumption driven by the belief that expressions of Muslim identity correlate with a propensity for terrorism.[9] Islamophobia is the modern progeny of Orientalism (analyzed in the next chapter), a worldview that casts Islam as the civilizational antithesis of the West and that is built upon the core stereotypes and baseline distortions of Islam and Muslims embedded in American institutions and the popular imagination by Orientalist theory, narratives, and law. Core to this book is the contention that Islamophobia is not an entirely new form of bigotry, but rather a system that is squarely rooted in, tied to, and informed by the body of misrepresentations and stereotypes of Islam and Muslims shaped by Orientalism.

Underlying this definition are three dimensions of Islamophobia: private Islamophobia, structural Islamophobia, and dialectical Islamophobia, the ongoing dialogue between state and citizen that binds the private Islamophobia unleashed by hatemongers like Craig Hicks to the war-on-terror policies enacted by Presidents George W. Bush, Obama, and Trump.

Furthermore, the definition of Islamophobia advanced by this book seeks to collapse the wall between private and structural Islamophobia that perpetuates the latter as a legitimate form of Islamophobia. Current popular discourse and the political moment have cemented a broad understanding of Islamophobia as an exclusively deviant and aberrant private violence. State policy and policing targeting Muslims is viewed as entirely divorced from the private hatemongering sweeping throughout the United States today. This limited framing diminishes grassroots, political, and legal challenges to Islamophobia, which must contemplate the state's manifold role in advancing Islamophobic policies and emboldening private violence. Therefore, my definition of Islamophobia frames the state as a potent collaborator that influences and (periodically) drives the acts of individual hatemongers, or Islamophobes, making it complicit in the range of hate crimes and hate incidents targeting Muslim individuals and institutions. A complex and multidimensional form of bigotry requires an equally complex and multidimensional conceptualization. Indeed, one cannot effectively counter or combat a system of hate without thoroughly understanding it and uncovering the myriad sources from which it originates.

It is important to recognize that Islamophobia does not exclusively rise from the right. Contrary to popular caricatures and flat media portrayals, Islamophobes are not always conservatives, far-right zealots, "lone wolf" killers, presidential hopefuls—or presidents—using hateful rhetoric, evangelical ideologues, or Trump voters. Moving beyond a narrow conception of Islamophobia requires dismissing these common caricatures. Islamophobes are also Democrats and liberals, libertarians and progressives, city dwellers and Ivy League graduates.

For example, liberal comedian and talk show personality Bill Maher, of HBO's *Real Time with Bill Maher,* referred to the Qur'an as "Islam's hate-filled holy book." Maher callously conflates the whole of Islam with the deviant interpretations of the faith subscribed to by terror groups such as Al Qaeda and the Islamic State of Iraq and Syria (ISIS), and in front of a live audience in the heart of Los Angeles he routinely vilifies Muslims and Islam to rousing applause. With little knowledge of Islam, and panels that seldom include Muslims when discussing Islam, Maher pawns off expertise about the faith and its people on an audience that knows just as little, or even less, about Islam. Bill Maher, an Islamophobe by any measure, illustrates that a figure championed by the left can be wed to the trite stereotypes and monolithic view of Islam that drive Islamophobia. His large following indicates that he is hardly alone.

Hamid Dabashi, a professor of comparative literature at Columbia University, writes that liberal Islamophobes like Maher "talk about the 'battle of ideas' without a single citation of any living or dead Muslim theologian, philosopher, mystic, poet, artist, or public intellectual evident in their vertiginously vacuous prose." Condemnation of Muslims is engaged in without Muslims sitting across from Maher as studio guests, and it masquerades as intellectual critique without even a rudimentary understanding of the faith and its various schools of thought.[10] Certainly, ignorance of Islam feeds Islamophobia. But an intimate familiarity with the damaging tropes and flat narratives propagated by news media is a more potent source, and in the case of Maher, is passed off as adequate enough expertise to engage in a "battle of ideas" that frequently sounds more like a "clash of civilizations" (discussed in chapter 3) than informed critique.

Furthermore, it must be noted that Barack Obama, a Democratic president heralded by many as the most progressive in U.S. history, embraced counter-radicalization policing and expanded the surveillance state beyond that of the Bush administration, under the supposition that Muslim identity was presumptive of terror threat. Hillary Clinton, the 2016 Democratic nominee defeated by Trump, generally referred to Muslims with qualifiers such as "terror hating" or "peace loving," implying that the word "Muslim" alone would conjure up images of terrorism and therefore be too politically costly to utter without some kind of modifier.[11]

Islamophobia coming from the left (and center) is often more latent and harder to detect than that which emanates from the right, and particularly the far right. However, it is still there. The news media covering the (first) Muslim ban vividly illustrated this. From January 30 through February 3, 2017, cable news coverage of the immigration order featured predominantly white men weighing in on an issue that targets Muslims, with Muslims watching from the sidelines. "Aligning with the spirit of the immigration order, mainstream news media effectively excluded

Muslims from the airwaves. This was not exclusive to 'conservative' media outlets like Fox News, but even more extreme on outlets commonly perceived as liberal mediums," I wrote in an op-ed in the wake of the ban.[12]

Research by media watchdog Media Matters confirmed my observation.[13] Only seven of the ninety commentators (7.8 percent) CNN featured to discuss the ban during this five day span were Muslim analysts. MSNBC, widely perceived to be the most progressive of the three major cable news networks, only featured two Muslim analysts out of the twenty-eight (7.1 percent) invited to speak during that period. Fox News, on the other hand, had the highest proportion of Muslims on air, with five out of the fifty-eight contributors (8.6 percent) identifying as Muslims. The effective exclusion of Muslim analysts from a concern that directly impacts their communities and very lives demonstrates not only latent Islamophobia but also the corollary belief that others (overwhelmingly white men pegged as "Muslim experts") are more qualified to speak on Islam and Muslims than Muslims themselves. Islamophobia is not merely fear or animus toward Muslims, but also erasure of Muslims. In the case of the Muslim ban, they were not only denied the lead on addressing concerns that directly impact their lives, but even materially barred from involvement in the discussion. Whether latent or patent, liberal or conservative, rural or urban, Islamophobia is a system carried forward by private and state actors and by the ongoing dialectic between the two.

PRIVATE ISLAMOPHOBIA

Private Islamophobia is the fear, suspicion, and violent targeting of Muslims by private actors. These actors could be individuals or institutions acting in a capacity not directly tied to the state.

Craig Hicks's murder of the three Muslim American students in Chapel Hill is a clear example of private Islamophobia. Another example is Fox News, which has built its brand in great part around demonizing Muslims, capitalizing on "scaremongering about Islam" to help solidify and even expand its share of the American television news market during an era of rising Islamophobia.[14] The Gatestone Institute in New York City, a right-wing think tank focusing on the Middle East, Muslims, and Islam's incompatibility with Western societies, is another example of a purveyor of private Islamophobia.

Private Islamophobia can target specific individuals, as in the case of the students in Chapel Hill, and it can home in on collective communities, institutions, and even non-Muslims. For example, the wave of armed and unarmed anti-Muslim protests held across the United States in September 2015 were staged in front of, and targeted, community mosques—centers where Muslims congregate and worship, particularly on Fridays, Islam's holy day.[15] Islamophobes also vandalized, desecrated, and burned down mosques, the most salient symbols of Muslim American life, during the same year, which witnessed a horrific uptick in attacks on U.S. mosques.

The Council on American-Islamic Relations (CAIR) reported seventy-eight attacks on U.S. mosques in 2015, the highest number since the immediate aftermath of the 9/11 terror attacks.[16] Many of these attacks took place in heavily concentrated Muslim neighborhoods and enclaves, indicating that the culprits were not necessarily targeting specific institutions, but rather the entire communities that surrounded them. Muslim Americans, and the faith they practice, were under attack, and the most visible representations of Islam bore the brunt of the frightening uptick in hate crimes recorded in 2015.

Incidents of private Islamophobia continued to proliferate during the following year. There were 2,213 anti-Muslim hate incidents recorded in 2016, a 57 percent increase from the preceding year.[17] In addition, the Southern Poverty Law Center found that the number of anti-Muslim hate groups rose from 34 in 2015 to 101 in 2016, becoming more common than neo-Nazi, white nationalist, and anti-LGBTQ outfits, and growing at a far faster clip.[18]

Again, mosques were frequent targets of private Islamophobia, and in 2017, an average of nine mosques were being vandalized, desecrated, or bombed per month—a frightening number that highlights that private Islamophobia in the U.S. is still on a violent incline.[19] Even more frightening was the lack of attention from the mass media and, not surprisingly, the Trump administration, which is hardly an innocent bystander but rather a propagator of rhetoric and policy that incites hate and emboldens the private targeting of Muslim Americans, which proliferated by a staggering 584 percent from 2014 to 2016.[20] Individuals and families, businesses and mosques were the targets, including the Dar Al-Farooq Muslim Center in Bloomington, Minnesota, which was bombed early Sunday, August 6, 2017, only minutes before morning prayer.

Non-Muslims are also vulnerable to private Islamophobic animus and violence. Since Muslim identity is racialized as Arab or Middle Eastern, an embedded caricature of Muslims (closely examined in chapter 3) guides how private Islamophobes imagine and identify adherents of the faith.[21] A wide swath of non-Muslim groups and communities, most notably non-Muslims from South Asia, the Arab world, Middle Eastern nations, and Latinx states, and particularly Sikhs, are often profiled as Muslims and victimized by private Islamophobes. Muslim men are stereotypically perceived as brown, bearded, and turbaned—a caricature few Muslim American men actually comport with but one that aligns with the physical appearance of a specific non-Muslim demographic, Sikh men. In America, the trouble with wearing turbans, a spiritual mandate for Sikh men, is their nexus to the ingrained stereotype of the Muslim terrorist[22] and the hatred that stereotype activates.

The murder of Balbir Singh Sodhi, a Sikh gas station owner in Mesa, Arizona, six days after the 9/11 terror attacks is a lasting reminder of how Sikhs—a non-Muslim faith group with origins on the Indian subcontinent—are often the victims of private Islamophobia. Sodhi, who wore a turban and kept a full beard in line with his religious convictions, fit the caricature of the Muslim terrorist subscribed to by many Americans. Frank Roque, the man who killed Sodhi, was guided by this caricatured portrait and shouted, "I stand for America all the way!" after taking Sodhi's life. Sodhi, a non-Muslim, became the first victim of private Islamophobic murder in the wake of 9/11.[23]

Well after 9/11 and the violent murder of Sodhi, Sikh men continue to be routinely perceived as Muslims and targeted by private Islamophobia.[24] Arjun Sethi, a Sikh American civil rights lawyer and professor, states, "In post-9/11 America, Sikhs have become an easy target. Our articles of faith—a turban and beard—make us acutely vulnerable to profiling and bigotry, Islamophobia and hate violence. But we continue to resist and push back, alongside other communities of color, in particular Muslim Americans."[25]

This private dimension of Islamophobia dominates popular and even scholarly understandings of the term and is the form that monopolizes mainstream media framing and coverage of Islamophobia. However, if we confine our understanding of Islamophobia to the irrational actions of hatemongers like Craig

Hicks or Frank Roque, or the economic or political agendas of institutions like Fox News or the Gatestone Institute, how do we account for the laws and policies that similarly cast Muslims as unassimilable, suspicious, and potential terrorists? Are these policies part and parcel of the broader system of Islamophobia, or are they distinct and exempt from condemnation?

STRUCTURAL ISLAMOPHOBIA

Structural Islamophobia, the second dimension, is the fear and suspicion of Muslims on the part of government institutions and actors. This fear and suspicion are manifested and enforced through the enactment and advancement of laws, policy, and programming built upon the presumption that Muslim identity is associated with a national security threat. These laws, policies, and programs may be explicitly discriminatory, like the first and second Muslim bans, which explicitly restricted immigrants from Muslim-majority nations from entering the United States. Others may seem neutral, having been framed in generally applicable terms, when in practice they are disproportionately enforced against Muslim subjects and communities.

Although thought to be a novel form of bigotry against Muslims, close investigation of structural Islamophobia illustrates that it is anything but. Again, Islamophobia is the modern progeny of Orientalism, "a master discourse that positions Islam—a faith, people, and imagined geographic sphere—as the civilizational foil of the West."[26] Connecting Islamophobia to Orientalism is a vital first step toward understanding that Islamophobia is deeply entrenched, fluidly remade and reproduced, and deployed by the state to bring about intended or desired political ends.

Structural Islamophobia is manifested by historic policy and state action against Islam and Muslims, and most visibly today, by the abundant laws, policies, and programs enacted to police Muslims during the protracted war on terror. Chapter 2 examines the formative racial classifications and immigration policies that narrowly caricatured Muslims as Arab or Middle Eastern and stifled their attempts to become naturalized citizens from 1790 until 1944. Chapters 4 and 5 examine the extension and expansion of structural Islamophobia in the modern American context, exploring law and policy enacted to police, prosecute, and punish Muslim immigrants and citizens on the grounds of protecting national security.

Following 9/11, law scholar Leti Volpp observed how terror attacks involving a Muslim culprit spur the immediate "redeployment of Orientalist tropes."[27] These tropes are embedded within popular representations of Muslims, such as news coverage or depictions in film.[28] But more saliently, they are embedded within the institutional memory of government agencies, including the judiciary,[29] the legislature, and the executive branch—most notably, in the Department of Homeland Security and anti-terror law enforcement during the protracted war on terror. These foundational stereotypes, which portray Islam as irreconcilable with American values and society and Muslim identity as foreign, subversive, and harboring an inherent propensity for terrorism, move state agencies to enact policies that profile and closely police Muslim citizens and immigrants. Such policies assign the presumption of guilt to Muslims at large, and in turn diminish the civil liberties of Muslim Americans.

While a number of government policies fit within the structural Islamophobia classification, the PATRIOT Act, counter-radicalization programming, and first and second Muslim bans are four of the most vivid examples. In the aftermath of 9/11, the Bush administration established the Department of Homeland Security with the mission of not only expanding its domestic counterterror program, but also entirely overhauling and restructuring it in specific response to "Islamic extremism." Modern American national security and the counterterror state were remade to reflect the belief that Muslims pose a threat, and to reflect how that threat is imagined and exaggerated. Structural Islamophobia is not exclusive to the federal government; it is also advanced on the state and city levels. However, state and city governments typically follow in the footsteps of the federal government, as illustrated by war-on-terror policy and strategy.

President Obama ushered in the second phase of the war on terror. His administration extended the restrictive immigration policies enacted in the wake of 9/11 by President Bush (the National Security Entry and Exit Registration System, or NSEERS) and formally installed counter-radicalization policing in 2011, which expanded the surveillance state and "localized" state scrutiny of Muslim subjects by enabling local law enforcement to monitor "homegrown radicalization."[30] Although Obama was heralded as a progressive president who declared that "America and Islam are not exclusive, and need not be in competition" during his celebrated Cairo speech on June 4, 2009,[31] his administration expanded the surveillance of Muslims beyond the degree established by the Bush administration.

Finally, structural Islamophobia was made more transparent and brazen during the third phase of the war on terror, ushered in by the Trump administration on January 20, 2017. By issuing the executive orders on immigration, promising to enact a Muslim Registry (and to revitalize NSEERS),[32] remaking Countering Violent Extremism into the more hardline Countering

Islamic Violence, and seeking to designate the Muslim Brotherhood as a terrorist organization—a measure that would severely cripple Muslim American civic and advocacy organizations with tenuous, imagined, or fabricated ties to the transnational political group[33]—Trump made the war-on-terror objectives of the state the most explicitly anti-Muslim they have ever been. However, the Trump administration should not be viewed as a marked departure or outlier, but rather as a more transparent and brazen step in a progression that has been, in great part, enabled by the stated war-on-terror aims and programs of the previous two administrations.

Perhaps the best way to think about structural Islamophobia is by analogizing it to structural racism. Both are cultures embedded within government institutions. Both have preexisting narratives and propagate stereotypes based on understanding a people in flat, damaging, and subhuman terms, stories that are then institutionalized at every level of public and private organizations, institutions, and agencies. These stories are manifested in seemingly benign decisions or routine functions that bring about a discriminatory end, and sometimes through actions whose explicit intention is to bring about a discriminatory end.

How do we explain the relationship between private and structural Islamophobia? How does the latter endorse or influence the actions of individuals and actors that participate in the former? What do we make of the dynamic, or dialectic, between the state and its polity with regard to authorizing and emboldening Islamophobia? And how does the fluid exchange between government structures and citizens perpetuate Islamophobia as a broad system of bigotry and violence? I explore these and additional questions next.

DIALECTICAL ISLAMOPHOBIA

The final dimension of Islamophobia is the least detectable, but it is the very thread that binds the private and structural forms together. Dialectical Islamophobia is the process by which structural Islamophobia shapes, reshapes, and endorses views or attitudes about Islam and Muslim subjects inside and outside of America's borders. State action legitimizes prevailing misconceptions, misrepresentations, and stereotypes of Islam and communicates damaging ideas through state-sponsored policy, programming, or rhetoric, which in turn emboldens private violence against Muslims (and perceived Muslims).

Islamophobia at its core is the presumption of guilt assigned to Muslims by state and private actors. But it also must be understood as a process, the one by which state policies endorse popular tropes. This ongoing process is most intense during the aftermath of terrorist attacks like the 9/11 attacks or the April 15, 2013 Boston bombings,[34] points in time when structural Islamophobic policies are typically enacted, advanced, or zealously lobbied for.

Moments of national mourning, particularly after a terror attack committed by Muslims or individuals perceived as outsiders,[35] also spark a desire to exact revenge and perpetrate violence against anybody and everybody perceived to be Muslim, or more generally, not American. This mass anger, typically enforced through acts of vigilante violence directed at innocents, is also often endorsed and emboldened by formal policy that deems Muslims to be suspicious and to be members of a faith that ties them to the terror acts. For example, four days after a suicide bombing in England's Manchester Arena on May 22, 2017, a man shouted that "Muslims should die," then lunged toward two girls, one of whom was Muslim, on a train in Portland, Oregon, with a knife, and fatally stabbed two of the men who stepped in to defend the girls.[36] Only hours after an ISIS-inspired attack in London on June 3, 2017, a headscarved Muslim American woman, Rahma Warsame, was savagely assaulted by an Islamophobe in Ohio, leaving her with missing teeth and a broken nose and jaw.[37] These victims were a continent away from the terror incidents that drove Islamophobes to attack them.

Stories like these are all too common, particularly in the wake of terror incidents, and exhibit the Islamophobic base narrative that holds all Muslims guilty of every terror attack. Expectations that Muslims disavow or apologize for acts of terror[38] highlight this narrative. Mainstream media coverage is replete with headlines such as "Muslims Must Do More against Terrorism" and "Why Aren't Muslims Condemning ISIS?" confirming the baseless tie between terrorism and Muslim identity, and further emboldening the private backlash against any and every Muslim.

The state's rubber-stamping of widely held stereotypes of Islam and Muslims, through the enactment of surveillance programs, religious and racial profiling, restrictive immigration policies, and the war-on-terror campaign, is the cornerstone of dialectical Islamophobia. This exchange—by which citizens absorb the suspicion and demonization the state assigns to Muslims by way of (structural Islamophobic) law or state action—is an ongoing dialectic that links state policy to hate and violence unleashed by private citizens.

While Craig Hicks's murder of the three Muslim students is generally framed as a deviant act committed by one deviant actor entirely divorced from the state, dialectical Islamophobia reveals an underlying thread that connects the (seemingly) deviant actions of hatemongers like Hicks with the state's repeated message that Muslim identity alone is grounds for suspicion that justifies vigilante action by private citizens. If the law is laden with damaging stereotypes of Islam and Muslims, and American citizens are expected and instructed to obey the law, the dialectic between the state and the citizen—and the hostility the state authorizes—is made clear.

Most of the attention devoted to Islamophobia fixates on sensational stories of private Islamophobia. Stories about "intensifying calls for the exclusion of Syrian refugees,"[39] anti-Muslim rallies spearheaded and staged by fringe militants, mosque arsons, and the spike in violence against *hijab*-clad Muslim women that took place after Trump's presidential victory[40] dominate mainstream news, social media, and even academic research. This preoccupation with sensational stories of private Islamophobia obfuscates the process by which structural Islamophobia authorizes and mobilizes private bigotry toward Muslims. Like other forms of bigotry, Islamophobia is contingent on media representations, political rhetoric, and most saliently, formal law, policy, and programming. The fluid expansion of structural Islamophobia, through the advancement of the war on terror, communicates to the broader citizenry that Islam is to be viewed with suspicion. And under a president who openly states, "I think Islam hates us,"[41] it is easy for many people to believe that Islam is utterly irreconcilable with American culture, and that those who identify as Muslims are not part of the collective "US" or "we." Structural Islamophobia marks Muslims and Muslim Americans as, at best, possible threats, and at worst, as terrorists in our midst. These state designations prompt the passions and stir the suspicion of private citizens, increasingly motivating them to take action.

In "A Rage Shared by Law," written in the wake of the 9/11 terror attacks, Muneer I. Ahmad of the Yale Law School observes,

"Like the post–September 11 perpetrators, the state claims an intimate relationship with the nation....Moreover, the state has purported to act in the names of the victims of the terrorist attacks, invoking their memory as justification for a broad range of antiterrorist policies." In this passage, Ahmad articulates one dimension of the dialectic, whereby the state—or the government—takes action against the enemy in the name of the fallen victim, on behalf of the people living in the United States, which Ahmad calls the nation. He continues, "Through its policies of racial profiling and racially targeted immigration enforcement, the state has ... adjudged all 'Muslim-looking' people to be terrorists, and carried out acts of retribution against them."[42] Here, Ahmad is loosely explaining the gist of dialectical Islamophobia.

This very dialectic continues following the Paris, San Bernardino,[43] Brussels,[44] Orlando, Manchester, and London terror attacks, wherein the nation's intensifying private Islamophobia drives the Countering Violent Extremism policing programs expanded by the state. In turn, structural Islamophobic policy and state action communicate to private Islamophobes that their fear and anger toward Muslims are justified. During moments when structural Islamophobia is broadened to address (real or imagined) Muslim extremism, structural Islamophobic policies embolden the private passions of Islamophobes to partake in the national project of policing and punishing Muslims, in the name of revenge, citizenship, and patriotism—which, in the wake of terror attacks, are virtually indistinguishable.

Therefore, structural Islamophobia should also be viewed as a latent (and in the case of Trump, a patent) call to action transmitted from the state to its citizens. The state is alerting the American people to be on the lookout for suspicious Muslims, and when the time comes, to take action. Craig Hicks, after all, was just acting on what war-on-terror policy instructed him about the threat posed by Muslims like Deah, and particularly Deah's new bride Yusor and her sister Razan, who wore "the flag of Islam" around their heads.[45] Even if they were backpack-toting, pizza-eating, wide-eyed college kids, driven by the very same aspirations held by non-Muslim students at high schools and college campuses across the country, Yusor, Razan, and Deah were ultimately Muslims, which meant that according to the highest laws of the land, they were members of an enemy bloc bent on menacing America. As Muslims, the three students gruesomely murdered in Chapel Hill were said to be part of an enemy race, a caricature of Muslims embedded within the memory of American institutions centuries before it was implanted in the mind of Craig Hicks.[46]

CHAPTER TWO

The Roots of Modern Islamophobia

I think Islam hates us.

> Donald Trump, March 9, 2016

The intense hostility of the people of Moslem faith to all other sects, and particularly to Christians, affected all their intercourse.

> Judge Stephen Field, U.S. Supreme Court, May 25, 1891

The sun's familiar rays crept through the crack of the door. The lord's voice, synchronized with the sun, summoned Omar Ibn Said from his slumber. With a water-pot near his bedside, Omar performed the customary ablutions in Fayetteville, North Carolina, as he had every day in Futa Tooro, West Africa.[1] He meticulously cleansed his dark brown skin in line with the ancient Islamic custom, beginning with his feet and finishing with his face. Omar then set out on foot for the first of the five daily prayers.

The *fajr* summons grew louder.[2] Omar marched alongside his companions to heed his overlord's call. He paused when he reached his assigned plot on the green field, pointing his wiry brown frame east toward Mecca, the Holy City on the other side of the world. He fondly reflected on his daily prayers on the banks of the Senegal River, where he once sourced the water to cleanse his body every day before worship. Flanked by Muslim brothers to his immediate right and left, Omar bowed his head and dug his black, wrinkled hands into the North Carolina fields—not to pray, but to pick.[3]

Picking cotton simulated a choreography that Omar knew only as prayer before the Middle Passage—when he and many other men, both Muslim and non-Muslim, were densely packed onto slave ships en route to a distant, foreign land. Far from home, Omar repeated these prayer motions diligently and hypnotically. Although picking cotton resembled the Islamic prayer prostrations, the law that marked him as a slave because of his blackness and made him the property of his white master conflicted with the dominion of the Qur'an, Islam's holy book. Although he presented himself as a Christian to the slave masters and the white world, his outward conversion was a shield from punishment, one that enabled him to continue to observe Islam, his native faith. He remained lodged between the clashing identities of Muslim and black slave until his death in 1864— one year before the abolition of slavery and the legal dissolution of the legal line that segregated both halves of his identity.

. . .

More than two centuries before a "Muslim ban" headlined the *New York Times* or led to the detainment of thousands of Muslims at airports across the United States, Muslims were statutorily barred from becoming American citizens. They were deemed threatening to and unassimilable within American values and society. In line with the demonization of this entire bloc of immigrants, the courts prohibited Muslim immigrants from becoming naturalized citizens from 1790 to 1944. During this span, Muslim identity, by law, was viewed as contradictory with American citizenship.

Days after then-candidate Donald Trump doubled up on his plans for enacting a Muslim ban on the campaign trail, I wrote in the *Washington Post* that "Donald Trump's calls for a ban on Muslims entering the United States and, more recently, for 'extreme vetting' of anyone seeking to immigrate to the United States have been condemned as breaks from this nation's traditions of religious tolerance and welcoming immigrants. Actually, Trump's proposal reflects a long-standing, if ugly, strain of U.S. immigration policy, one that restricted the entry of Arab and South Asian Muslim immigrants and barred them from becoming citizens until the middle of the 20th century."[4] For Trump, "Make America Great Again" was not forward looking, but instead sought to weaken multiculturalism, which his proponents deemed a threat to America's national identity.[5] It also sought to revitalize backward policy that explicitly conflated extremism with Islam, and to codify both goals in immigration policy.

Trump's Muslim ban proposal, which he advanced by way of three executive orders, was driven by the same discourse and stereotypes that prohibited Muslims from becoming U.S. citizens from 1790 through 1944. The characterization of Muslim immigrants as an enemy race during this period of American history, called the naturalization era, is echoed by the modern characterization of Muslim immigrants as fundamentally different and unassimilable, as potential terrorists, and, in the case of Syrian refugees fleeing war, as cloaked "ISIS terrorists."[6]

During the naturalization era, immigrants seeking citizenship were bound by the prerequisite of being found to be "free

white persons" by a civil court. However, what defined whiteness was not allowed to extend beyond Christianity, and especially Protestantism, and Islam stood as its rival and thus was
considered irreconcilable with whiteness. Therefore, up until
1944, Muslim identity precluded one from being deemed white
by law and therefore eligible for citizenship. Furthermore, the
Naturalization Act of 1790 also curbed the migration of Muslims
to the United States, as they were largely aware of the opposition their religious identity would spur at ports of entry like
Ellis Island. The Naturalization Act persuaded many Muslims
considering emigrating to the United States to stay home, while
those who did travel across the Atlantic for the promise of a better life were largely destined to become lifelong aliens in a new
land, restricted from becoming naturalized citizens on account
of their Muslim identity.

   In addition to the mandate that no one who was not "white by
law" could become a U.S. citizen,[7] America's first Muslims were
also enslaved and reduced to chattel. Muslims comprised a sizable portion of the population of Africans kidnapped, shipped,
and auctioned off to slave masters on the other side of the world.
One study has estimated that 46 percent of the slaves in the
antebellum South were kidnapped from Africa's western region,
encompassing modern-day Nigeria, Niger, Cameroon, Senegal,
Ghana, and neighboring states, which boasted "significant numbers of Muslims."[8] However, the racial construction of blackness
and the legal enforcement of slavery not only eroded and ultimately extinguished the Islam they brought with them and
practiced on plantations, but the vantage point of American law,
institutions, and individuals also prevented the recognition of
these pioneer Muslims for who they were: bona fide observant
Muslims. They not only established the first Muslim communi-

ties in the American colonies, but they also helped build the very economic and infrastructural foundations of the United States.

In conjunction with the racialization of blackness as synonymous with property and slave, during the eighteenth and nineteenth centuries Orientalism manufactured a racially narrow understanding of Muslim identity as exclusively Arab or Middle Eastern.[9] Thus an entire religion was remade into a racial identity. If black meant property and slave, and Muslim meant Arab or Middle Eastern, then black Muslim was a legally contradictory and impossible identity in early American history. This contradiction of racial constructions erased the pioneering Muslim American population from the pages of mainstream American history and, as examined in chapter 6, continues to drive the dissonance between black identity and Muslim identity that grips the minds of far too many.

This chapter investigates the deep and old roots of modern Islamophobia, roots that wove through the foundations of American state and private structures, from antebellum Southern plantations to Northeastern federal courts. More closely, it examines the intersection between Orientalism, blackness, and whiteness, probing Orientalism's dynamic system of dehumanization and the place where that system meets the race-making project of constructing blackness to designate property, a project that could not exist without the mirroring project of constructing whiteness to signify the heights of humanity and the gateway to the full-blown privileges of citizenship. While the architects of Orientalism were European, and the white supremacist racial taxonomy became the backbone of American law as framed by legislators, judges and statesmen, the two systems overlapped to manufacture two narrow and dissonant definitions of black and Muslim identity.

Orientalism informed not only how race was understood during the formative stages of American history, but also how it was constructed. Orientalism helped guide, and fluidly tweak, the parameters of whiteness. And in the same way that blackness stood as the racial antithesis of whiteness, the necessary other without which whiteness would not exist, the Orientalist construction of Islam marked the faith as the civilizational foil of the West, a contrast that was necessary for the emerging United States to envision itself as an extension of Western civilization. In order to solidify itself as part of the West, and an extension of Europe in the Western Hemisphere, the United States had to follow in the footsteps of Europe and establish itself as the mirror opposite of the Muslim world.

UNDERSTANDING ORIENTALISM

The most trenchant and influential critic of Islamophobia, in both its past and modern configurations, was not a Muslim. He was, rather, a man born to a Palestinian Christian family who eventually crafted the foundational theory and framework that not only uncovered the roots of modern Islamophobia, but provided the intellectual language and tools to combat it.

Edward Said (Sa'eed), one of the most influential intellectuals of the past century, seldom (if ever) used the word "Islamophobia" in his writings or lectures. Said passed away on September 25, 2003, just over two years after the 9/11 attacks, a time of intensifying hostility toward Arabs, Muslims, and other peoples from the Middle East, which would ultimately give rise to the system of bigotry that we currently know as Islamophobia. He committed much of his life as an academic and intellectual to grappling with Orientalism, the system that preceded and mothered Islamophobia, challenging a long line of thinkers who fed the discourse that the West, and particularly the United States, was rightly locked in a cultural, civilizational, and military crusade against Islam. Said's landmark book, *Orientalism,* is "one of the most oft-quoted texts across the various disciplines engaged in studying the Middle East or Islam" and has immortalized him among thinkers and activists grappling with the caricaturing of Islam and the demonization of Muslims.[10] One cannot understand Islamophobia until one has thoroughly examined Orientalism, and every project aimed at demystifying or deconstructing Islamophobia must begin with Said's work.

I met Edward Said six months before his untimely death, following a public lecture he gave at UCLA. Said spent some of his address warning the audience about a "new era of Orientalism" following the 9/11 attacks, an era characterized by a war on terror built upon the epistemological, normative, and legal architecture of Orientalism. Said addressed the illegality of wars launched in the name of "defeating terror" and the counterterror dragnets that implicated Arab and Muslim Americans on account of their ethnic or religious identities. His lecture was more than simply a contextualization of Orientalism within the challenges of the post-9/11 era; in retrospect, it was a lecture that highlighted the intimate nexus between Orientalism and Islamophobia. Muslims in the United States, and indeed the world, lost Said when they needed him most.

Well before Islamophobia was devised and deployed to explain the demonization of Islam and Muslims, Said's *Orientalism* illustrated the extensive history and complex process by which Islam and its adherents were *othered,* or more specifically, constructed and cast as inferior and subhuman, unassimilable and savage, violent and warmongering. Islam was everything the West was not, and it was assigned these and other damning attributes in order to elevate the West and characterize it, and its people, as progressive, democratic, and modern.

The fundamental baseline of Orientalism was casting the Muslim world as the mirror opposite of the West. Said opens *Orientalism* with this: "The Orient has helped to define Europe (or the West) as its contrasting image, idea, personality, experience."[11] The process of characterizing and vilifying the Muslim world, which Orientalists dub the Orient, became the very way in which the West, as well as its principal thinkers, statesmen, and tastemakers, came to define itself. This mirrored identity was very much a fluid dialectic, whereby the shifting characterizations of the Muslim world—informed by political engagements with Muslim-majority nations, colonial interventions and projects, and most intensely, clashes—would also inform how the West saw itself.

Anthropology scholar Daniel Martin Varisco, the author of an excellent analysis of *Orientalism*'s strengths and shortcomings, articulates that "This radical distinction between East and West is labeled by Said as both ontological and epistemological," pointing to the depth to which this system impacted individual and institutional views of Islam and its adherents.[12] Orientalism penetrated every sphere of European, and later, American life, from art to pedagogy, from foreign policy to domestic law. Its foundational thesis and attendant stereotypes drove a grand narrative and "discourse with supporting institutions, vocabulary, scholarship, imagery, doctrines, even colonial bureaucracies and colonial styles."[13] Orientalism was a discourse first, and then the narrative and its attendant ideas gradually morphed into material objects in the form of literature, art, formal state policies, academic disciplines and departments, and most saliently, the very worldview from which state leaders and governments engaged Muslim-majority states and their inhabitants.

Based on a binary that made Europe the antithesis of the "Orient" and "Orient" synonymous with the "Muslim world,"[14]

Orientalism spawned the corollary view that Muslims were a monolithic racial or ethnic bloc, imagined in the narrow form of an Arab or Middle Eastern. Critical race theorists call this process "racialization,"[15] and contend that "races are not biologically differentiated groupings but rather social constructions."[16] Races, and racial categories, therefore, are fluid and dynamic constructs that are shaped and reshaped in line with political, economic, and cultural interests. In line with this process of racialization, Orientalism (re)made "Muslim" into a race. This conversion of Muslim identity from a religion into a race changed a diverse population represented in every corner of the globe to the narrow form of the Arab, or as stated by Islamophobia scholar Erik Love, anybody "who looks Middle Eastern."[17] Orientalists limited the geographic and civilizational bounds of the Muslim world to the majority-Arab regions in North Africa, the Levant,[18] the Gulf, and the Arabian Peninsula. These contiguous regions, also home to sizable non-Muslim and indigenous non-Arab populations, were consolidated into one region called the "Middle East," itself a product of Orientalist perspective, creation,[19] and geographic ambiguity.

AMERICAN ORIENTALISM

Orientalism was essential to Europe's colonialist, imperialist project; it was the fuel without which foreign conquest into Muslim-majority nations could not have run—and the early colonists carried it with them into what would become known as the United States. Orientalist discourses have shaped state policy since before American independence. Many formative statesmen viewed, "Islam as the antithesis of the 'true faith' of Protestant Christianity,"[20] illustrating just how pervasive this worldview was during the embryonic stages of American history, and how well it was embedded at the very top of American government.

Notable figures in early American history also regarded Islam, and the Muslim world, as the civilizational foil of the United States. Republicans and Federalists used Islam and its most important prophet, Muhammad, to caution against threats to liberty and "unbridled despotism."[21] In *The Crescent Obscured,* Robert Allison observes, "Americans regarded Muhammad as a dangerous false prophet and as the creator of an evil religious and political system.... Islam, as the Americans saw it, was against liberty, and being against liberty, it stopped progress."[22]

The parameters of American democracy and the bounds of liberty would be measured against how the framers of the Constitution imagined Islam. This was Orientalism in action. The architects of the United States adopted wholesale the Orientalist worldview and its attendant representations and misrepresentations. These distorted stereotypes of Islam and its followers would shape the contours of the law and policy that would engage Muslim-majority nations and states, and just as potently, domestic law and policy.

While the framers disagreed about and hotly debated matters ranging from the breadth (or limits) of federal power to the sovereignty of the states, anti-Muslim animus was not a wedge issue. It was a matter that unified the fiercest rivals at the Constitutional Convention and beyond. As Allison writes, "Both Republicans like Mathew Lyon and Thomas Jefferson, who welcomed the progressive libertarianism of the French Revolution, and Federalists like John Adams, who feared the consequences of unchecked democracy, agreed that liberty and human progress were good things and the unbridled despotism of the Muslim world was a bad thing for preventing it."[23]

If America wanted to be democratic and free, then purging every manifestation of Islam—whether in the form of ideas, institutions, or individuals—was a mandate, the Republicans and Federalists generally agreed. These views held by early statesmen at the federal and local levels would eventually, inevitably, evolve into law, policy, and institutional memory and drive the state's perception of Islam and its policing of both real and imagined Muslims.

Although Muslims toiled inside and outside of plantations in antebellum America, some of them perhaps owned by the very men who framed formative U.S. institutions and charters—thereby living in close proximity to the men claiming to be experts on Islam—Muslim identity in the minds of the founding Americans was less about religious identity and more about racial, cultural, and civilizational identity. Muslims were not adherents to the world's second largest religion, in the mind of founding American Orientalists, but rather an alien, unassimilable people from the Middle East.

American Orientalism is hardly a relic of the past. It is, rather, a phenomenon that lives on today and steers how politicians, journalists, and everyday citizens think about Muslims and frame Islam. It is fluid and potent. It is the root system that gave rise to and drives Islamophobia. Justifying fear of and violence against a people requires a foundational system that actively dehumanizes that people. We cannot understand American Islamophobia without understanding its predecessor, American Orientalism.

ANTEBELLUM ISLAM

An enslaved African and a devout Muslim, Omar, whose story opens this chapter, exemplifies members of the first, yet largely forgotten, Muslim communities in the United States. Research affirms that Muslims were not a negligible element, but an integral segment of the enslaved African population in the antebellum South. Social scientists estimate that 15 to 20 percent, or, "as many as 600,000 to 1.2 million" members of the aggregate enslaved African population were Muslims.[24] That is a staggering figure, particularly when juxtaposed with the dearth of attention given to, and public knowledge of, enslaved African Muslims in that time period of American history.

Although these enslaved Muslims prayed, observed Ramadan, maintained pious lifestyles, and forged spiritual communities while bonded to slave code and slave master, the law preempted *seeing* them as bona fide Muslims.[25] Blackness, the antithesis of whiteness, was constructed to justify and perpetuate the enslavement of African peoples, and systematically reduce them to property. But this was by design. In her landmark treatise *Whiteness as Property*, UCLA law professor Cheryl Harris observes, "The hyper-exploitation of Black labor was accomplished by treating Black people themselves as objects of property. Race and property were thus conflated by establishing a form of property contingent on race—only Blacks were subjugated as slaves and treated as property."[26] The creation, construction, and consignment of blackness onto the bodies of Africans washed away, from the eyes of the law and those expected to abide by and enforce it, the spiritual identities of enslaved Africans. Enslaved African Muslims were black, the law held, and thus property. And property could not adhere to any organized religion, let alone believe in Islam. Furthermore, the enslaved black population hailed from the western regions of Africa, an area beyond what Orientalism had demarcated as the "Muslim world."

Eliminating the religious identities of slaves was central to the process of bifurcating black from Muslim identity during the antebellum era. Although Africans thrust into the American slave market hailed from a diverse range of tribal, ethnic, and religious backgrounds, their heterogeneity had no relevance to the law's conversion of them into property. Legal recognition of the religious identities of Africans would amount to a concession to their humanity and undermine the project of converting them into subhuman beings whom it was ethically permissible to enslave.

Criminalizing religion was vital to the project of stripping the humanity of Africans and reducing them to "beasts of burden" pushed to inhuman limits to maximize revenue for their slave masters. Frederick Douglass observed that "elevating" a slave through better treatment gave witness to the humanizing effect of religion and the dehumanizing effect of keeping a person's religion from them. Douglass famously stated, "Beat and cuff your slave, keep him hungry and spiritless, and he will follow the chain of his master like a dog; but feed and clothe him well, work him moderately, surround him with physical comfort, and dreams of freedom intrude."[27] Part of the "spiritlessness" Douglass speaks of had to do with barring slaves from feeding their spirits with the soul food of religion. Denying slaves religion kept them bound to their condition. Religion, and in this instance Islam, would inspire the enslaved to question their condition, contemplate resistance, and as illustrated by a series of slave narratives from within and beyond the United States, rebel, revolt, and seek liberation.[28]

The narrow construction of black and Muslim identities drew a sharp line between the two racial classifications, which preempted seeing both as coexistent identities. Slave codes codified the belief that slaves were a godless people incapable of practicing religion, while formative immigration and citizenship policy restricted the naturalization of an alien bloc of people from the Muslim world, which it classified as Muslims (or during the naturalization era,

"Mohammedans"). Enslaved Muslims occupied the intersection of these two irreconcilable racial configurations. Although they were black and Muslim, the law furiously denied conjoining these identities, because doing so would undo the subhuman blackness branded upon the bodies of the enslaved, while also disrupting the narrow way in which Muslim identity was racially configured.

Although black Muslim identity was denied to enslaved Muslims by law, they still strove to practice their faith while in bondage. Sylviane Diouf writes, "A double minority—religious and ethnic—in the colonial world, as well as in the enslaved community, the West African Muslims did not succumb to acculturation but strove hard to maintain their traditions, social values, customs, and particular identity."[29]

The common practice of Islam and the observation of its traditions moved Muslim slaves in close proximity with one another to reconstruct spiritual communities while enslaved. These reconstructed Muslim communities were built across tribal and ethnic lines, and even brought in converts from among the enslaved and emancipated Africans of different faiths. Prayer, observing Ramadan,[30] making charitable donations, and striving to meet Islam's "Five Pillars" remained a core pursuit for many Muslim slaves.[31] Faith was also a bond between enslaved Muslims that spurred frequent communication within and without the boundaries of individual plantations, fostering new Muslim communities among the disjointed slave populations in a given region of the antebellum South.

Despite slaves' observation of Muslim traditions and Muslim lifestyles, historians (both Muslim and otherwise) examining Muslim American history have largely fallen short of recognizing Muslim slaves as the first Muslim American communities. The legal construction of black and Muslim into separate racial classifications, rooted in American Orientalism and racism, brought about the erasure of the first Muslim population in the United States. It continues to be the driving force behind a failure to recognize their descendants—today's African American Muslims, the biggest subset of the Muslim American population—as bona fide Muslims. The marginalization of African American Muslims in the face of rising Islamophobia today is connected to the legacy of erasure that started centuries ago in antebellum America, anchored in the notion that black identity and Muslim identity are clashing and irreconcilable.

AMERICA'S FIRST MUSLIM BAN

Judge George H. Hutton peered across his bench in the direction of George Shishim. Shishim, a longtime resident of California and native of the Mount Lebanon Province (modern-day Lebanon) of the Ottoman Empire, had come to Hutton's court to petition for American citizenship. After living in Los Angeles as a resident alien and serving as a policeman for the LAPD, he was poised to finally become a naturalized citizen and a formal member of the country he served and for which he felt a great affinity.

An immigrant from Canada, Hutton was elected to preside over the Los Angeles Superior Court in 1906. During the naturalization era, judges like Hutton held unfettered discretion over deciding which immigrants fit within the statutory definition of whiteness mandated by law, and therefore, authority over deciding whether petitioners like Shishim could become citizens. In 1909, when Shishim filed his petition, it was impossible to become a naturalized citizen unless you were white. From 1790 until 1952, whiteness stood as the legal dividing line between inclusion and exclusion from the range of privileges and benefits that came with formal citizenship. *Whiteness* and *citizen* were made synonymous by law, and the courts were the enforcers and the final gatekeepers.

Weeks before his appearance in Los Angeles Superior Court, a naturalization and immigration agent had moved to deny Shishim's citizenship petition on the grounds that his "Arab identity," synonymous with Muslim identity, did not meet the legal mandate of whiteness. Judge Hutton seemed persuaded by the immigration examiner's position, which deemed immigrants from the region Shishim originated from as hostile to American democracy and values, unassimilable, and Muslim unless proven otherwise. However, although Shishim was an Arab, he was also a Christian. In fact, the overwhelming majority of Arabs in the United States in 1909 were Christians.

Short on rebuttals, Shishim closed with the lone argument that he hoped would resonate with Judge Hutton and save his petition. It was a Hail Mary, a final plea. He rose from his seat, stood firmly with his LAPD badge glistening from his jacket, and testified, "If I am Mongolian, then so was Jesus, because we came from the same land."[32] Shishim was effectively stating that if Jesus were white, the court would also have to find him to be white, or render an admission that Jesus was not white—an admission that would undermine the construction of Jesus as a white man and of Christianity as a portal toward whiteness. Christianity was one of the primary hallmarks of whiteness in the United States in the early twentieth century, and Shishim's spirited appeal insisted that although he was from the Muslim world, he was not a Muslim but in fact a Christian, and therefore white.

Hutton, conditioned to believe that anybody who hailed from the Middle East was Muslim, struggled with this dissonance. But Shishim's brilliant appeal to Christianity managed to persuade

Hutton, and Shishim became the first immigrant from the Middle East to be naturalized as an American citizen and judicially ruled white by law.[33] "When the court finally determined Shishim to be a white person, thus allowing for his acquisition of citizenship," a *Los Angeles Times* reporter wrote that "it made every feature of his dark, swarthy countenance radiate with pleasure and hope."[34]

Civil judges like Hutton were responsible for interpreting the statutory meaning of whiteness during the naturalization era. In *White by Law,* law scholar Ian Haney López observes:

> The individuals who petitioned for naturalization forced the courts into a case-by-case struggle to define who was a "white person." More importantly, the courts were required in these prerequisite cases to articulate rationales for the divisions they were creating. Beyond simply issuing declarations in favor of or against a particular applicant, the courts ... had to explain the basis on which they drew the boundaries of Whiteness. The courts had to establish by law whether, for example, a petitioner's race was to be measured by skin color, facial features, national origin, language, culture, ancestry, the specialization of scientist, [or] popular opinion.[35]

Most saliently for immigrants from the Middle East, the courts could also determine whiteness on the basis of religion. American whiteness, therefore, was very much a social construction, endorsed by law and subject to revision. In the words of James Baldwin, "No one was white before s/he came to America. It took generations, and a vast amount of coercion, before this became a white country."[36] And just because race is a social construction does not mean that racism is not real, a tenet as true during the naturalization era as it is today.

Whiteness was not merely a race during the naturalization era, but a "material concept imbued with rights and privileges."[37] The greatest right, citizenship, was inscribed into it. Thanks to the deeply embedded narrative of a rivalry between Orient and Occident, Muslims and Christians, this brought forth the functional enactment of a Muslim naturalization ban that stood in place for 154 years. In other words, Muslims have been banned from becoming citizens for the bulk of the existence of the United States as a sovereign nation. What can be labeled as the structural Orientalism that prevailed during the naturalization era is akin to the structural Islamophobia reflected in today's laws, programs, and policies targeting Muslims; indeed, those early institutional roots shaped how law understands Muslim identity, as well as how Muslims are policed by the state.

The Muslim naturalization ban that prevailed during this era also impacted Christians and Jews from the Middle East. Although George Shishim successfully petitioned for his naturalization, not all Christian Middle Eastern petitioners overcame the suspicion that hailing from the Middle East made them Muslim. A 1913 case involving an immigrant petitioner from modern-day Lebanon, *Ex parte Shahid*, illustrates how Muslim identity was acutely racialized and deeply institutionalized during this time. Following George Shishim's lead, Faras Shahid, a Maronite Christian, asserted his Christian faith to rebut the presumption that he was a Muslim. Judge Henry Smith engaged in his own brand of in-court eugenics, describing Shahid to be "about [the color] of a walnut, or somewhat darker than is the usual mulatto of one-half mixed blood between the white and the negro races."[38] According to Judge Smith, Shahid's dark skin signaled that he was either Muslim or the product of racial miscegenation with Muslims that diluted his Christianity and ultimately undermined his petition for American citizenship. The appeal to miscegenation demonstrates that Judge Smith understood Muslim identity in pointedly racial terms, and as in the infamous *Plessy v.*

Ferguson "separate but equal" case, used the language of the "one-drop rule" to hold that any modicum of Muslim blood made Shahid, before the eyes of the court, a Muslim.

Before denying Shahid's petition, Judge Smith drilled home the Orientalist baseline that Muslim identity was indeed a racial one. In his opinion, he wrote, "What is the race or color of the modern inhabitant of Syria it is impossible to say. No geographical area of the world has been more mixed since history began. Originally of Hittite or non-Semitic races ... then again followed by another Semitic conquest in the shape of the Arabian Mahometan [Muslim] eruption."[39] Smith's framing of Ottoman rule as the "Mahometan eruption" illustrates his aversion to Islam, which today would be characterized as an example of structural Islamophobia. More than a century before immigration officials, politicians, and pundits would view with suspicion and fear the Muslim identity of Syrian refugees fleeing civil war and persecution from ISIS, the South Carolina court viewed Islam the same way.

In the early twentieth century, the vast majority of immigrants coming to the United States from modern-day Syria and Lebanon were Christians, not Muslims, who were nevertheless suspected to be Muslims. Some Christian immigrants, like George Shishim, were able to overcome that presumption, while others, like Faras Shahid, were not (see table). Then, in 1915, the fate of Christians from the Middle East, and specifically the Levant (modern-day Lebanon, Syria, Jordan, Israel, and Palestine) would be resolved once and for all.

In *Dow v. United States,* the Fourth Circuit Court of Appeals established that "Syrian Christians fit within the statutory definition of whiteness"[40] and as a class of immigrants could be naturalized as American citizens. Muslim immigrants from the same region, however, were still prohibited from citizenship, as were

Naturalization-Era Cases Involving Immigrant Petitioners from the Middle East

Case	Petitioner Identity and Court Ruling
George Shishim v. United States (1909), Los Angeles Superior Court	A Lebanese (Maronite) Christian resident of Los Angeles, California, was granted citizenship on grounds of religious identity.
In re Najour (1909), Circuit Court for the Northern District of Georgia	A Lebanese (Maronite) Christian, Costa George Najour, who resided in Georgia, was granted citizenship on grounds of religious identity.
In re Mudarri (1910), Massachusetts Circuit Court	A Syrian Christian born in Damascus who settled in Massachusetts was granted citizenship on the grounds of physical appearance and religious identity.
In re Ellis (1910), District Court of Oregon	Ellis (who likely changed his name from the Arabic Elias to enhance his naturalization petition) was a (Maronite) Christian from Beirut who settled in Oregon. He was granted citizenship on the grounds of religious identity and physical appearance.
Ex parte Shahid (1913), Eastern District Court of South Carolina	A (Maronite) Christian from Lebanon who settled in South Carolina was denied his petition for citizenship on the grounds of physical appearance, specifically, his dark complexion.
Ex parte Dow (1914), Eastern District Court of South Carolina	George Dow was a (Maronite) Christian from Batroun (Lebanon) who settled in South Carolina. His petition for naturalization was denied on the grounds of his Middle Eastern origins.
In re Dow (1914), Eastern District Court of South Carolina (Appeal)	Dow's appeal was denied by the South Carolina court, which affirmed that he was not white and could not become a naturalized citizen.

Dow v. United States (1915), Fourth Circuit Court of Appeals	Dow won his appeal in the Fourth Circuit Court, establishing the precedent that Syrian Christians as a class fit the statutory definition of whiteness and could become naturalized American citizens.
In re Ahmed Hassan (1942), Eastern District Court of Michigan	A Muslim petitioner from Yemen was found to be non-white on account of his religious identity and his petition for naturalization was rejected.
Ex parte Mohriez (1944), District Court of Massachusetts	Mohriez was a Muslim from Saudi Arabia who filed his petition for naturalization after the United States brokered strong economic/political relations with his country of origin. The court granted Mohriez citizenship in the interest of not disrupting "friendlier relations between the U.S.... and other nations."

Muslims from throughout the rest of the region that Orientalists dubbed the Middle East. *Dow* was a landmark decision because it emphatically held that as long as they were Christians, immigrants from the Levant were white by law, thus broadening the parameters of whiteness in the same way that earlier developments had assimilated Jewish, Irish, and Italian people. In addition, it established an early rule that Christians from the Arab world were racially different from Muslims from the very same lands, further illustrating how deeply conflated religion and race were during the naturalization era, and more specifically, how closely tethered Christianity was to whiteness and Islam was to otherness.

The Muslim naturalization ban continued until 1944.[41] This had the effect of suppressing Muslim migration into the United States and of encouraging religious conversion or "passing as

Christian" on the part of many who did migrate.[42] In 1924, approximately 95 percent of the immigrants who resettled in the United States from the Arab world were Christians, while only 4 percent identified as Muslims.[43] This illustrates the immense impact of the Muslim naturalization ban not only on who could and could not become a citizen, but also on who did and did not emigrate to the United States. Many Muslim immigrants, aware of the judicial animus toward their faith, chose not to migrate to the United States. Others likely converted or passed as Christians in order to stave off anti-Muslim animus and enhance their prospects of assimilation and naturalization.

Muslim immigrants who confirmed their religious identity, like Ahmed Hassan of Yemen, were denied naturalization when they sought it.[44] In Hassan's case, litigated in Michigan, Judge Arthur J. Tuttle's opinion centered on the belief that Muslims "as a class would [not] readily intermarry with our population and be assimilated into our civilization."[45] Marriage was a proxy for assimilability, and for Judge Tuttle, the belief that Muslims would not intermarry with Christians, or should not intermarry with Christians, confirmed the Orientalist baseline that Muslims could not be integrated. Although Muslim immigrants began to trickle into the United States at a higher clip in 1942, the Michigan court rejected Ahmed's petition. In addition to Hassan's religion, Yemen's distance from Europe and Hassan's "darkness of skin"[46] were arguments Judge Tuttle cited in rejecting Ahmed's petition for citizenship.

Anticipating Ben Carson's 2015 claim that "Islam is inconsistent with the Constitution"[47] and Louisiana governor Bobby Jindal's statement, that same year, that Muslim immigration is part of an attempt to "overtake the culture" of the West,[48] the *Hassan* court's framing of Islam as threatening to American values and society carried the Muslim naturalization ban forward. Indeed, the very stereotypes instrumental to the courts' understanding of Islam have been echoed, in virtually identical terms, by today's Islamophobia-peddling politicians.

The Muslim naturalization ban lasted until American geopolitical interests in the Muslim world shifted, specifically when the need for Saudi oil facilitated its judicial dissolution in 1944.[49] The case that spurred the dissolution of the longstanding Muslim ban involved a Saudi Muslim immigrant petitioning for citizenship in a Massachusetts court. Mohammed Mohriez walked into court with his quintessential Arab physical features, dark skin kissed and colored by the scorching Saudi sun, fully candid about his religious beliefs. To borrow a phrase that prominent Muslim American civil rights activist Linda Sarsour has often applied to herself, Mohriez arrived in court "unapologetically Muslim."[50] His prospects for citizenship would fall or advance without his shrinking from his religious identity.

His case came before Judge Charles Wyzanski eleven years after the United States, and President Herbert Hoover, formed the Arabian American Oil Company (ARAMCO) with the fledgling Kingdom of Saudi Arabia, which had recently unearthed phenomenal reserves of crude oil—oil needed to fuel automobiles, a booming economy, a two-front war (World War II), and American foreign policy aspirations. Judge Wyzanski's ruling would impact far more than the citizenship fate of one Muslim immigrant. It had the potential to disrupt or enhance the economic interests of the United States in Saudi Arabia and its political aspirations within the broader Middle East—a region rising from colonialism and coveted by both the United States and its emerging rival, the USSR. On that day in 1944, when the world and America's position in it were radically changing, the naturalization interests of

Mohriez, a Muslim immigrant, converged with the foreign policy and economic interests of the United States.[51] The court's ruling would impact far more than the fate of one Muslim immigrant.

Judge Wyzanski granted Mohriez's petition for naturalization, and so at long last Muslim immigrants could become citizens. However, political interests were more important than principle in delivering the formal dissolution of the longstanding Muslim naturalization ban. As a result of this case, Middle Eastern historian Sarah Gualteiri writes, Arab Muslims became "'honorary whites,' those accepted into the nation but still under suspicion that they did not quite deserve it. Whereas the Christian identity of Syrian applicants in the racial prerequisite cases had been central to their argument for whiteness, Muslim Arabs were at their whitest when stripped of their religious identity"[52] —and, as exemplified by the Mohriez case, when the citizenship interests of Muslim immigrants aligned with the foreign and economic policy interests of the state.

The two cases that established that Syrian Christians and Arab Muslims were to be legally considered white, *Dow* (1915) and *Mohriez* (1944), are the basis of the modern legal classification of Arab and Middle Eastern Americans as white by law. This is a paradoxical designation considering the sociopolitical and legal stigmatization of Arab and Middle Eastern identity today,[53] as well as the rise of structural Islamophobia. This has pushed activists, civic organizations,[54] and scholars, including myself and law scholar John Tehranian, to advocate on behalf the "Middle Eastern and North African" (MENA) box that the United States Census Bureau may add to the 2020 census.[55]

Although the Naturalization Act of 1952 encouraged more Muslims to come to the United States, the Immigration Act of 1924, which had instituted quotas on immigrants from nations in

Africa, Asia, and the Middle East—home to sizable Muslim populations and many Muslim-majority nations—was still in effect. Despite a spike, from 1948 until 1965, in the number of students from Muslim-majority countries studying in the United States,[56] strict immigration quotas continued to stifle Muslim immigrants' ability to enter the United States, and suppressed their numbers within the country.[57] On one front, immigration restrictions against Muslims were eroding, but the Orientalism that fed the restrictions fluidly mutated into other forms of state policy and programming.

The Civil Rights Act, signed into law by President Lyndon Johnson in 1964, opened the door for the dissolution of these immigration quotas by way of the Immigration and Nationality Act of 1965, and it subsequently opened the door for Muslims to migrate to the United States and pursue citizenship without the obstacle of racial mandates or in-court religious vetting. As historian Kambiz GhaneaBassiri, author of *A History of Islam in America,* writes, "Thanks to the Civil Rights Movement, ... these new Asian and African Muslim immigrants came to the United States [and] did not have to change their names or dissimulate their religion."[58]

And yet, though the rights granted in 1964 and 1965 did change conditions in many positive ways, Islamophobia was not magically removed from the United States, but rather morphed into new forms, as it had in the past. The Islamophobia that pervades government structures and the minds of Americans today rises from a bleak history, judicial memory, and a naturalization ban that stood for 154 years—a ban that was enforced by the courts long before Trump proposed another while campaigning for the presidency and rode the tide of Islamophobia all the way to the White House.

CHAPTER THREE

A Reoriented "Clash of Civilizations"

There can be no true friends without true enemies. Unless we hate what we are not, we cannot love what we are.

Samuel P. Huntington, *The Clash of Civilizations and the Remaking of World Order*

One always has exaggerated ideas about what one doesn't know.

Albert Camus, *The Stranger*

"This is the deadliest terror attack on U.S. soil. A U.S. government source has told CBS News that it has Middle Eastern terrorism written all over it,"[1] reported Connie Chung minutes after the Alfred P. Murrah Federal Building in downtown Oklahoma City was bombed on April 19, 1995. The words from Chung were uttered with the certitude that the culprits of what would become known as the Oklahoma City bombing were "Middle Eastern," a people from a region broadly conflated with Islam and, over and again, terrorism.

The swift reporting of "Middle Eastern terrorism" did not come from the mouths of lay citizens or reactionary hatemongers, but were the words of Connie Chung, a journalistic icon who spoke only when she was entirely certain—or so my sixteen-year-old mind believed, because she spoke from behind one of the nation's most respected media desks. This country, of which I was a citizen, had been attacked by the region my family hailed from, which indicted my family and me and drove a sharp wedge between both halves of my identity, Muslim and American. In the immediate wake of the Oklahoma City bombing, I felt obligated to choose between them.

I ran to my mother, who was still sleeping, echoing what Chung reported live on television. "Mama, a government building in Oklahoma City was bombed by Muslims," I relayed, instantly causing her to jump out of bed and race over to the television. It had only been two years since the 1993 World Trade Center bombing, an incident that spurred considerable backlash against the Arab, Middle Eastern, and Muslim American communities concentrated in the metropolitan Detroit area where we lived. Mosques were vandalized, children accosted, women with headscarves attacked—the robust underbelly of anti-Muslim attitudes and hatred were fully exposed. However, this attack in Oklahoma City was far bigger in scale than the World Trade Center bombing, claiming the lives of 168 men, women, and children, injuring 680 more, and destroying hundreds of other buildings near the federal building.

"This was the deadliest attack on American soil," several news anchors repeated, with many prominent journalists rushing with lighting speed to proclaim that the Oklahoma City attack had "every single earmark of the Islamic car-bombers of the Middle East" and that "the betting here is on Middle East terrorists."[2]

How could they be so certain that the culprits were Muslims only minutes after the attack had taken place? Did these journalists, and the handful of "self-proclaimed 'terrorism experts'" they routinely relied upon (none of whom were Muslims)[3] swiftly compile evidence from the scene of the explosions to substantiate their findings? Or were their *expert* conclusions driven more by their imaginations, laden with ideas and images of terrorism that conflated it deeply with Islam and the Middle East, instead of the circumstantial evidence typically needed for good-faith assessments?

"The hate toward us is going to get far worse," my mother whispered in Arabic as she absorbed the words coming from the screen, and I nodded in agreement, fearing she and my older sister, Khalida, would be more vulnerable to the looming hate violence because they wore headscarves. We braced ourselves for the backlash, particularly after hearing stories of an elderly Muslim man being assaulted at a community grocery store, the Al-Fajr mosque in Indianapolis being shot up, and an editor of an Islamic newspaper being threatened, "We'll shoot you! We'll send you back. You don't belong here."[4]

Everybody, most notably my mother, was on high alert, frightened that our community mosque, or worse, one of us, would fall victim to a bigot. A seamstress and single parent, my mother feared what the world had in store for her and her three children. The following morning, she ordered my brother Mohammed and me, with her piercing eyes and words, to come "right back home after school," and gave special instruction to my sister to "be sure you are always with somebody, don't stay by yourself," fearing that Khalida's headscarf would isolate her, make her a target.

This experience was not unique to my family or within the Muslim American community concentrated in the metropolitan Detroit area, but was akin to the fear and storyline that united Muslims who were summarily cast as accomplices in the Oklahoma City bombing. It was years before 9/11, but the animus and violence that descended on our hometown felt a lot like what was to come six years later.

Minutes after the Oklahoma City attack, and well before a formal investigation into the bombing had commenced, the mainstream media, the majority of the American public, and soon after, the state ruled that "Middle Eastern terrorists" were the culprits, focusing the collective rage on Muslims at large. Regardless of our status as citizens, the faith that held us collectively culpable made us vulnerable to the backlash and scapegoating that was sure to come. Just as swiftly as leading journalists blamed Muslims for the Oklahoma City attack, our status as Americans was materially diminished to second- or third-class citizenship,[5] if not entirely stripped from us. This was further illustrated by how the external allegations of blame converged with the internal swelling of fear, promptly denying Muslim Americans of the opportunity to partake in the national mourning for the scores of lives lost that Wednesday in Oklahoma City.

Before we could fully absorb the magnitude of the attack and brace ourselves for the collateral hatred that would come our way, investigators found the real culprits. Two days after the bombing, Attorney General Janet Reno revealed the name and identity of the culprit. He was not Arab or Middle Eastern, but white. He was not Muslim, but Christian. He was not even an immigrant, or the child of immigrants, but a born-and-bred citizen from the American heartland.

Timothy McVeigh was a former military man who attended Ku Klux Klan protests, wore white power T-shirts, and conspired with other white supremacists to carry out the Oklahoma City bombing on April 19, 1995. McVeigh's identity clashed with the strategically crafted and furiously deployed caricature of the Middle Eastern Muslim extremist, an image that had become synonymous with terrorism in the minds of most Americans. This, despite studies indicating that 77 percent of "terrorism and related events" in the United States in the 1980s were committed by U.S.-based white men.[6] However, for journalists who were quick to indict Muslims, the force of stereotypes trumped the weight of these statistics. Perhaps they did not take the time to check who was actually responsible for terrorizing Americans; journalists, like people at every level of public and private life, allowed themselves to be swept up in prejudice and stereotypes.

There were no "Middle Eastern terrorists," despite what Chung and a myriad of reputable journalists reported on that day. Mainstream news anchors incessantly stoked fears about and warned of subsequent attacks by Muslim boogeymen who were nowhere to be found in Oklahoma City. The boogeyman in their midst was a white Christian man, aided and abetted by other white Christian men.

But it did not matter. The conflation of terrorism with being Muslim and Middle Eastern was deeply institutionalized within CBS, ABC, CNN, and the rest of the American media industry, which endorsed a stereotype already stamped on the minds of the millions of Americans who collected in front of television screens to watch the carnage in Oklahoma City. Even after revealing McVeigh as the culprit, journalists like CNN's Wolf Blitzer desperately peddled the notion that "There is still a possibility that there could have been some sort of connection to

Middle East terrorism,"[7] even after the highest-ranking lawyer in the land ruled that no Muslims or people of Middle Eastern descent had been involved. And so the backlash continued in Dearborn, Michigan; Patterson, New Jersey; Chicago; Los Angeles; and other concentrated Muslim communities across the country. In many ways, the violence was even worse against Arabs, Muslims and Middle Easterners living outside of such communities. While concentrated Muslim communities were easy targets for hatemongers, they had the networks, institutions, and leadership to soften the blow and brace for the backlash. Muslims and Muslim families in areas where they stood alone, or in scarce number, had no immediate sources of support or refuge.

This chapter examines the period immediately before the formal emergence of modern Islamophobia on September 11, 2001. This era witnessed the rearticulation of the Orientalist binary that pitted Islam and the Middle East—imagined as one monolithic civilization—against the West, a geopolitical theory known as a "clash of civilizations." The theory became an immensely influential essay-turned-book by Harvard University political scientist Samuel P. Huntington.

This clash between the United States (as proxy for and guardian of Western civilization) and Islam revitalized and redeployed the stereotypes rooted in Orientalism and armed the state with a supposed reason to mount a pre-war on terror against Muslims on the domestic front and Arab and Muslim-majority countries abroad. The conversion of clash of civilizations theory into formal national security strategy and policy was enabled by the media misrepresentations of Islam, which primed the polity for the war on Muslims long before the war on terror.

MADE IN THE IMAGE OF OUR ENEMY

A wall once bisected Berlin. The western half of the city belonged to the Federal Republic of Germany, a sovereign nation wed to the same democratic and capitalist principles as its European neighbors to the west, and the United States. The eastern half of Berlin was a satellite of the Soviet Union, guarded from 1961 to 1989 by the iron curtain of communism. West versus east. Good versus evil. The German city with a wall dividing it, smack in the heart of the European mainland, stood as a vivid symbol of the familiar binaries that have long driven the politics of empire and the propaganda campaigns crafted to fuel them.

American identity during the Cold War (1947–1991) rested heavily on detesting the Soviet Union and the ideas, images, and icons that represented it. Performances of this hate validated one's citizenship, patriotism, and Americanness. Hollywood and television glorified the savior state (the United States), armed with the humanitarian mandate to vanquish a nemesis that threatened not only its own citizenry, but also the stability of the world at large. Freedom-loving soldiers like Rambo and fighting archetypes like Rocky battled rival communists in battleground nations, the boxing ring, or wherever the threat loomed and lingered.[8] Being American during the Cold War rested largely on hating the Soviet Union and communism, and *performing* that hate through political rhetoric, associations, and opposition to anything affiliated with the Soviet Union. Our identity, as Americans, was defined by who and what we hated. And for those aspiring to become American, performance of this hate was a vital part of the process of becoming American.

American Cold War policy, and the real and fictive narratives it inspired, flatly saw the world as two halves: the free world and the communist world, the United States and the Soviet Union. Then, on November 9, 1989, everything changed. Berliners rushed toward the wall from both east and west, destroying a divide that had long segregated families, friends, and country-men. Images of families reuniting, couples embracing, and bits of the crumbled wall lifted up in the Germany sky were broad-cast all over the world, signaling that the Soviet Union was no more, that the "evil empire" the United States had battled for generations was finally defeated.

President Ronald Reagan famously declared, "Here's my strategy on the Cold War: we win and they lose." His vice presi-dent and successor, George H. W. Bush, delivered on that prom-ise. But what, and who, would come next? In a political system dependent on the binary of good and evil, someone or some-thing had to play the role of villain. Who would be the next villain?

The fall of the Soviet Union and the global decline of com-munism left a sociopolitical and existential void for the United States. After decades of saber-rattling, competition, and strife, the United States was the undisputed victor of the Cold War, inspiring celebration in Washington, D.C., and American cities and towns far from it. And now American policy needed a new geopolitical villain to facilitate its foreign policy objectives and carry forward political interests on the home front. The thrill of victory was momentary, ultimately creating a vacuum. The project of expanding the U.S. sphere of influence rested on iden-tifying an archrival and manufacturing the state-sponsored and popular narratives that this archrival's mission was the downfall of the United States. Again, *we are what we hate;* lacking that exis-tential archrival and cultural antithesis created confusion about who *we,* Americans, are and aspire to be.

As evidenced by the breathtakingly swift indictments of "Islamic extremism" minutes after the Oklahoma City bombing, politicians and pundits did not have to look far. The Muslim world would succeed the Soviet Union as the next geopolitical embodiment of evil, the counterimage of America—the Cold War replaced by the formative stages of the eventual war on terror. By resurrecting Orientalist tropes and gazing toward the events unfolding in the Middle East, the United States not only found a suitable replacement, but a more visually foreign and religiously inspired archrival.

Pitching Islam as the new American nemesis did not require much convincing. Stereotypes of Islam as totalitarian, backward, and hostile were deeply embedded in the American imagination, supported by news coverage that regularly showcased airplane hijackers from the Middle East, angry mobs of Arabs collecting in city squares shouting at the camera, and Iran's Ayatollah Khomeini—whom the media and policy positioned as the symbol of the faith at large (although he presided over one nation and was a member of a minority sect of Islam, Twelver Shi'ism) shouting on television, "Death to America, the Great Satan."[9] Indeed, "at the end of the Cold War, Islam became deeply entangled in America's most recent search for a national identity" and was anointed as its new rival in the formation of this new identity.[10] The United States had identified its new geopolitical enemy, and at Harvard University it found the scholar who would help justify the war it would eventually declare against that enemy.

A NEW ORIENTALISM

In 1993, Harvard University political scientist Samuel P. Huntington observed a "new phase" of American geopolitical tension and rivalry. Four years after the fall of the Soviet Union, Huntington would formally declare Islam, and the billions of people it encompassed, to be the existential threat that threatened American harmony and hegemony. In a widely read essay published by *Foreign Affairs* in the summer of 1993, Huntington wrote, "The fundamental problem for the West is not Islamic fundamentalism. It is Islam, a different civilisation whose people are convinced of the superiority of their culture and are obsessed with the inferiority of their power."[11]

Building off of the very East versus West paradigm that framed the Cold War, and revitalizing the tropes that Orientalists ingrained in the minds of Americans and the memory of state institutions during the naturalization era, Huntington theorized that "the most important conflicts of the future will occur along the cultural fault lines that separate these [Islam and the West] from one another."[12] The line in the sand was drawn, and the Muslim world, once again, would be cast as the very image of threat, evil, and therefore everything un-American.

Huntington's clash of civilizations theory did not narrowly pit the United States against "Islamic fundamentalism" or "Middle Eastern terrorists." Rather, the clash Huntington theorized was against the whole of Islam, a faith practiced by 1.7 billion people, millions of them in the United States. Like his Orientalist predecessors, Huntington viewed Islam as a malignant monolith, writing that "Islam's borders are bloody and so are its innards." In the same way that Europeans and Americans invented the Orient, Huntington constructed an "Islamic civilization" that was based on essentialist myths, arcane stereotypes, and most absurdly, a homogenization of a supremely diverse region.

Huntington's reductionist position enabled the attendant ideas, discourses, and propaganda that Muslims were backward, warmongering, and inclined toward terrorism. This flat characterization of Islam allowed the United States, and the broader "Western civilization" it which it belongs, to continue to uphold itself as the bastion of modernity, progress, and liberalism. Revitalizing the principal Orientalist binary of "us versus them" and "they are everything we are not," Huntington echoes, "Unless we hate what we are not, we cannot love what we are." Huntington appropriated the basic theoretical tenets of Orientalism, dressing them with new phrases like "bloody borders," "civilizational clashes," and "Islamic extremists" to explain the Middle East and the world as he saw it.

Huntington's theory was immensely influential both in private American households and, far more deeply, in American halls of power. *The Clash of Civilizations,* initially an influential article that three years later was expanded into a book, was the political theory du jour of the 1990s and beyond. It was broadly assigned in undergraduate and graduate courses across the country, became a *New York Times* best seller, and beyond the academic and popular spheres, steered policy on both the international and domestic fronts.

In addition to recasting Islam—which it falsely contended was a civilizational, sectarian, and ideological monolith—as the geopolitical rival of Western civilization, Huntington's *Clash of Civilizations* equipped policymakers and pundits with a new lexicon for analyzing Islam and Muslims. It included, most notably, the phrase "war on terror." Huntington shaped and advanced this and other terms that would become staples of the political and popular discourse. While the Bush and Clinton administrations initially resisted the framing peddled by Huntington, its ideas, concepts, and language proved immensely resonant in Washington.

Huntington's lexicon dominates how the war on terror is characterized today; much of the mainstream language used to explain the threat of "Islamic extremism" or "fundamentalism" finds its origins on the pages of *The Clash of Civilizations.* The book offers a geopolitical paradigm and terminology that primed the state and society for the war on terror, a paradigm and terminology still operative more than two decades later.

Like American Orientalists of the eighteenth, nineteenth, and twentieth centuries, who enacted policy on the grounds of Islam being an enemy race, Huntington lobbied that Islam was not simply a religion, but a rival civilization and violent ideology that—despite regional wars in the Muslim world, sectarian tension and divide, and more than fives times the number of Muslims living outside of the Middle East than within it—had coalesced to stage war against the United States. More than simply a competing and inferior ideology, like communism, Islam posed a far greater civilizational threat, Huntington warned. The "bloody borders" separating Islam and the West were far older, wider, and more violent than the rift separating the United States and its fallen Cold War foe, and were rooted in a religious crusade that Muslims were bent on revitalizing. As Orientalists yesterday and Islamophobes today routinely proclaim, "Islam is not even a religion; it is a social, political system that uses a deity to advance its agenda of global conquest."[13] The famous American Orientalist and Princeton University scholar Bernard Lewis echoed in his bestselling 2003 book, *The Crisis of Islam,* that Islam is not merely a religion, but a "civilization that grew up and flourished under the aegis of a religion."[14]

Columbia University professor Hamid Dabashi reflects on the work of Lewis, who contends that he, and not Huntington, modeled the clash of civilizations theory. Dabashi observed, "As early as the 1950s he [Lewis] had envisioned the clash of civilizations, and to this day he remains incensed that the idea is credited to Samuel Huntington. Since the early 1960s, he has published books which repeatedly rattle on about the opposition of the two sides, including *The Middle East and the West* (1964), *Islam and the West* (1994), *Cultures in Conflict* (1996), *The Muslim Discovery of Europe* (2001), and *What Went Wrong* (2003), laying the groundwork for [Francis] Fukuyama and Huntington."[15] So although he popularized the phrase "clash of civilizations" and gave it momentum in the public and political spheres, Huntington was not an isolated actor peddling the worldview that the United States was on a civilizational collision course with Islam. These scholars, Orientalists of the highest order, were simply dressing old Orientalist ideas and arguments in modern terms and catchy phrases.

It did not take much for Washington to buy what Huntington, Lewis, and their ideological counterparts were selling. "By 2000, the ideas of Fukuyama and Huntington had so utterly stormed Washington that militant Islamism had moved to the center" of its agendas.[16] The rhetoric that argues that Islam is not simply a religion, but a menacing political ideology and rival civilization, is regularly uttered by politicians, illustrating Huntington's (and Lewis's) influence in Washington and the staying power of Huntington's clash of civilizations theory.

It's important to note that Huntington's theory did not gain resonance because of its intellectual rigor; he was, after all, scathingly denigrated by scholars within political science, law, and other academic disciplines. Rather, his theory gained momentum because of its political expediency on two key fronts: first, because it filled the void for a new geopolitical nemesis left by the Soviet Union; and second, because Huntington's simplified construction of a menacing Islamic civilization was deeply familiar, having already been embedded within the collective American imagination and the halls of power. With a new civilizational rival in place, and the theoretical framework and lexicon developed to push it forward by way of policy, the next step was peddling the threat of this repackaged menace to the American public by way of news, television, and film. A new evil empire, even more extreme and ominous that the communist threat that came before it, was conspiring to bring down America.

Muslim Americans and Muslim residents of the United States found themselves in the crosshairs of this new civilizational standoff. And unlike Russian citizens or immigrants during the Cold War, who could generally find safe haven on account of their whiteness and ability to blend in to mainstream society, Muslim Americans were generally more conspicuous and consequently more vulnerable to private and structural bigotry. As immigration and citizenship scholar Linda Bosniak argues in *The Citizen and the Alien,* "Formal citizenship status often fails to protect people from exclusion and violence directed at those perceived to be 'foreign' in character, habit, or appearance."[17] And for Muslim Americans, amid the buildup toward a "clash of civilizations" and the war on terror it facilitated, their faith, again, became the very marker of foreignness and menace.

COVERING ISLAM

Six months before Donald Trump announced his presidential run, Clint Eastwood's modern wartime drama, *American Sniper,* hit American theaters nationwide. The film, starring Hollywood heartthrob Bradley Cooper in the lead role and based on a true story, centers on one soldier's exploits and precision as a sniper in the Iraq War. This film was released well after the war on terror became formal state policy, but it provides a compelling case study that illustrates the resonance of the core ideas and binary seeded by Orientalism and *The Clash of Civilizations*. *American Sniper* would become emblematic of this new era of American Islamophobia and a lasting and lurid representation of the deep and robust connections between Islamophobia and the systems that came before it.

The Iraq War, a campaign of misdirected vengeance launched less than two years after the 9/11 terror attacks, provided the context for the film. In the film, "Iraqis are nothing more than fodder and foes, whom Chris Kyle [the American sniper] is hell bent on gunning down."[18] And that is precisely what he does, throughout the film, with extraordinary efficiency and a cold-blooded trigger finger. One Iraqi after the other, Kyle systematically shoots down Muslims wearing headscarves and other traditional clothing, mowing down "raghead" after "raghead."

Kyle finishes his celebrated career as a wartime sniper with 255 victims. Not a single one of them is assigned a name or given a voice; pictured from a distance and stripped of any agency, they are presumed by the sniper—and the American viewer he tacitly represents—to be guilty and worthy of death. "Whether a veiled mother, young boy, or the fictitious rival Mustafa—the black-clad, brooding embodiment of [the terrorist]" is dedicated to Kyle's demise, and more broadly, the downfall of the United States.[19] Every Muslim who appeared on the screen was a probable culprit, giving Kyle license to shoot him or her.

The film, which generated over $350 million in North America and roughly $500 million globally, was a box-office smash and a critical hit. *American Sniper* became the highest-grossing war film in Hollywood history[20] and helped prime the American electorate for the Islamophobic rhetoric Trump peddled at his raucous campaign rallies, during the Republican Party debates, and during interviews with CNN, Fox News, and other media outlets. Indeed, many of the audiences that rushed to the theaters to watch *American Sniper* later raced to the voting polls to vote for the candidate who, like Kyle, spoke about Islam and Muslims in the most vile, subhuman terms.

Showcasing Islamophobia was big business, essential for currying popular support for formal law and government programs enacted to push and promote wars abroad and police and punish Muslims at home. Before 9/11, the war in Iraq, and the global war on terror, mass media centered on America's new civilizational nemesis, Islam. Hollywood produced a range of blockbusters, including 1994's *True Lies,* starring Arnold Schwarzenegger; 1996's *Executive Decision,* featuring Kurt Russell and Steven Segal; and 2000's *Rules of Engagement,* with Samuel L. Jackson and Tommie Lee Jones. A long line of films re-created Huntington's civilizational rivalry on screen: the American hero swooping into the desert to conquer Islamic extremism, or safeguarding Americans on the home front from the dark-skinned terrorist toting the Qur'an in one hand and a machine gun in the other. The narrative championed in these movies featured our most beloved movie stars espousing racist and religious slurs, and for two hours or more, beating, bashing, and killing Muslims.

The heroes and villains on screen were molded in the image of their counterparts on the news. Evelyn Alsultany, one of the nation's foremost experts on representations of Arabs and Muslims in the media, observes that,

> Significant shifts toward portraying Arabs and/or Muslims as terrorists in the 1970s are evident not only in Hollywood filmmaking but also in U.S. corporate news media.... [The] Americans'

association of the Middle East with the Christian Holy Land or Arab oil wealth shifted to a place of Muslim terror through news reporting on the Munich Olympics (1972), the Arab oil embargo (1973), the Iran hostage crisis (1979–1980), and airplane hijackings in the 1970s and 1980s. The news media came to play a crucial role in making the Middle East, and Islam in particular, meaningful to Americans as a place that breeds terrorism.[21]

The images and ideas filtered by the news media were virtually indistinguishable from film, and vice versa, affirming and reaffirming the ideas that the United States was at war with Islam and Muslims were vested in killing Americans at home and abroad.

The Muslim world presented in this American media is one contiguous and consolidated territory, gripped by endless war and irredeemable turbulence, a perfect vacuum for cultivating terrorism and terrorists. Its inhabitants are backward and static, nameless and angry, violent and irrational. They are not people to be engaged or judged in individual terms, but rather a faceless bloc that can be explained with sweeping ease and reduced to a fundamental essence.

A series of new stories arose in the 1980s and 1990s, priming Hollywood and television for a new wave of Orientalist propaganda. I will examine two: the Iran hostage crisis of 1979–1981 and the Persian Gulf War of 1991.

The Iran hostage crisis, which lasted from November 4, 1979, to January 20, 1981, cast the new Islamic government of Iran and its charismatic bearded and turbaned leader, Ruhollah Khomeini, as the modern embodiments of Islamic evil. The overthrow of Shah Mohammed Reza Pahlavi in 1979 gave way to the rise of a new Islamic theocracy in Iran, unseating one of the strongest *U.S.* allies in the region with a regime it would anoint as one of its greatest adversaries.[22] The turnover of power also led to the takeover of the U.S. embassy in Tehran and the holding of fifty-two American diplomats as hostages. President Jimmy Carter, who ultimately lost his bid for reelection in 1982 because of the events that unfolded in Iran, dubbed the takeover of the American embassy an "act of terrorism."[23]

News coverage of the hostage crisis echoed Carter's words to a captive American audience that watched the news in record numbers. Special programming such as ABC's *America Held Hostage* communicated the message that America at large, and Americans everywhere, were being victimized by the brown, bearded Muslim extremists in the Middle East. The fear stoked by the mainstream news also warned of a Muslim takeover stateside, corroborated in the minds of viewers by the rising Muslim population and the "significant rise in the number of mosques and Muslim associations in the 1970s and 1980s."[24] Again, citizenship did not protect Muslim Americans from being roped into guilt and conflated with an incident that was neither representative of Islam nor unfolding domestically, but one perpetrated by a specific nation-state on the other side of the world.

The hostage crisis lasted for 444 days, and mainstream television and print media capitalized on each day to deliver story lines, images, and narratives that drove the fear of Islam and a new encroaching Muslim threat into the private confines of every American home. Although the Soviet Union still stood as the primary geopolitical threat to the United States throughout the duration of the hostage crisis, coverage of the crisis alerted Americans to the threat that would eventually supplant it. Indeed, "the Islamic revolution of Iran and the hostage crisis became emblematic of the 'threat of Islam,'"[25] which news coverage readily and regularly delivered to an American public that could not turn away from its television screens. As Nathan Lean tells in his compelling book *The Islamophobia Industry*, reporting on the hostage crisis netted considerable revenues for television news networks and newspapers, and in CNN's case established it as a major cable news station and commodity.

The collateral revenue generated by other franchises, most notably the 1991 drama *Not without My Daughter* (based on the book of the same title), starring Sally Field and Alfred Molina, was considerable. In the film, Molina plays Moody, the Iranian American (and tritely named) lead who transforms from a loving secular husband while in the United States into a violent extremist when his wife (played by Field) and daughter visit Iran with him. The film, based on a true story, capitalizes on the very stereotypes the news showcased during its coverage of the Iran hostage crisis, garnering a broad audience, syndication, and for the filmmakers, a proven story line for commercial success.

The nine years between the Iran hostage crisis and the Persian Gulf War in 1990 witnessed seismic reform in the geopolitical landscape and drastic changes on the American home front. The Soviet Union and the global threat of communism were no more, Iran's Ayatollah Khomeini passed away in June of 1989, and following Ronald Reagan's two terms in office, George H. W. Bush continued Republican dominance of the White House.

In his second year in office, President Bush formally kicked off the transition toward making the Muslim world the new geopolitical foe of the United States by launching Operation Desert Shield against Iraq and its secular dictator, Saddam Hussein. Hussein's army had taken over the nearby state of Kuwait on June 2, 1990, and threatened to move into the Kingdom of Saudi Arabia, one of the strongest U.S. allies and its primary supplier of crude oil. In response, Bush deployed American forces to

Saudi Arabia, and the media machine turned against Saddam Hussein, who only years before had been Washington's close friend and ally during Iraq's bloody eight-year war with Iran. According to historian Kambiz GhaneaBassiri, "The event that most significantly affected the history of Islam in America at the outset of the 1990s was the Persian Gulf War."[26]

Coverage of the Persian Gulf War bolstered the modern image of the menacing Arab, synonymous with Muslim, in the mind of the American viewer. The Iranians at the center of the hostage crisis were not Arab, and the Iranian government the United States tapped as the embodiment of Islamic fundamentalism was a Shiite-controlled state, whereas Hussein himself was a secular Sunni Muslim. But these distinctions were unimportant to most Americans, who conflated Iranian with Arab and had no clue what Sunni or Shiite meant. Saddam Hussein, whom the news media focused on by way of special reports, vignettes, and documentaries, succeeded his old foe, the Ayatollah Khomeini, in becoming the new embodiment of Muslim terror.

For ABC, NBC, CBS, and the upstart CNN (the only major American network that provided twenty-four-hour news coverage), the fact that Hussein was an ardent secularist and alleged pan-Arab nationalist, again, was of no importance. He was dark, Arab, and from a region tethered to the maligned faith of Islam, so he fit the role. News outlets consistently emphasized the Iraqi dictator's identity as Muslim, shaping the narrative in line with the "clash of civilizations" binary.

Hussein, however, was no innocent bystander. He abetted the process, launching scud missiles toward Israel, adding *'allahu akbar* ("God is greater") to the Iraqi flag, and claiming "to be the religious warrior or *mujahid* who was going to unfetter Mecca from its American shackles."[27] While "the whole world was watching" news coverage of the Persian Gulf War,[28] the American audience was getting to know a dictator and the strategically crafted civilizational threat he allegedly represented, a civilizational threat it would meet again after 9/11 and the formal declaration of the war on terror. Hussein and his regime survived the first U.S. incursion against it. However, news coverage of the first war in Iraq would stay in the American public's consciousness, and in 2003, George H. W. Bush's son, George W. Bush, would tap into that consciousness and declare a second, and much more prolonged, war on Iraq.

Hollywood, television, and news media were—and continue to be—indispensable collaborators in the broad project of casting Islam as a civilizational threat. In *Covering Islam,* Edward Said observes, "To make 'our' attitudes to Islam very clear, a whole information and policymaking apparatus in the United States depends on these illusions and diffuses them widely."[29] Indeed, the "clash of civilizations" theory shaped the direction of state structures, the rhetoric of government officials, and foreign and domestic policy, and the media delivered to a primed American public the familiar stereotypes and tropes that Orientalism had originally ingrained. All of this set the conditions for the structural and private Islamophobia that would emerge after the 9/11 terror attacks.

But the state adopted policies targeting Muslim citizens and immigrants long before the structural reforms and strident laws enacted in the wake of 9/11. Almost a year to the day after the Oklahoma City bombing, the law would follow the anti-Muslim animus peddled by scholars, reported by news anchors, and featured in film. On April 24, 1996, with broad bipartisan support, President Bill Clinton signed into law the Antiterrorism and Effective Death Penalty Act, which focused on policing Arab and Muslim elements within the United States, and which stands as a principal pre-9/11 example of structural Islamophobia.

The law, on its face, aimed to "deter terrorism, provide justice for victims, [and] provide for an effective death penalty" for culprits of terrorism. However, its enforcement disproportionately targeted Middle Eastern and Muslim subjects, the very same demographic Connie Chung, the media at large, and most Americans presumed to be terrorists. The vast majority of designated foreign terrorist groups were of a Muslim character or based in the Middle East. Muslim Americans who traveled back to their homelands, sent remittances to support family members, or were involved with religious or political organizations found themselves being profiled or suspected of "abetting terrorism," while immigrants were viewed with heightened suspicion.

The United States was locked in a "clash of civilizations" with Islam, prominent academics theorized and news anchors reported, pushing the state to enact laws and policy that aligned with this binary. Never mind the racial or religious identity of the Oklahoma City bomber, Timothy McVeigh, who represented the demographic that commits the vast majority of terror attacks on U.S. soil.[30] Stereotypes, not statistics or specifics, mattered most to Orientalists, proponents of the clash of civilizations, and Islamophobes who would beat the war-on-terror drums in the era to come. Terrorism, for the state, was not defined generally or neutrally, but focused exclusively on Islam and Muslims.

CHAPTER FOUR

War on Terror, War on Muslims

> Our war on terror begins with Al Qaeda, but it does not end there.
>
> President George W. Bush, September 20, 2001

> It's not right to respond to terrorism by terrorizing other people.
>
> Howard Zinn, *Terrorism and War*

"America is a wonderful place," Harjit Sodhi would routinely tell his older brother, Balbir Singh Sodhi, trying to coax him to follow in his footsteps and move from Punjab, India, to California. Balbir loved his home country, and the people and places that colored the only life he knew. Leaving India, and everybody behind, would be extremely difficult. But his brother, Harjit, would lobby him every time they spoke.

His brother finally convinced him in 1988. Holding back tears while packing his bags, Balbir left India to reunite with his brother in California. He left home for a brave new world, where his appearance was no longer a common sight but the object of stares, suspicion, and in the years to come, fear.

Like many other immigrants, thirty-seven-year-old Balbir worked odd jobs to make ends meet in Los Angeles. He worked at a 7–Eleven convenience store for several years, and after hearing that he could earn more for himself and his family as a cab driver in the San Francisco Bay Area, moved north to Walnut Creek, east of Oakland, to join the ranks of the city's fleet of cabbies. "He worked 12, 14 hours a day, and saved his pennies," his brother Harjit shared,[1] testifying to the grit and determination his brother had in providing for his family, purchasing a home, and converting the dream that lured him to the United States from his beloved India into a reality.

In 2000, he took major strides toward that dream, purchasing a beautiful home in Mesa, Arizona, and a gas station that he paid for with his hard-earned savings. His new business enabled him to provide for his two daughters in ways that were once unfathomable for the Sikh immigrant from India and, in line with a promise he made to himself before leaving for the United States, he regularly sent money back to family members relying on him back home.[2] Balbir Sohdi had made it: he was a living example of the American dream realized, an immigrant who left everything behind to come to a new country, with nothing except a willingness to work hard and make a better life for himself and his loved ones. Twelve years after his arrival in America, he was a citizen, a homeowner, and the head of a thriving business. He loved the country that afforded him the opportunity to realize these goals.

Like all of America, Balbir watched the events of 9/11 unfold with shock and fear. Al Qaeda terrorists crashed three passenger planes into the World Trade Center in New York City, a city he had visited and loved, and the Pentagon in Washington, D.C. The terrorists killed 2,977 innocent victims, and the images of people leaping out of windows, recounting harrowing tales of near-death, and sharing stories of loved ones lost in the attacks stayed with Balbir. He was, after all, a father of two young daughters, and he could not imagine the pain of losing a loved one to a horrific terror attack. As with millions of other Americans, the 9/11 attacks strengthened Balbir's patriotism and his love for a country that had taken him in as one of its own. He flew an American flag on his home in solidarity with the victims of 9/11, and four days after the attacks, on Tuesday, September 15, he decided to sell American flags at his Chevron gas station.

While gardening and arranging the flags in front of his station, a Chevrolet S 10 pickup pulled up to one of the pumps. The man driving the truck looked in Balbir's direction, sizing up the brown man wearing a turban, black beard, and friendly smile. He remained inside his truck, staring squarely at Balbir. The Sikh American assumed the man was just another customer. However, this was the furthest thing from the truth, and Balbir realized this when he heard the first shot ring out from the truck. He would not hear the next four.

Balbir was not a Muslim. But according to his killer and scores of Islamophobes, *he looked Muslim*—he wore the same beard, had the same dark skin, and donned a turban similar to those the terrorists on television wore. Was he part of the Taliban, the extremist Muslim group that controlled much of Afghanistan, blew up ancient Buddhist temples, forced its women to wear burqas, and adopted the arcane form of Sunni Islam peddled by U.S. ally Saudi Arabia? Or was Balbir a member or sympathizer of Al Qaeda, the transnational terror network behind the 9/11 terror attacks? No. He was neither, nor was he Shiite or Sunni Muslim, Arab or Middle Eastern. He was Indian American, and his religion was Sikhism.

But it did not matter. Because to Frank Roque, who murdered Balbir on September 15, 2001, Balbir *looked* the way so many non-Muslim Americans imagined Muslims to look. To Frank Roque, and the growing ranks of Islamophobes, Balbir's skin color, beard, and dress were enough to mark him as Muslim, and being Muslim was enough to mark him as evil.

After 9/11, the American legal system would embolden the public rage against Muslims (and dark-skinned non-Muslims) to usher in an era of structural Islamophobia. Seeded by the Orientalism of the past and justified by the World Trade Center terror attacks, scrutiny of and institutionalized prejudice against Muslim Americans would dramatically intensify. "For most Americans, any mention of the presence of Muslims in the United States today is bound to conjure up thoughts of 9/11 and its aftermath,"[3] which tightens the bond between Muslim identity and terrorism, the stereotype that drives both private and structural Islamophobia. This also holds true for Sikh Americans and other communities wrongly stereotyped as Muslims.

The violent backlash against Muslim Americans carried out by the state and private hatemongers was intense in the months and years after September 11, 2001. The current phase of the war on terror is just as ominous. On December 7, 2015, Donald Trump called for a "total and complete shutdown" of Muslims coming into the United States.[4] His proposal, which he made good on during his first week as president with the (first) Muslim ban, galvanized his supporters and mobilized his detractors. Trump's proposals, rhetoric, and—once he claimed the presidency—his policies marked a new era of American Islamophobia, one marked by brazen vitriol against Islam. But were Trump and his routine deployment of explicit Islamophobia aberrational? Or a transparent extension of the two administrations that came before his?

The Trump administration ushered in the third era of the protracted war on terror. It followed the Obama administration, a regime celebrated for its outward celebration of multicultural-ism but critiqued for its expansion of the surveillance state; and before that, the Bush administration, the original architect of the war on terror. While the Trump administration promises that the war on terror will be escalated to a third, patently more hostile and brazen stage, what is palpably clear is that the "with us or against us" binary echoed by Trump binds him to George W. Bush, who first uttered those words, and to the administra-tion that launched a war that spawned Islamophobia as we know it today.

WITH US OR AGAINST US

Nine days after the 9/11 terror attacks, President George W. Bush addressed a shaken, angry, and permanently transformed nation. In his address, President Bush declared, "This is not, however, just America's fight. And what is at stake is not just America's freedom. This is the world's fight. This is civilization's fight. This is the fight of all who believe in progress and plural-ism, tolerance and freedom.... The civilized world is rallying to America's side. They understand that if this terror goes unpun-ished, their own cities, their own citizens may be next.... We are in a fight for our principles."[5]

President Bush's speech, which specified that America's target were terrorists who "practice[d] a fringe form of Islamic extrem-ism," was saturated with appeals to an ideological, cultural, and civilizational war—indeed, the very standoff Huntington wrote about in *The Clash of Civilizations*. The speech was more than just a demonstration of resolve to the American people and the world at large; it was, most fundamentally, a declaration of war, a "war on terror," as it came to be known, against an enemy the state explicitly identified as Al Qaeda and the "Islamic extremists" who supported it. In practice, the war on terror has been against Islam as a civilization, and a war on Muslims everywhere.

This war is dramatically distinct from its predecessors and unlike conventional wars in general. Its target is not a nation-state or empire, but rather the vague and amorphous concept of terrorism, conflated with Islam and the billions of its believers presumed to be sympathetic to or in cahoots with terror. The state has linked Muslims, whether immigrants or citizens, living in the United States or abroad, to the suspicion of terrorism, and it has formally enacted a two-front war: the foreign war, and the surveillance, policing, and cultural wars deployed within the country.

This two-front war spurred the creation of the Department of Homeland Security (DHS), led by Republican Tom Ridge, who would oversee the vastly broadened surveillance, prosecutorial, and punitive measures the state could enforce against those it deemed to be terrorism suspects. The wholesale restructuring of the state's national security system; centralization of surveillance, immigration, and terror policing within one entity; and the sweeping counterterror policing programs that followed would be politically enabled by the unfathomable terror that unfolded on our television screens on 9/11 and the gut-wrenching images of mothers holding up photos of their sons or daughters to television lenses, makeshift memorials springing up in American cities large and small, and most poignantly, the stories of the 2,996 people whose lives were taken.

Not too long after the tragic events of 9/11, the American public forgot the specific identity of the individuals and faction that committed the largest terror attack on American soil. This forgetting was abetted by presidential declarations of civilizational wars, politicians who internalized the rhetoric and lexicon of "Islam's bloody borders," and a public hungry for revenge and already intimately familiar with the images and ideas of "Islamic extremism." As the days passed, the nineteen culprits of the attack on the World Trade Center became an afterthought. The state and the public were more keen on prosecuting and punishing all Muslims for a conspiracy perpetrated by a handful of terrorists.

It did not matter that fifteen of them were Saudi nationals, or that all of them were committed to Salafi-jihadism, an extremist interpretation of Sunni Islamic thought that brands entire Islamic sects as "apostates." It did not matter that they were hired guns carrying out an Al Qaeda conspiracy. None of the specifics of the story or the nuances of the narrative seemed to matter. They were, simply, Muslim, indistinguishable from all the other Muslims in the world.

By the foundational principle of American criminal law that holds only the people guilty of committing crimes responsible for them, only the nineteen men and their aiders and abettors were convicted. And yet, at every level of American public and private life, Muslims were increasingly considered collectively culpable. Two law scholars even made the claim that "Saudi Arabia's dedication to building Wahhabism globally should make Saudi Arabia civilly liable for at least some small part of the harm caused by the Wahhabist-inspired terrorists."[6] The cornerstone principle of American rule of law was turned on its head for the 1.7 billion Muslims across the globe and the 8 to 10 million living in the United States, now presumed to be guilty until proven innocent. "Guilty until proven innocent" forms the fundamental definition of Islamophobia. War-on-terror policies have rolled it out by law, expansive surveillance, policing programming, and outright war.

After 9/ 11, America's vengeance was instantly unleashed on two Muslim-majority countries. President Bush rolled out his global war on terror in 2001 by first invading Afghanistan, home to the Wahhabi-inspired Taliban, which gave safe haven to many of the perpetrators of the 9/11 terror attacks. Two years later, Bush declared war on familiar foe Saddam Hussein, driven by the baseless claims that the Iraqi dictator had collaborated with Al Qaeda and was developing weapons of mass destruction that the Bush administration baselessly speculated could fall into the hands of Al-Qaeda and other terrorists.

With the capture and execution of Saddam Hussein on September 30, 2006, President George W. Bush finished the first leg of the civilizational war his father had launched more than a decade before. He put an end to the standoff with the Iraqi dictator, making way for the broader war to come. Iraq was sent into a spiral of bloody sectarian civil war, chaos, and division, making it the perfect vacuum for Al-Qaeda terrorists and the more menacing ISIS terrorists born on its battlegrounds (examined in chapter 5).

The second front of the war on terror was at home. In his September 20, 2001, speech, President Bush addressed Muslims and Muslim Americans directly, claiming, "We respect your faith. It's practiced by millions of Americans, and by millions more in countries that America counts as friends. Its teachings are good and peaceful, and those who commit evil in the name of Allah blaspheme the name of Allah.... The enemy of America is not our many Muslim friends ... our enemy is a radical network of terrorists." However, his appeal to a civilizational war overshadowed his distinction between "peaceful" Islam and the extremism manifested by Al Qaeda and the 9/11 terrorists and his delineating between good and bad Muslims. And more immediately, his revelation of the surveillance and policing measures on the horizon signaled that Muslim American life would never be the same.

"We will come together to give law enforcement the additional tools it needs to track down terror at home," Bush declared in the same address, foreshadowing the passage of the USA PATRIOT Act, which was signed into law a month later. The PATRIOT Act devastated the civil liberties of Muslim citizens and immigrants, enabling the "addition of roving wiretaps [and] the ability to secretly survey email communications," generally without warrants or a basis for suspicion, even of American citizens.[7] Although the act specifically stated that "Arab Americans, Muslim Americans, and Americans from South Asia are ... entitled to nothing less than the full rights of every American" and that their "civil rights and civil liberties ... must be protected," in practice the disproportionate surveillance, collection of computer and phone data, and prosecution diminished the citizenship and civil rights of these groups. The fact that this had to be stated indicated a purpose to police these specific groups. The PATRIOT Act's broad and vague definition of "terrorism" was religiously neutral, but it envisioned Muslims as its targets and was subsequently enforced against this population.

"We will come together to strengthen our intelligence capabilities to know the plans of terrorists before they act, and find them before they strike," President Bush continued, signaling that the privacy rights Muslim Americans, tenuously held before 9/11, would be further eroded. A year later they would be eroded further still with the enactment of the National Security Entry and

Exit Registration System (NSEERS), a Muslim immigrant registry that remained on the books for fourteen years. Twenty-four of the twenty-five countries of interest listed in the NSEERS legislation were Muslim-majority nations, which was a clear manifestation of the structural Islamophobic presumption that Muslim identity was correlative with terrorism. NSEERS was predominantly concerned with tracking the activity of Muslim immigrants, particularly while they were within the United States, as evidenced by the nations it honed in on and the arrests made after its enactment. Immediately after it went into force, 80,000 men were entered into the NSEERS registry, the vast majority of them Muslims, "2,870 of whom were detained and 13,799 placed in deportation proceedings within two years after 9/11."[8]

The domestic war on terror ushered in the era of full-fledged, state-sanctioned Islamophobia, complete with the foundational structures, signature policies, and all-hands-on-deck governmental will to police virtually every dimension of Muslim American life. Although the rhetoric coming out of the White House insisted that the target of the war on terror was Al Qaeda and, in the words of President George W. Bush, "the governments that supported it,"[9] the actions taken and the injuries inflicted revealed that the war was also being waged against Muslim citizens and immigrants.

More than ever before, the war on terror made Arab, Middle Eastern, and especially Muslim identity a proxy for terrorism. Any manifestation of Islam, whether at the individual or institutional level, at the level of ideas or expression, triggered fear of terror. And this fear invited suspicion, surveillance, and possible prosecution by the state. Muslim American households, communities, and mosques were closely monitored, and religious organizations, political groups, student associations, and more were surveilled by DHS, federal agents, and informants. Structural Islamophobia was in full swing, and the laws and programs installed by the state communicated to the American people that Muslims were suspicious and their faith the source of terrorism that threatened national security.

The mainstream media corroborated this and related messages. In her book *Arab and Muslims in the Media: Race and Representation after 9/11*, Evelyn Alsultany observes, "Xenophobia and outright racism flourished on the airwaves; the pundits of Fox News were always a reliable source of antagonism. At the same time, a slew of TV dramas cashed in on the salacious possibilities of Arab and Muslim terrorist threats and assured viewers with depictions of the U.S. government's heroic efforts to combat this new, pulse-quickening terrorism. These shows, from network and cable channels, alike—include—but are not limited to—*24, Sleeper Cell, NCIS, JAG, The Grid, The Threat Matrix*."[10] In his landmark book *Reel Bad Arabs*, Jack Shaheen observes, "A far-too-common scene shows a mosque with [Muslims] at prayer, then cuts away to showing civilians being gunned down,"[11] which affirms, emphatically, the conflation of terrorism with Islam—the very crux of Islamophobia.

A personal experience of mine illustrates the point. Richard Alvarez, a classmate from law school, revealed to me one day, "If not for you, I would probably have the worst opinions of Muslims. You guys are always the bad guys in the movies I love." This admission did not surprise me—even from a Mexican American law student who would eventually become one of my closest friends. Damaging images of Muslims were ubiquitous when I was in law school, and perpetuated (to great profit) by news media and, as highlighted by Alsultany, by entertainment media. "Growing up in West Sacramento, I did not know any

Muslims, or anybody who came out and said they were Muslims," Richard said, reflecting on his upbringing in the largely working-class Chicano neighborhood in northern California. Law scholar John Tehranian echoes Richard, observing that "The average American has little direct contact with the Middle East or even with Middle Easterners [or Muslims]. Instead, popular perceptions are driven by indirect contact through the mediating force of mass communications. In news and entertainment programming, fear is reflected, cultivated and magnified to devastating effect."[12]

The lines between news and entertainment media were often blurred, as representations of Muslims in television dramas and on the big screen matched the religious and racial profiles of the Muslim terrorists the Bush administration hotly pursued; they were almost always Arab or Middle Eastern (the two are routinely conflated), bearded, male, and Muslim. These male representations were sometimes coupled with female representations of the subordinate mother or wife (or wives), whose role was to aid, abet, and harbor the terrorists. Although the portrayals of Muslim women on screen were flatter, less frequent, and less damaging than the depictions of their male counterparts, the tropes were recurring and were directly or indirectly linked to terrorism. This private Islamophobia, unfolding on screen, was triggered by the structural Islamophobia made more expansive and explicit by the Bush administration, which spurred a second wave of private Islamophobia.

The Bush administration's war-on-terror policies authorized and emboldened private vigilante violence against Muslims, and perceived Muslims like Balbir Singh Sodhi, violence that skyrocketed after 9/11. In 2001, the FBI reported that "hate crimes against Arabs and Muslims multiplied by 1,600 percent from

2000 to 2001."[13] This figure, frightening on its own, does not include "hate incidents," acts that do not rise to the level of a crime and that are unreported, sometimes because of fear on the part of the victim. Hundreds of mosques were targeted and attacked, neighbors of Muslim (or perceived Muslim) families began making baseless reports to the FBI and law enforcement, and individuals were removed from airplanes without any kind of process or justification.

The wave of hate crimes and hate incidents inflicted on Muslim individuals and institutions was not confined to the immediate aftermath of 9/11. Structural Islamophobic policies characterizing Muslim citizens and immigrants as a dangerous fifth column continued to fuel private Islamophobia for years after. In 2007, the Council on American Islamic Relations reported receiving about 1,900 complaints of abuse and held that anti-Muslim physical violence rose by 52 percent between 2001 and 2003.[14] Many assumed that private Islamophobia would decline after 9/11's immediate aftermath, but the continuing wave of attacks on mosques, unarmed and armed rallies and anti-Muslim protests, and violent attacks against Muslims and perceived Muslims proved otherwise.

Indeed, the structural Islamophobia enacted by the Bush administration, and confirmed by media channels "redeployed [the embedded] Orientalist tropes" that Muslims were vile, violent, and bent on destroying the United States.[15] The national security policies of the war on terror were far more than merely protective actions taken to bolster the country's ability to preempt and prevent terrorism; they were a resounding call to action. They were a call to the broader polity to stand on guard and keep your eyes open, to participate in the national project of defeating terrorism by reporting suspicious activity, to enlist as informants, and, as demonstrated by the horrendous uptick in hate crimes and hate incidents, to take the law into your own hands if need be.

Although 62 percent of Americans "don't happen to have a friend who is a Muslim" and 87 percent admitted to never having been inside a mosque,[16] private Islamophobes acted upon what the media told them about Islam and Muslims. Violent, warmongering, immutably alien and unassimilable, brown, hostile to anything and everything America—that's what Americans saw and heard, incessantly and in heavy doses, which mobilized a vengeful public to pounce on a people, and a faith, they were overwhelmingly ignorant of. Droves of innocent citizens and immigrants were victimized, and modern Islamophobia—the system of bigotry we know today—was not only born, but rampant and rife.

In many ways, the signature stamp and enduring legacy of the Bush administration are the infrastructure, policies, and strategy of the war on terror. For eight years, the administration would tweak and enhance its surveillance programs, its scrutiny of immigration and restrictions on Muslim immigrants, and its brutal and prolonged war in Iraq—which would claim the lives of hundreds of thousands of Iraqis and scores of American soldiers.

The war on terror did not end with its architects, and neither did Islamophobia. Both would enter a new phase with the landmark election of Barack Obama, the first African American elected to the highest office in the land, and the president who would shift the counterterror model to focus more closely on Muslim American communities.

STRUCTURAL ISLAMOPHOBIA AND THE STATES

"What is shariwa law?" Steve asked me. I seemed to be considered the resident expert on everything Islam and Muslim.

"Do you mean Shari'a law?" I responded, wondering why the middle-aged white international lawyer took a sudden interest in Islamic jurisprudence, or the faith at all.

"Yes, Shari'a law!" he confirmed, stumbling through the pronunciation. "I don't know, I just hear it popping up again and again on the news, especially with this Ground Zero mosque debate out of New York City."

"Well, I'll start by saying this," I began, prepping my old work colleague for an explanation free of the typical loaded sound bites and flat misrepresentations of the complex body of Islamic jurisprudence. "First off, it isn't a codified system of law, but rather scripture that is up for interpretation."

"So, sort of like the Constitution," he responded.

"Yes, in many respects, both documents have general and sometimes vague ideas that can be construed differently and are open to debate. Some provisions are clear, but more are contingent on the perspective of the reader. That's why relying on experts and scholars is important, but like constitutional law scholars or Supreme Court justices, there are diverse positions and varying interpretations of Shari'a."

"That makes sense," Steve responded, with a tone indicating that I had changed his view of the widely misunderstood phrase, a phrase that has been contorted by the media and their pundits into some sort of call for an Islamic takeover or violent war, which is completely upside down.

Shari'a law is not monolithic. It is not a menacing body of uniform law ordained by a state, "or one book or a single collection of rules. Shari'a is divine and philosophical."[17] Interpretation of Shari'a, or *Fiqh*, ranges depending on the degree of education and expertise of the individual, the individual's method of construction, age, gender, race, and a wide range of other variables. Mirroring the diversity of the global Muslim population, interpretation of Shari'a is heterogeneous. And "Shari'a law" as characterized by the likes of Sean Hannity or Ben Carson is a tool used to stir up more fear and confusion about Islam and Muslims, like "jihad," "fatwa," and other Arabic words that have been distorted and deployed to incite Islamophobia.

Fear of Shari'a law proliferated again in 2011, resulting in a series of bills being introduced in states across the country. Capitalizing on the intense Islamophobia spurred by debate over a possible Muslim community center near Ground Zero, the congressional hearings on "Islamic radicalization" called by Representative Peter King, and the extended war on terror, a number of states introduced legislation that sought to ban Shari'a law. The proposed bills were not standalone or isolated, but part of a broader movement driven by a partnership between conservative think tanks and politicians, which looked to convert the private Islamophobia saturating the country into structural policies adopted on the state level. The movement to ban Shari'a law, debated within and carried forward by state legislatures, illustrates how structural Islamophobia also unfolds beyond the federal level and within state governments.

Proponents of anti-Shari'a legislation defined Shari'a law as "'totalitarian ideology' and 'legal-political-military doctrine,' committed to annihilating Western civilization as we known it today." Relying on principal Islamophobic baselines that frame Islam as a competing political ideology (sometimes referred to as "Islamo-fascism") as much as religious scripture, Shari'a law abolitionists authored a model statute that "would prohibit state judges from considering foreign laws or rulings that violate constitutional rights in the United States."[18] The model statute, titled "American Law for American Courts," was passed on to allies within state legislatures and subsequently rewritten into bill form. Using this template, conservative legislators sought to pass copycat bills in their respective states, bills that, depending on enforcement, could materially infringe upon a range of civil liberties for Muslim Americans and endanger Muslim American life.

Anti-Shari'a bills became prominent items of discussion in state legislatures across the country. "As of June, 2011, there were forty-seven bills in twenty-one states that were seeking to ban the use of Shari'a and/or any category of international law."[19] Spearheaded by the Louisiana and Tennessee legislatures, nearly half of the country's states entertained the idea of banning Islamic law. One state, Wyoming, even engaged the idea of prohibiting its courts from citing other states that might permit the use of Shari'a law. In addition to crippling the ability of judges and juries to engage the religious and cultural dimensions of Muslim subjects coming before the courts, anti-Shari'a legislation conflicts with the Establishment Clause and, perhaps more acutely, the Free Exercise Clause of the First Amendment, thereby endangering the rights of Muslim Americans to freely practice their religion of choice. These bills disregarded the constitutional cornerstone of separation of church and state and scoffed at the foundational right of free exercise.

A number of states passed explicit anti-Shari'a legislation or superficially neutral but de facto Islamophobic measures that restricted state courts from considering foreign, international, or religious law. While not explicitly including the words "Islam" or "Shari'a," these laws are specifically aimed at the faith and the citizens who observe it. The 2016 presidential race and the induction of the Trump administration facilitates even more opportunity for states to pass anti-Shari'a bills. Indeed, the prolific spike in private Islamophobia since Trump was inaugurated, emboldened by the structural policies enacted by him on the federal level, have furnished the anti-Shari'a movement with momentum and support from Washington to introduce more bills, and very likely, enact more state laws.

While this legislation conflicts with the First Amendment's principle of separating church and state and preventing the states from meddling in the religious affairs of their citizenry, the ferocity of Islamophobia in America today, at both the federal and state levels, reveals that there is always an *Islamophobic exception:* violating core constitutional principles is deemed justifiable or permissible as long as the target is Islam or Muslims.

The anti-Shari'a movement that reached its climax in 2011 illustrates that Islamophobia was just as pervasive during the Obama administration as it was during the George W. Bush era. And while the charismatic and fresh-faced politician came into office promising an end to the war on terror, what came to pass was entirely different.

A TALE OF TWO MOSQUES:
THE OBAMA ADMINISTRATION

In 2008, Kameelah Mu'min Rashad was all in: "The first black president or first woman president? Wasn't a hard choice for me,"[20] reflected the African American Muslim woman and prominent activist, who backed the man who inspired so many and rode "hope" all the way into the White House and the history books.

Like many, she did not believe that she would see a black president in her lifetime. Rashad explained, "Honestly, I never imagined a black president before Obama. It seemed so far-fetched or something that would only be possible in Hollywood.

For me, Barack Obama was an appealing candidate not because of his individual competence or brilliance. I was equally if not more impressed by Michelle Obama. The fact that he was married to this incredibly accomplished, well-educated, honest, unapologetic black woman was really all the convincing I needed."[21] A black president and first lady seemed a fantasy only years before for Rashad, and for millions more who shared her view, but the sudden emergence of Barack Obama as a presidential contender pushed the black Muslim mother of two to be part of his historic campaign.

An Obama administration also meant newfound hope for Rashad's two children, Laila and Bilal, who were five and three at the time. She canvassed homes in Philadelphia, the symbolic and demographic capital of the African American Muslim experience in the United States, lobbied friends and colleagues, and pushed mosque congregations to vote for the transcendent black man with the Muslim middle name. Her efforts, part of a grassroots presidential campaign like no other, lifted Barack Hussein Obama to the White House.

·   ·   ·

On February 3, 2015, President Obama finally visited an American mosque. His stop at the Islamic Society of Baltimore came seven years into his presidency, a span that encompassed the rise and fall of the Arab Spring, escalating private Islamophobia, and a protracting war on terror targeting Muslims abroad and Muslim Americans stateside. Obama's lengthy avoidance of American mosques is made even more glaring when juxtaposed with his famous speech at Cairo's Al-Azhar University, a global center of Islamic education and thought, delivered a year into his first term.

On June 4, 2009, in Cairo, Obama openly challenged the "clash of civilizations" rhetoric and policies advanced by the Bush administration. In front of an audience of thousands at Al-Azhar University, and watched by billions more around the world, the newly elected president stated, "I have come here to seek a new beginning between the United States and Muslims around the world; one based upon mutual interest and mutual respect; and one based upon the truth that America and Islam are not exclusive, and need not be in competition. Instead, they overlap, and share common principles—principles of justice and progress; tolerance and the dignity of all human beings."[22]

His words were a direct rebuttal to the war on terror carried out by his predecessor, George W. Bush, for eight years. And for those watching, particularly Muslim Americans at home, the speech signaled a rebuke of the structural Islamophobia established and expanded by the Bush administration, and the private Islamophobia it authorized. It was a new day, or at least it seemed that way.

Following his Cairo speech, Obama was celebrated by Muslims and Muslim Americans as a transformative leader who could undo the damage wrought by previous administrations and reconcile tensions between Muslims and the United States. However, the seven years between Obama's historic Cairo speech and his address to Muslim Americans in Baltimore witnessed the expansion of structural Islamophobia (with the formal establishment of Countering Violent Extremism [CVE] policing, discussed in chapter 5) within his administration and a growing opposition among Muslim Americans.

Criticized by many Muslim Americans as long overdue, President Obama's first visit to an American mosque climaxed with a speech that condemned private Islamophobia. But behind the words was a counterterror mandate that drove that private

Islamophobia forward. Mirroring his own relationship with Islam and Islamophobia, defined primarily by resisting allegations that he himself was an undercover Muslim, President Obama's engagement with the faith can be best characterized as strategic accommodation and intentional distance.

While campaigning for the presidency, Obama's opponents, most notably Donald Trump, called Obama a Muslim in order to undermine his campaign and deepen perceptions that he was a foreigner. Perceptions that Obama was Muslim continued into his second term, illustrating how years-old allegations developed into widely held beliefs. Certainly, "the prominence of Obama's middle name as a signifier of his Arab/Muslim identity would not leave him until the last days of the presidential campaign, if ever."[23] These beliefs had a considerable impact on Obama; as a result of them, he chose to limit his outreach and engagement with the Muslim American community.

Political aversion to mosques, in President Obama's case, exhibits a less conspicuous brand of Islamophobia. And under what circumstances did Obama—during the final quarter of his second term—finally enter a mosque and speak to its congregation? That his visit took place during his second term, and at the close of his administration, meant that the political stakes were far lower. The damage the visit could have done to his administration was minimal; he was setting his sights beyond his presidential post. He dodged American mosques and close association with Muslims until it was no longer politically expedient to do so, namely when he sought to advance his signature structural Islamophobic program: CVE policing.

The expansion of CVE policing in the aftermath of the San Bernardino, Paris, and Orlando attacks strongly suggests another motive: interest in enlisting Muslim Americans as strategic supporters of expanding counter-radicalization programming and CVE policing. And so the latent political Islamophobia of Obama's decision to steer clear of mosques was fused with the anti-Muslim underpinnings of his cornerstone anti-terror policy, CVE policing, which Hillary Clinton would likely have expanded if she had been elected president.[24]

While "celebrat[ing] the contributions Muslim Americans make to our nation" was the motive issued to the media for Obama's mosque visit,[25] enlisting Muslim Americans as CVE policing interlocutors and informants was the likely reason for the visit. In line with this aim, Obama made "a direct appeal to America's Muslim youth... asking Muslim communities to be 'partners' in state and federal campaigns [CVE policing] to combat militant groups that try to recruit young followers of Islam."[26] In a speech that probably would not have been given if not for the San Bernardino shooting, President Obama called for closer collaboration with Muslim Americans to combat and counter radicalization.

Mobilizing Muslim American support for CVE policing, Obama's cornerstone structural Islamophobic program, certainly would be bolstered by the symbolic force of the president speaking inside an American mosque. And it would strategically tap into what had been unprecedented Muslim American support for a presidential candidate, which, after controversial foreign policy decisions and the expansion of Muslim American surveillance, had been gradually eroding since 2012.

President Obama condemned the "inexcusable rhetoric" from Republican candidates and implored that "we can't suggest that Islam is the root of the problem."[27] And yet, in direct conflict with these words was the primary political objective of his historic address, to promote a counterterror program that suggests Islam is the root of radicalization and Muslims are the lone demographic prone to becoming radicalized. The Baltimore speech, essentially, was an exercise in masterful doublespeak—President Obama used the laudatory rhetoric about Islam that Muslims so desperately wanted to hear, while warning about the threat of Islamic radicalization to mitigate the fears of everybody else.

Whereas speaking at a mosque before the Paris attacks and the San Bernardino shootings may have symbolized a connection with Islam in the minds of those who believed that Obama was Muslim, speaking in a mosque after these tragedies signaled the state mandate for expanded CVE policing. What appears to be an official acknowledgment of Islam becomes, upon deeper investigation, a calculated presidential maneuver driven by fear. This time, instead of fearing damage to his reputation or political career, President Obama pivoted—seven years later—to carry forward counterterror policies exclusively focused on Muslim American bodies and communities, policies rooted in a fear as old as the nation itself.

While the Republican Party, particularly with Trump's ascent, became the party of blatant and explicit political Islamophobia, the Democratic Party under President Obama stood as the party of expanding structural Islamophobic policy and programming. The latter, mirroring Obama's masterful speech at the mosque in Baltimore, used benign and gracious language toward Muslims to enlist them as informants in programming that invites great dangers into Muslim American communities. President Obama also appointed a White House Muslim American liaison in May of 2016, in part to build strategic bridges and partnerships with Muslim leaders and stakeholders, partnerships that would that enable the state to further establish and expand CVE programming in Muslim communities across the country.[28]

Above all, this strategy of engagement within Muslim American communities not only carried forward the baseline presumption that Muslim identity is correlative with terrorism, but also localized it by deputizing police officers to lead the charge in unearthing potential radicals and preventing them from taking action.

A tale of two mosques, beginning with a lofty speech in the heart of one of Islam's most important religious centers in Cairo and concluding with a long overdue appearance in a Muslim American mosque eight years later, form the axes of President Obama's administration of structural Islamophobia. His presidency began with much optimism and concluded with the bitter realization that Obama did not put an end to the war on terror launched by his predecessor, but mutated, modernized, and marched it forward. With a fresh new face, rhetorical smoke signals, and the pacifying effect afforded by his racial identity and strategic deployment of progressive ideas and language, the war on terror was craftily pushed forward for another eight years under the Obama administration, and Islamophobia swelled right alongside of it.

Obama, a landmark president who broke the racial barrier to the highest office in the land, did not usher in post-racial America, as illustrated most vividly by the Movement for Black Lives that unfolded during his second term. Nor did his administration put an end to the war on terror. The very mosques where Obama opened and closed his historic presidency were the sites on which his surveillance programming focused, where the assessment of good Muslim, bad Muslim was unfolding most furiously.

Kameelah Rashad was among the guests invited to President Obama's Baltimore mosque visit on February 4, 2016, along with her two children, Laila and Bilal, now thirteen and eleven years old. "As a black Muslim, over the eight years of his presidency, it was difficult at times to reconcile how I felt about his presence with his foreign and domestic policies, which were detrimental to many of the communities of which I am a member," recalled Rashad.[29] The hope that pushed her to canvass for the black candidate with the middle name Hussein had, eight years later, devolved into disappointment and concern, particularly as her two children became more and more vulnerable to the CVE programming that came to define President Obama's relationship with Muslim America.

GOOD MUSLIM, BAD MUSLIM

The feeling of being perpetually out of place characterizes my life best. Born to a Shiite Muslim father from Lebanon and a Sunni Muslim mother from Egypt, I was ignorant to the differences between the two sects until my early teenage years growing up in a predominantly Shiite community, where I was singled out as "not Shiite enough" by friends. Later on, during college, acquaintances and classmates profiled me based on my last name and hometown origins and concluded that I was not Sunni enough. In addition to faith, I straddled ethnic and racial margins as an Arab living in a predominantly black neighborhood in Detroit, right outside of Dearborn's borders, and being the target of proxy racism from Arab classmates who called me "ghetto" and warned me, "Beware of the '*abeed*,'" the Arabic equivalent of the N-word, as they dropped me off at my house after school or playing basketball.

I seldom felt fully integrated as a youth in Muslim and Arab American spaces, and later in college, among generally upper-middle-class and affluent friends whose parents were lawyers, doctors, and corporate executives. I was the first in my family to leave home for college, and my mother—who came to my dorm almost every weekend with bags full of groceries—worked at a Laundromat during my sophomore year. While my closest friends led political organizations and plotted the next march or campus protest, ate at expensive restaurants and immersed themselves in college culture, I was more concerned with helping my mother pay her mortgage, partitioning my financial aid to help her and make my own ends meet, and making the forty-five minute drive home as often as I could. I left home for my studies, but home never left me, and that existential feeling of being perpetually out of place stayed lodged within me in college and beyond.

I could empathize entirely with Meursault, the protagonist in Albert Camus's *The Stranger*, when he said, "I noticed then that everyone was waving and exchanging greetings and talking, as if they were in a club where people are glad to find themselves among others from the same world. That is how I explained to myself the strange impression I had of being odd man out, a kind of intruder."[30] Intruder and imposter syndrome stayed with me throughout my time at the University of Michigan, a public university that in practice catered to students from middle-class and affluent origins who explored radical politics as some sort of cultural tourism or transient experimentation, only to retreat back to the comforts of suburban life. My circumstance was the very opposite, although Ann Arbor and college life offered little retreat from the difficult realities at home, which continually loomed over me.

Many years later, my most politically radical college friends, who had the luxury of dedicating the time to activism that I did not have, retreated to the lives of their parents, shelving political activism for a quiet life in the suburbs and the professional upward mobility that a quiet, apolitical life enabled. Struggle, again, was a social fad that many of my classmates could opt out of as easily as they opted in, while the challenges I faced were no extracurricular activity, but the only life I knew.

I recall reading Edward Said's memoir, *Out of Place,* as a college junior.[31] His experience as a stateless Palestinian, living in the United States but always longing for the home from which he was displaced, resonated deeply with me. I was not Palestinian, but an Egyptian and Lebanese American, raised on the west side of Detroit, and unlike Said, a man I consider an intellectual hero, I grew up on welfare and without the means he had. But his story spoke to me, and his experience made sense of that incessant circumstance, feeling, or spirit of perpetually being out of place: not Muslim enough in some spaces, not Arab enough in others; not Shiite or Sunni enough, cultured or sophisticated enough, or down or radical enough. Gloria Anzaldúa, the Chicana feminist and one of my favorite thinkers, articulated this feeling of perpetual flux best, writing, "Living on borders and in margins, keeping intact one's shifting and multiple identity and integrity, is like trying to swim in a new element, an 'alien' element."[32] These intellectuals articulated what I was, at that point, unable to, and just as importantly, they gave me community.

But as I approached my mid-twenties, the pressures of living at the intersection of multiple borders mattered less and less. I rebuffed them and ultimately learned that that feeling of being out of place was empowering, and more fundamentally, offered a portal toward full-fledged freedom and independence. As my friend and mentor Hisham Aidi would later tell me, "There's might at the margins!" Not having to appease an individual, placate a gatekeeper, or conform to a narrowly defined community marked the essence of liberty and the pathway toward the person I wanted to be. And indeed, the only individual, student, activist, and Muslim

I knew how to be. *Being out of place was my only place*, so I rejected the binaries that surrounded me and rejected the binds and burdens that compromised others and compelled them to conform.

While I was rejecting the social scripts of existential binaries, the war on terror was expeditiously crafting a new binary-driven script. You are "either with us or against us," President Bush stated emphatically nine days after the 9/11 terror attacks, speaking explicitly to foreign nations, but also to Muslims in the United States and abroad. Many years later, President Obama echoed a similar message to Muslim Americans, claiming that "Muslims around the world have a responsibility to reject extremist ideologies that are trying to penetrate within Muslim communities."[33] This was, again, an appeal, if not a mandate, for Muslim Americans to be part of the profiling and surveillance programs installed by the Obama administration, programs that rely heavily on Muslims to serve as informants, watchdogs, and data collectors within mosques, community centers, student groups, and other places Muslims gather, including social media platforms.

The message from both Bush and Obama to Muslim Americans was clear: there were good Muslims and bad Muslims. The latter were not only the terrorist groups and their agents, such as Al Qaeda and ISIS, but also Muslims and Muslim Americans who might be suspected of sympathizing with these groups. The former were citizens who heeded the call of the war on terror to participate in identifying terrorists and "homegrown radicals," which not only showcased their patriotism, but also excluded them from suspicion of terror.

Although Muslim Americans are bona fide citizens, their religious identity induces scrutiny of their citizenship status, patriotism, and belonging. This scrutiny is strongest after national crises, and specifically in the direct aftermath of a terror attack committed by a Muslim culprit. As constitutional law scholar Kenneth Karst writes, "In times of trouble ... fears tend to focus on particular groups of cultural outsiders as a source of danger."[34] This is particularly true for Muslim Americans, whose religious affiliation can negate any legal or material claim to Americanness and hold them out to be threatening interlopers.

September 11 functioned as the great modern juncture that "increase[d] awareness of Muslim culture and practice" in the United States,[35] ushering in intensified private and structural Islamophobia. The deployment of Islamophobia after 9/11 presumed that, by virtue of their faith, Muslim Americans would prioritize their allegiance to Islam over their allegiance to their country. This assumption had implicit in it the demand that Muslims prove allegiance to the United States through performance of vivid, recurring, and over-compensatory acts of patriotism. The alternative was exposure to the full-fledged might of state and societal suspicion and violence. Leti Volpp of the University of California Berkeley School of Law theorizes that "terrorist and citizen are opposition terms. Thus the 'terrorist citizen' seems also an impossible subject. Putative terrorists are not considered deserving of the protections of citizenship."[36] Thus, as putative terrorists, Muslim Americans must actively perform their patriotism and (outwardly, at least) under-perform their Muslim identity to mitigate the suspicion tethered to their religious identity.

Law scholar Natsu Saito wrote that, after September 11, "Arab Americans and Muslims have been 'raced' as 'terrorists': foreign, disloyal, and imminently threatening. Although Arabs trace their roots to the Middle East and claim many different religious backgrounds, and Muslims come from all over the world ... these distinctions are blurred and negative images about either Arabs or

Muslims are often attributed to both."[37] This is particularly true for private Islamophobes, who largely latch on to the idea that Muslim identity is a racial identity or a civilization. Meanwhile, the state and structural Islamophobic policy, over time, has become more adept at distinguishing between Arab, Middle Eastern, and Muslim identities.

Because Muslim and American identities are constructed as opposable, any performance of Americanness requires downplaying Muslim identity. Devon Carbado and Mitu Gulati list some examples of Muslim American expressions of patriotism: "[A man] shaving before taking a plane trip. Or for a woman it might mean refraining from wearing a headscarf. For the family, it might mean placing an American flag outside the home. It also might mean refraining from doing the traditional Muslim prayers at work."[38] In addition to collaborating in the war-on-terror effort to identify terrorists in the community, performing Muslim identity in line with what the state deems "moderate" or "non-threatening" is another avenue in which the state pushes Muslim Americans to perform the "good Muslim" role.

Law scholar Karen Engle observes that those who forsake their Free Exercise rights in exchange for demonstrations of American patriotism are deemed "good Muslims" by the state.[39] Those who refuse to make the trade-offs demanded by structural Islamophobia are branded "bad Muslims" whose identity signals subversion and warrants suspicion of terrorism. In this way, the war on terror and the Islamophobic policies and private behaviors it induces compel Muslim Americans to perform Muslim identity in ways that conform to the state-sanctioned perception of the "good Muslim," concealing "negative" traits or expressions linked to subversion or terror threat, and in some instances, entirely concealing their Muslim identity. Muslim

Americans who freely exercise their faith are suspected of being "bad Muslims," and those who diminish or forsake that civil liberty are likely to be cast as "good Muslims."[40]

One of the many assumptions embedded in imagining Muslim Americans as subversive is presuming that their allegiance lies with a foreign actor bent on harming the United States—in particular, allegiance to transnational terror networks like Al-Qaeda, the orchestrator of the 9/11 terror attacks, or ISIS, the emergent terrorist organization DHS holds culpable for "inspiring" homegrown radicalization and acts of terror. Under Presidents Bush and Obama, Muslim Americans were expected to rebut these presumptions by disavowing every terror attack that involved a Muslim, assisting the state as interlocutors and informants, and—in conflict with their Free Exercise rights—practicing their faith in ways that mitigated the suspicion of structural Islamophobic policies like the USA PATRIOT Act and CVE policing.

In a May 2016 article for Al Jazeera English, I wrote,

> For Muslim Americans, demonstrations of good citizenship are tied to terrorism. Namely, condemning any and every act that involves a Muslim culprit. Apologizing for the actions of a deviant, distant few. And routinely on deaf ears, collective statements against the savage acts of savage actors such as ISIL.... Muslim Americans are riddled with the assignment of collective guilt that obliges them to disavow or apologize for entirely unrelated actors, or completely unconnected actions.... Unfortunately, there are only two sides, and selecting the wrong side leaves one vulnerable to identification as a bad Muslim, followed by the surveillance and state violence attendant with that classification.[41]

Being a "good Muslim" is hard work during the war on terror, and the binary was on vivid display during the 2016 presidential election. In addition to the brazen Islamophobia coming from the political right, the good Muslim / bad Muslim binary was also actively promoted by Hillary Clinton's campaign.

Journalist Nesrine Malik pinpointed how Clinton carried forward the central Islamophobic narrative that tethers Muslim identity tightly to terrorism, specifically, through the tokenization of Khizr and Ghazala Khan, the gold-star parents of fallen Army captain Humayun Khan. The Khans lost their son to a suicide-bomber attack in Iraq in 2004. Like thousands of other American families, the Khans had to move forward without a child lost to war. The Clinton campaign seized on their story and sought to showcase it and the Khans during the 2016 presidential campaign. In response to this, Malik observes, "Take the Khans of Hillary Clinton's campaign, for example. They are liberal America's final answer to the right's toxic messaging and Trump's 'Muslim Ban' electioneering. Rather than countering simplistic and reductionist views of Muslims, they confirmed them—something that was not lost on many, despite how desperate the situation was."[42] Clinton, and the Democratic Party at large, advanced Islamophobia by projecting a specific image of the "good Muslim," indirectly instructing Muslim Americans to condemn terrorism, endorse American foreign and war policy, and more broadly, abstain from dissident and critical behavior. The message was to be like the Khans, who were projected as the Democratic Party's sanctioned models for Muslim American to conform to.

Declan Walsh of the *New York Times* echoed this very point: "The manner in which Mr. Khan was lionized in the American media also aroused discomfort and debate among other American Muslims. Some say it has resurrected the specter of the 'good Muslim'—the idea, born of the fertile post-2001 era, that

Muslim American patriotism can be measured only by the yard-stick of terrorism and foreign policy. That raised a question: Did Mr. Khan's testimony, determined and powerful as it was, show that it takes the death of a son, in a disputed war in a Muslim land, to prove you are a good American?"[43]

The liberty that comes with being out of place, during the war on terror, exposed Muslim Americans who freely expressed their religious identity to the conjoined Islamophobia of the state and the citizenry. This dynamic, in turn, incentivized Muslim Americans to find their place on the safe side of the good Muslim / bad Muslim binary—or face the steadily expand-ing suspicion that they may be linked to terrorism, or, in line with the new language of counter-radicalization policing, that they may be "homegrown radicals."

CHAPTER FIVE

A "Radical" or
Imagined Threat?

Since Islam is "against us" and "out there," the
necessity of adopting a confrontational response of
our own toward it will not be doubted.

Edward Said, *Covering Islam*

Minneapolis is worlds away from Mogadishu, Somalia. It feels
especially distant during the cold and seemingly endless Minnesota winters. And yet, the eastern Twin City is home to the
largest and most concentrated Somali population in the United
States, a predominantly Muslim diaspora that migrated en
masse to Minnesota following the 1993 civil war, with waves of
newcomers gravitating toward the Somali hub every year since.
Minneapolis has been dubbed "Little Mogadishu" by many, a
title that, depending on who you ask, is linked either to the large
presence of Somalis in the midwestern city or to the images of
turbulence and terror the capital city of Somalia conjures up.

In the last two decades, Minneapolis has become the center
of the Somali American experience, and because Islam is central
to Somali identity for so many, one of the epicenters of the

broader Muslim American experience. While Detroit and its Michigan neighbor, Hamtramck, the first officially Muslim-majority city in the United States, have garnered attention from media and scholars as the lifelines of the Muslim American experience, any accounting of Muslim Americans that does not dedicate ample attention to Minneapolis, and Somali American life in this city, is incomplete. A short stroll through Little Mogadishu reveals that the most salient dimensions of Muslim American life, from surveillance to systematic racism to the struggles of negotiating assimilation alongside spiritual identity, are vividly showcased on these streets.

Ahmed was born in Little Mogadishu two years after his parents settled in Minnesota, building community with other Somalis seeking refuge in the heart of the American Midwest.[1] It is the only home he has ever known. Today, Ahmed studies biology at a nearby college, regularly attends a local mosque, and, in line with his parents' request, sends some of the money he earns from his part-time job to family members in Somalia. He also helps his parents, who live on a modest income supplemented by federal assistance and food stamps, pay their rent each month. A diehard Minnesota Timberwolves and Vikings fan, Ahmed's social media timelines are flooded with posts about the teams' latest victories and losses, and from time to time, status updates about the political and economic tumult in Somalia—a nation that he has never visited, but like many first-generation Somali Americans living in the city, has a strong affinity for.

Ahmed is every bit Somali and American, effortlessly switching from English to Somali, blending both beautifully into a distinctly harmonized tongue. Indeed, both languages, and the cultures they represent, make Ahmed neither Somali nor American alone. He is both, coexistent and combined to form a distinct identity shared by the thousands of Somali American youth and twenty-somethings living in Minneapolis and throughout the country.

The year 2014 marked a critical turning point for Ahmed. During the holy month of Ramadan, when Muslims are obliged to abstain from food and water from sunrise to sundown, Ahmed found himself spending more time in the mosque. He would make the short walk over when he found time between classes and his work shifts, and he became a fixture at the mosque in the early morning, when brothers and sisters convened to make *taraweeh,* the special Ramadan prayers. Like many young people of faith, whether Christian or Jew, Hindu or Buddhist, Ahmed was drawn to Islam at the crossroads of his teenage and adult years, smitten by the beauty of the Qur'an he finally picked up to read closely, and drawn in by the tight-knit community that surrounded him. Ramadan drew him closer to Islam and closer to the community, and he found himself drawn to maintaining a more pious lifestyle beyond the Holy Month. Faith changed Ahmed from the inside, and gradually his enhanced spirituality would become more manifest on the outside. Ahmed always knew Islam and was always around the mosque, but months before his nineteenth birthday, he fully embraced it as a way of life.

At the end of Ramadan in 2014, Ahmed kept a beard to signify his piety. He skipped spending weekend nights with friends at downtown clubs in favor of evenings discussing politics, community concerns, and faith at the "Somali Starbucks" on Riverside Avenue. His Facebook statuses began to reflect the spiritual growth and personal maturity Ahmed was experiencing, and in line with developing a stronger social justice bent, he began forming critical opinions of American foreign policy and domestic counterterror policy. Quotes from the Prophet Mohammed and other important Islamic figures filled his Facebook page, while pictures of grand mosques in the Middle East, Africa, and beyond were the snapshots he featured on his Instagram account, instead of selfies or pictures of his dream cars.

Everybody around him noticed his shift for the better, particularly his family and closest friends. Apart from spiritual growth, Ahmed's academic performance dramatically improved, his professional drive and sense of purpose sharpened, and his commitment to social justice and community philanthropy strengthened. But this personal development, which would seem benign for young men of other faiths, spelled danger for Ahmed, a Muslim and a young black man; he occupied perhaps the most dangerous intersection of identity during the American moment in which he lived, a period of radical reform on the national security policing front.

In 2014, the Department of Homeland Security named Minneapolis as one of the pilot cities where Countering Violent Extremism (CVE) policing would be implemented. CVE was a recently established program, formally implemented by the Obama administration in 2011, whereby local law enforcement (the Minneapolis Police Department) collaborated closely with federal security agents to help identify prospective "homegrown radicals" and try to prevent them from enlisting with a terrorist organization or taking part in a terror attack. CVE policing focused almost entirely on Muslims and concentrated on Muslim communities like the Cedar-Riverside neighborhood in Minneapolis that Ahmed called home. Religious piety was considered by CVE policing policy to be one of the signals of a Muslim becoming radicalized, particularly when the shift toward religiosity was an abrupt one.

This left Ahmed, whose embrace of faith was in line with his quest for personal growth and theoretically protected by the Free Exercise Clause of the First Amendment, in the crosshairs of CVE policing and terror suspicion. To the Minneapolis Police Department and the DHS agents it collaborated with, Ahmed's spiritual growth signaled risk and prompted suspicion. His name made its way onto the list of "subjects of interest"—all of whom were Muslim men, whether Somali, Arab, black, or white—tallied by Minneapolis police officers as suspected of "being radicalized" by Al-Shabab, ISIS, or other Islamic transnational terror networks. Ahmed's spiritual growth and placement on the suspect list all happened in less than a year.

Ahmed had no idea he was a suspect until one Saturday morning when two police officers, who had been carefully observing him and his social media for weeks, stopped over at his family's home to question him. The officers were acting with the help of an informant, a school acquaintance who kept tabs on Ahmed in exchange for reduced probation time for a crime he had committed. Ahmed had done no wrong, he had no prior convictions, no criminal record at all, and yet he was deemed a subject of interest—a prospective radical on account of his nationality, neighborhood, and especially, his spiritual evolution from secular to devout Muslim. Like thousands of Muslim youth in Minneapolis, and millions more across the country, Ahmed's faith marked him as suspect of radicalization—not a crime or criminal activity, not hateful or violent behavior, but rather the Islamophobic, prejudice-driven fear that his faith might spur him toward terrorism.

CVE policing, the signature structural Islamophobic program implemented and enforced by the Obama administration, shifted the focus of the war on terror from foreign terrorist organizations to "homegrown radicals," in line with DHS's belief that Al Qaeda, and more potently, ISIS, was inspiring "homegrown radicalization." CVE policing extended the Islamophobic presumption that an expression of Muslim identity, whether through religious practice or observance, physical markers, or even political activity (perceived as Muslim-related), is indicative of radicalization and deserving of suspicion and investigation. This story is not Ahmed's alone, but a common tale of Muslim youth, men, and women throughout the country.

THE RISE OF ISIS

The bustling and narrow streets of Old Havana were a panorama unlike anything seen back home in the United States. The sounds of salsa reverberating and the chorus of Spanish coming from every direction signaled that I was very far from home. Cuba's communist foundation and its turbulent relationship with Washington, D.C., made home feel ever further away, even though I was only ninety miles away from Miami.

It was Thursday, May 25, 2017, two days before the holy month of Ramadan, and I roamed around the Old District in search of Havana's only mosque, the Mezquita Abdallah. My brown skin and ethnic ambiguity helped me blend in nicely and I was ignored by the street peddlers pestering tourists from Europe, Canada, and other origins. Yet I would soon learn that my religious identity would cast me as an outsider, as it did back home in the United States.

Confused by the maze of streets and limited by my lack of Spanish, I asked a passerby if he knew where the mosque was located. He paused, inspected my lightly bearded face and snickered, "Why, are you with ISIS?" For me, worlds away from home and momentarily free—I thought—from the continual looming presumption of suspicion and guilt attendant with American Islamophobia, this was no laughing matter. First, it signaled the obvious, that Islamophobia was indeed a global phenomenon; second, it showed with stark clarity that ISIS had become the preeminent global face of the Muslim terrorist not only in the United States, but also around the world. I could not escape the connections people made between Islam and ISIS, whether at home or on vacation.

On May 2, 2011, Navy SEALS in Pakistan killed Osama Bin Laden, the head of Al Qaeda, the terror network behind the 9/11 terror attacks. His death was celebrated all over the United States and marked a major political victory for the Obama administration. It also marked a critical turning point in the war on terror. The assassination of Bin Laden led to the gradual decline of Al Qaeda as the principal Islamic terror network in the world, opening the door for ISIS, its more violent offshoot, to assume that mantle. ISIS's mission was to establish, and expand, a caliphate, an Islamic state, in the heart of the Arab world. This caliphate became the primary theater for ISIS's two-front war, a war that also included staging terror attacks outside of the Middle East, most frequently in Europe. Simultaneously, the terror networks in Europe were busy recruiting thousands of disaffected youth and young adults to either join ISIS in the Arab world or carry out terror conspiracies at home.

While Al Qaeda and Bin Laden had been focused centrally on attacking the West, ISIS's objectives were grander and more complex. Fawaz Gerges writes that "conceptually and operationally, there exist important differences between Al Qaeda Central and ISIS, even though they belong to the same Salafi-jihadist family. Bin Laden and [current Al Qaeda leader] Zawahiri never wavered from viewing America as the real enemy and consistently reminded their followers that 'the focus should be on killing and fighting the American people and their representatives,' a mission ISIS and its leadership embraced and, to great horror, continued."[2] However, in addition to fighting this "far enemy," ISIS was also committed to a "near war" with what it considered a primary foe, Shiite Muslims in the region. Growing out of the tumult of the Iraq wars and the vacuum those left in Iraq, and the violent clashes and anarchy in Syria, ISIS gained considerable momentum in relative obscurity for nearly a decade.

The mainstream American news media finally turned its attention to ISIS in 2013, and most prolifically, in June of 2014, when the terror network took over the Iraqi city of Mosul. Although ISIS had been conspiring in the shadows for more than a decade, Mosul marked a critical turning point that signaled it was no trivial movement, but a rapidly expanding regional power bent on accelerating its territorial control, ideological influence, and, for nations far from the Arab world, its global terror reach. In *The Atlantic*, David Ignatius observed, "Like many consequential events, this one didn't sneak up on policymakers; they simply didn't see what was taking shape in front of them. ISIS told us exactly what it was going to do, and then did it. This was a secret conspiracy hiding in plain sight."[3] In relative obscurity, ISIS had enlisted and mobilized legions of followers, mounted successful offensives in Iraq and Syria, and chewed up more and more territory, capitalizing on regional tumult and global neglect to emerge as an unprecedented terror menace.

If its victory in Mosul was not enough to demand the attention of policymakers and the mainstream American media, its "pornographically violent" and vividly crafted videos of beheadings and executions, distributed through social media platforms, demanded attention.[4] Striking fear in the hearts of viewers was its primary aim, but ISIS also spent millions of dollars to use these videos as propaganda, hoping to inspire wayward youth, men, and women looking for a cause or a calling in the Arab world, Europe, and the United States.

The news became rife with stories asking, "Why did three American kids from the suburbs of Chicago try to run away to [join] the Islamic State?"[5] and headlines such as "The Americans: 15 Who Left the United States to Join ISIS."[6] Fixation on ISIS, and fear of its reach and resonance within Muslim American communities, became the subject of daily news stories. Although it never took much to trigger the embedded fears that conflated Muslim identity with foreign violence, the emergence of ISIS and the counterterror policing model it helped spur marked a critical shift in the framing of Muslim terrorism.

The primary profile of the Muslim terrorist was no longer that of the foreign actor who traveled to the United States to carry out an act of terror. The new image was the "homegrown radical," who was (likely) born and bred in the United States, by all measures American but vulnerable to recruitment and ideological conversion by ISIS on the basis of his or her Muslim identity alone. Thus any and every Muslim American (particularly Sunni Muslims, since radicalization is disproportionately linked to Sunni terror networks like ISIS) was presumed to be vulnerable to radicalization, and therefore subject to the suspicion and surveillance of the state.

The powder keg of war and sectarianism in Iraq and Syria have facilitated ISIS's expansion, and its systematic killing of Shiite Muslims, Christians, and ethnic minorities has added to that apocalyptic mix. The conflict in Syria and the crimes of the Assad regime have also played into the sectarian vision of ISIS, leading many to believe that its "power will only be enhanced ... by Assad's continued hold on power."[7] Moreover, its advances in the Arab world are accompanied by horror abroad, as illustrated on November 13, 2015, in Paris, when ISIS attackers, in separate but coordinated bombings and shootings, killed 130 people and injured roughly 400. This followed the Paris attacks in January 2015, when terrorists killed seventeen people at the offices of satirical magazine *Charlie Hebdo,* a kosher grocery, and in the suburb of Montrouge. These attacks helped fuel the rise of private and structural Islamophobia in a nation where both were already rampant, as demonstrated most vividly by the rise of the National Front's Marine Le Pen, who finished second in the May 2017 presidential runoff, claiming nearly 34 percent of the national vote. Like Trump, Le Pen capitalized on virulent Islamophobic rhetoric, claiming that Muslim and French identities are irreconcilable, echoing the longstanding rhetoric that Islam is unassimilable, hostile, and inherently at odds with the West—a rhetoric deeply embedded in the American imagination and, today, one of the latent drivers of CVE policing.

CVE policing was the new counterterror paradigm, and in terms of encroaching on the privacy of Muslim Americans and presuming guilt based on religious identity alone, the "new PATRIOT Act."[8] Actors with (real or nominal) Muslim identities, such as the perpetrators of the terror attacks in San Bernardino and Orlando, were instantly presumed to have ISIS ties and to be acting in furtherance of ISIS objectives. As with the Oklahoma City bombing more than two decades earlier, and the hundreds of attacks committed by Muslim and, overwhelmingly, non-Muslim actors since, mainstream media spun the same fantastic and trite narratives of Muslim terror conspiracies, basing them on the thinnest pieces of information or no evidence at all aside from the ethnic or religious profile of the actor.

Yet the private Islamophobia of the media was no aberration at all in this respect, but rather an extension of the structural Islamophobia shaped and enforced by the state, which likewise built its suspicion and surveillance of Muslim Americans, like Ahmed in Minneapolis, on the slimmest pieces of evidence, overwhelmingly focusing on the religious identity and lifestyle of the actor. In the words of my younger brother Mohammed, "The more you pray, the more you're prey."

THE THREAT OF "HOMEGROWN RADICALS"

In August 2011, President Obama formally implemented CVE policing, which would become the primary counterterror surveillance program and the signature Islamophobic policy of his administration. CVE theory contends that through collaboration between DHS and local law enforcement, individuals suspected of becoming radicalized can be identified, persuaded from adopting a "radical" ideology, and prevented from taking terrorist action. "To its proponents," writes New York University law professor Samuel Rascoff, "counter-radicalization begins with the uncontroversial proposition that manifestations of violent extremism are rooted in ideas and social-behavior processes. Understanding and addressing these ideas and processes will help prevent future attacks and thus should play an important role in American counterterror policy."[9]

Sahar Aziz, a Rutgers law professor and leading scholar on Muslim Americans and national security matters, adds: "Operationally, the objective is to stop people from embracing extreme beliefs (an inherently subjective and vague term) that might lead to terrorism, as well as to reduce active support for terrorist groups."[10] While "extremism" is framed in racially and religiously neutral terms, and CVE policing is theoretically focused on all culprits of extremism, it is disproportionately if not entirely focused on "ideas" and behavioral "processes" linked to Islam and expressions of Muslim identity. Radicalization, therefore, is theorized as an exclusively Muslim phenomenon, much like its precedent and related enterprise, terrorism.

Furthermore, "radicalization theory suggests that the path from Muslim to terrorist is a predictable one."[11] It links radicalization—or propensity for radicalization—with specific "religious and political cultures within Muslim communities."[12] In line with FBI guidelines, CVE policing philosophy breaks down the "identifiable and predictable process by which a Muslim becomes a terrorist into four stages: 1) preradicalization; 2) identification; 3) indoctrination; and 4) action."[13] During the first stage, the Muslim subject's radicalization potential is dormant, untapped; the second stage involves gravitation toward conservative religious expression; during the third stage, the Muslim subject has adopted or embraced an ideology deemed "extreme"; and finally, in the fourth stage, the subject is conspiring to take terrorist action. Since the Muslim subject is viewed as a greater threat at each successive stage, CVE policing seeks to apprehend the subject at the earliest stage possible.

According to DHS, the predictive pathway toward radicalization makes it preventable. And prevention is at the core of radicalization theory, which centers exclusively on Muslim subjects and geographies as presumptive sources of terrorism. Muslim Americans suspected of radicalization have engaged in no criminal act. And yet young Muslim men, like Ahmed in Minneapolis, are disproportionately vulnerable to the dragnet of CVE policing, which makes the Islamophobic leap that Muslim masculinity plus piety equals a desire to enlist with ISIS or another terror network. Muslim American women who exhibit the same piety are generally profiled as harborers of homegrown radicals, and with rising frequency, homegrown radicals themselves.

Today, CVE policing ranks among the most destructive forms of structural Islamophobia. Its strategy and enforcement, while framed in a facially neutral fashion, is "cloaked in expertise about the process by which Muslims become terrorists."[14] Individuals who maximize their Muslim identity, or "Muslimness," by freely expressing their faith and exercising their First Amendment rights, expose themselves to being profiled by the state as refusing to assimilate, as religiously conservative, as extreme or subversive, to name just some of the "bad Muslim" tropes that open the door to CVE suspicion. In short, the more Muslim one is, the more likely one will be pegged as a subject of CVE interest.

CVE policing is driven by the same fears that fuel private Islamophobes to vandalize and burn down mosques, isolate and attack Muslim men with beards or women with headscarves, and rally in front of religious centers and advocacy organizations. But instead of enforcing Islamophobia by way of vigilante violence, CVE policing plants informants in mosques and other spaces where Muslims congregate, and mobilizes local law enforcement to keep a watchful eye on Muslim communities. It also turns Muslim Americans against one another, and intentionally (or at minimum, consequently) divides Muslim communities.

In order to prevent radicalization among Muslims Americans, DHS is tasked with cultivating strategic partnerships with Muslim American communities. CVE could not succeed without robust and active Muslim American "engagement," specifically, community informants and stakeholders. Partnerships with individuals and institutions within Muslim American communities are vital for advancing CVE. This enables DHS to pivot from electronic surveillance to being deputized, on-the-ground watchdogs. DHS strategically "maps" gatherings and communities and then taps informants within mosques, organizations such as Muslim student associations on college campuses, community centers, and other "places for religious and political discussion and gathering."[15] In addition to monitoring subjects of interest through deputized informants, CVE also assigns FBI and law enforcement agents to monitor internet activity, piercing the privacy of Muslim Americans on the ground but also in virtual spaces.

Olivier Roy, a prominent French intellectual and critic of counter-radicalization theory and programs as they stand today, argues that "radicalization seems more linked to individual trajectories" than collective religious behavior.[16] Roy recommends that CVE strategy focus more on individual subjects and the societal conditions that give rise to radicalization, rather than on religious doctrine or religious groups at large. Societal symptoms include systemic poverty, declining education, disaffection, and hostility toward Muslims in the form of structural and private Islamophobia that isolates Muslim Americans and feeds into the propaganda of terror networks like ISIS.

Instead of seeking to mend the structural symptoms that give rise to extremism, CVE policing makes them worse by disproportionately targeting indigent, immigrant, and working-class Muslim communities. I echo Roy; I have closely researched and personally witnessed how CVE destroys communities, particularly poor and working-class neighborhoods—like the one I was raised in and still call home. If the real objective is prevention, then empowering youth instead of vilifying them should be the focus—particularly Muslim youth at the most distant and dire margins.

POOR AND MUSLIM IN
WAR-ON-TERROR AMERICA

In *The Souls of Black Folk,* W.E.B. Dubois writes, "To be a poor man is hard, but to be a poor race in a land of dollars is the very bottom of hardships."[17] DuBois's assessment points to the intersection poor blacks endured at the turn of the century, when "separate but equal" was furiously enforced by Jim Crow laws and a Supreme Court that authorized, and legally enabled, the structural racism and systemic impoverishment of black people. His words also speak to the experience of Muslim Americans during the war on terror, and more specifically, indigent and working-class Muslim Americans, a community sitting at the dangerous intersection of poverty, Islamophobia, and the mounting scrutiny and surveillance of DHS.

As I stated earlier this book, Muslim identity is *imagined* far more than it is *seen.* Rather than observing the genuine corporeal contours of the Muslim American population, the public, and oftentimes the state, frequently visualize individual and collective Muslim bodies through an Orientalist prism. Embedded tropes dictate how Muslims are imagined along racial, behavioral, ideological, and economic lines. Since Islam is conflated with the Middle East, an imagined sphere associated with infinite supplies of oil, sheikhs, and the gaudy wealth of Gulf states, Muslims are often stereotyped as an affluent and upwardly mobile population.

Once again, statistics deconstruct stereotypes. A 2011 Pew Research Center study, the first to closely examine poverty and wealth in the Muslim American population, found that 45 percent of Muslim American households reported a household income of less than $30,000 per year, compared to just 36 percent of the general American public.[18]

A 2017 study by the Institute for Social Policy and Understanding confirmed these figures and added insight into poverty experienced by Muslim Americans along racial lines and ethnic lines. That study reported that 44 percent of black Muslims reported an annual household income of less than $30,000 per year; for Arab Muslim American households the figure was 37 percent, and for Asian Muslim Americans it was 30 percent. Fourteen percent of black Muslims, 21 percent of Arab Muslim Americans, and 16 percent of Asian Muslim Americans reported an annual household income of $30,000–$50,000 per year. Combined, these statistics illustrate that sizable segments of the broader Muslim American population live below or dangerously close to the 2017 federal poverty level, defined as $32,960 for a family of six. These figures reveal that more than half of the black and Arab American Muslim households are either poor or working class, at 58 percent, while Muslim Asian American households figure in at 46 percent.[19]

Statistics show that Muslim Americans as a standalone faith group are comparatively poorer than the broader American polity, and according to a number of studies, poorer than any other faith group.[20] This doesn't just challenge the myth that Muslim Americans are overwhelmingly wealthy and upwardly mobile; it shatters it to pieces. And poverty for Muslim Americans comes with a range of other concerns and dangers, including those linked to how poverty enhances vulnerability to private backlash and state surveillance. The reality of pervasive poverty among Muslim Americans, particularly in immigrant-heavy communities, leads to their disproportionate targeting and victimization by war-on-terror policies, and, most frequently and furiously, CVE policing. It is trying to be poor in the United States, but exponentially more trying to be poor and victimized by the war on terror.

As a community marginalized on at least three tracks—poverty, religion, and race—poor Muslim Americans confront the brunt of both CVE and customary community policing. This was vividly evident in the New York Police Department's "stop and frisk" and "spying on Muslims" programs, which disproportionately targeted black and Latinx men and women, and poor, urban, and immigrant Muslim communities, respectively and intersectionally. Poor and working-class Muslim American communities, like Ahmed's Little Mogadishu neighborhood in Minneapolis, are indeed the locales DHS prioritizes and descends into to weaponize the structural Islamophobic vision that ties race, religion, and poverty to anticipated radical threat. Approximately 82 percent of the up to 80,000 Somalis in Minnesota live "near or below the poverty line."[21] The Somali community in Minneapolis has faced greater CVE scrutiny since scores of men were allegedly recruited by terrorist groups, many of them entrapped by the police on the basis of websites they visited, coerced admissions of guilt, visits to Somalia, or transfers of money to family members in Somalia.[22]

Furthermore, "Somalis tend to express their religious identity in traditions that resemble expression in their home country, generally maintain close ties with family and friends in Somalia, and tend to live and worship in predominantly Somali spaces. Therefore, CVE policing suspicion of Somali Americans is linked more closely to these 'immigrant' proxies to Muslim identity than it is to Blackness, while anti-terror suspicion of indigenous Black Muslims is more closely tied to conversion or political subversion."[23] The racial identity of Somali Americans also exposes them to conventional criminal profiling and policing, and the prospect of being gunned down by police on account of their blackness, as horrifically illustrated by the wildly disproportionate killing of black men by police around the country, including the killing of Philando Castille, a thirty-two-year-old black man shot by a policeman after a traffic stop in Minneapolis on July 6, 2016.

In 2014, DHS announced that Boston, Los Angeles, and Minneapolis would be the first cities assigned with hardline CVE policing programs. Boston was prioritized because of the 2013 Boston Marathon bombings, committed by the Tsarnaev brothers; Los Angeles was chosen because of its proximity to the Mexican border, and because California as a whole houses the largest population of Muslims in the country; Minneapolis was chosen because of its concentrated and large Somali population, the majority of which is Muslim, with strong ties to the homeland. While distinct events motivated DHS to make Boston, Los Angeles, and Minneapolis CVE pilot cities, what bound the three cities were Muslim communities that were overwhelmingly Sunni; that were presumptively vulnerable to transnational terror networks, principally Al Qaeda, ISIS, and the Somali terror group Al Shabaab; and that were home to concentrated indigent, immigrant, and/or working-class Muslim populations.

However, surveillance of indigent and working-class Muslims goes beyond these three cities, and even beyond the specter of formal CVE policing. The metropolitan Detroit area, home to the most densely populated Arab and Muslim American communities in the United States, many of them poor and working class, is among the most monitored areas in the country. In addition to preexisting DHS surveillance programs in Detroit and surrounding areas like Dearborn, Michigan, proposed and in-place CVE policies focus specifically on concentrated and poor Muslim communities within the city and its suburbs. Surveillance of these communities takes on a different form and flavor because of the ethnic, national, and sectarian divisions gripping the area.

For instance, Iraqi households centered largely in Dearborn and Detroit have an average household income of $32,075 per year.[24] Many of these Iraqi Muslims migrated to Michigan as a result of the 2003 Iraq War, an illegal war launched by the United States two years after the 9/11 terror attacks. Similarly, the median income of the Yemeni population is near the federal poverty threshold, standing at $34,667 per year.[25] Yemeni Muslim populations are mostly concentrated in large urban centers—principally in the San Francisco Bay Area, Detroit, and New York—where the NYPD operated a "spying on Muslims" program in the tri-state area that sowed the seeds for the informal and formal policing programs that followed, including Obama's 2011 formal implementation of CVE policing.

In addition, the metropolitan Detroit area is home to a sizable Lebanese American population, which, like the Iraqi community, is overwhelmingly Shiite. The sectarian demographics of the city have equipped DHS, and local law enforcement, with the added ability to turn Muslim American communities against one another—to mobilize Shiite Muslim Americans as informants or full-fledged partners against their Sunni Muslim American counterparts. In effect, this imports the sectarian divides of the Arab world into structural Islamophobic counterterror programming at home, in an effort to uncover the homegrown radical—who is far less real than imagined.

DIVIDE, CONQUER, AND
COUNTER-RADICALIZE

Turning Muslim Americans against one another is a direct effect, if not an intentional strategy, of CVE policing. This is particularly true in places like the metropolitan Detroit area, where divisions along national, generational, and most potently, sectarian lines arm DHS and its local interlocutors with the dangerous tools to carry forward CVE programming and policing. By pegging specific Muslim traditions, practices, and cultures, most notably Sunni Muslim populations, as prone to radicalization, the state is drawing clear economic, political, and sectarian divisions within the broader Muslim American population. Driven by clear articulations of the good and bad Muslim, CVE policing creates a landscape in which those who endorse CVE policing and partake in its programming as informants and collaborators are deemed good Muslims and good Americans, while those critical of it, and critical of structural Islamophobia at large, are not only perceived as bad Muslims, but more dangerously, are subjected to possible CVE policing.

CVE policing, therefore, not only capitalizes on preexisting divides within Muslim American communities, but also strategically exacerbates them and creates new rifts. For instance, DHS may emphasize the persecution of Shiite Iraqis by ISIS to engender sympathy among Shiite Iraqi Americans, or capitalize on the pointedly sectarian strife in Syria and the crimes of ISIS to resonate with Shiite Lebanese Americans. Whether motivated by sectarianism and regional politics, government grants and access to power, or some combination of these factors, DHS has exploited divisions within the Muslim American population to entrench and enhance surveillance of Muslim Americans. By recruiting Muslim American sponsors, or "native informants," the structural Islamophobic policy that is CVE policing is not only aided, but legitimized.

Hamid Dabashi argues, "For the American imperial project to claim global validity it needs the support of native informers and comprador intellectuals with varying accents to their speech, their prose and their politics. Supported by only white men and white women, the project would not have the same degree of narrative authority. But accents from targeted cultures and climes Orientalize, exoticize, and corroborate all at the same time."[26] CVE policing in particular, and structural Islamophobia at large, cannot be carried forward without the endorsement of a cadre or cohort of Muslim Americans that rubberstamp it. Without their legitimization, these programs are plainly and painfully exposed as patently Islamophobic. Muslim faces and voices make them seem reasonable, sanctioned by the idea that if a Muslim deems CVE policing to be legitimate, then the public at large should find no problem with it.

When CVE policing was inaugurated, the state had a ready supply of native informants in place—Muslim Americans who endorsed the structural Islamophobic policies of the state for personal gain. Examples include Ayaan Hirsi Ali, Asra Nomani, and Brigitte Gabriel, who trades on her Lebanese Christian identity (which, for the broader public, is synonymous with Muslim identity) as the basis of her expertise; these people have helped carry forward the narrative of "Islamic extremism" that supports the war on terror and programming like CVE policing. They have built careers castigating Islam, casting Muslim Americans as domestic threats, and endorsing strident war-on-terror policies.

Zuhdi Jasser, one of the most prominent and damaging Muslim informants, claims, "There can be no better way to ebb the tide of fear of Muslims in the West than for Muslims to demonstrate that we are the most important asset in defeating the very ideologies that attacked us 11 years ago [in the World Trade Center attacks]. This requires an embrace of a public critique of our faith leaders and institutions. All other approaches have been proven failures."[27] Public positions like this confirm the notion that Islam is some sort of religious or ideological monolith and that Muslim Americans are collectively responsible for not only condemning acts of terror, but also participating in the project of fighting against it. While extreme, Jasser's position echoes the logic of CVE policing, which binds Muslim Americans with the responsibility for fighting homegrown radicalization in their neighborhoods and places of worship, households and schools. Wherever Muslim Americans congregate is deemed the front line of radicalization.

Extreme native informants, those with no meaningful Muslim American following and largely viewed as "sell-outs" by the community, were more burdens than boons for President Obama's CVE policing program. Therefore a new crop of native informants, far more moderate and with resonance within Muslim American communities, was needed. DHS, the State Department, and other state agencies that pushed CVE policing abroad and domestically enlisted Muslim Americans from the political left and center, who became formal, subcontracted proponents of CVE policing. Many of them were located in Washington, D.C., but some were members of Muslim communities across the country where soft and hardline CVE programming was being promoted. In those communities, the Obama administration dangled huge sums of money, access to government,

government jobs or the prospect of government jobs in front of those willing to endorse CVE policing and facilitate its implementation. Again, in order for CVE policing to work to its optimal effect, robust Muslim American support was necessary.

Scores of Muslim American organizations took the bait, including a "Dearborn group led by Lebanese-Americans,"[28] which changed its name from the Lebanese American Heritage Club to Leaders Advancing and Helping Communities (LAHC), a decision motivated in large part by access to CVE funds from DHS. Led by its executive director, Wassim Mahfouz, the community organization had limited much of its previous activity to local political and cultural events. Then, in 2017, it received $500,000 to lay the groundwork for CVE policing in Dearborn, Michigan, home to a concentrated and sizable Muslim American population. Almost overnight, LAHC went from being a local cultural organization to a de facto policing outfit, making structural changes in order to carry out the groundwork for CVE policing in Dearborn-area schools, community centers, and meeting places. The makeover would create a slew of new jobs for LAHC staff, higher salaries, and direct reach into Washington, D.C.

Mahfouz stated, "The funding will be specifically used to sustain existing programming ... [including] youth development, nurturing parenting, substance abuse prevention."[29] But these seemingly benign programs were given greater clarity by the DHS secretary, who released a statement the week before the LAHC announcement, declaring that "in this age of self-radicalization and terrorist-inspired acts of violence, domestic-based efforts to counter violent extremism have become a homeland security imperative.... The funding will go for activities that include intervention, developing resilience, challenging the narrative, and building capacity."[30] These ambiguous aims, which sound innocuous and even well intentioned, are code-speak for programming that would educate students about the threat of radicalization, develop a "see something, say something" culture in schools, and, ultimately, deputize school administrators and students to be watchdogs on the lookout for homegrown radicals—radicals, absurdly, that were as young as eleven years old and profiled because of their religious identity.

However, the funds were awarded to LAHC after the election of Donald Trump, which dramatically changed the equation. Under the administration of a president who declared that "Islam hates us," LAHC was expected to carry out programming in elementary, junior, and high schools in Dearborn that centered on signaling forms of Islamic extremism, reporting suspicious activity by classmates, and developing informants and deputizing teachers as watchdogs—inside public school classrooms, no less, where young, impressionable minds are supposed to learn and be given a safe haven in which to grow.

CVE policing in a setting like Dearborn, with its sectarian diversity, would have capitalized on already profuse tensions among Shiites and Sunnis to advance its strategy. For example, Lebanese or Iraqi Shiites would have been sought as informants against Yemeni or Palestinian Sunnis, since radicalization is generally understood and enforced as a Sunni phenomenon. LAHC's identity as a largely Lebanese Shiite organization made it an attractive CVE policing partner for CVE policing, and the large sum of money it was set to receive would be compensation for stirring sectarian divides to facilitate the state's witch hunt for Muslim radicals among children. While LAHC, like the Muslim Public Affairs Council (MPAC) and other groups, would have garnered ample criticism for carrying forward CVE programming under the Obama administration, doing so under a Trump administration was untenable, opening the floodgates for public shaming and condemnation. And that's exactly what followed.

News of LAHC's receipt of these funds instantly spread through the metropolitan Detroit community and, soon after, across the country. Activists, including Abed Ayoub, Asha Noor, and myself, took action, using social media to critique the organization's role as a subcontractor in CVE policing, particularly under an administration that openly vilified Muslims, proposed a range of damaging policies, and claimed the White House, in large part, under the banner of brazen Islamophobia. Ayoub, a Dearborn native and acting legal director of the American Arab-Discrimination Committee in Washington, D.C., posted on Facebook on January 13, 2017, "Lebanese American Heritage Club. Will say it publicly. This is beyond disappointing. I've always respected the organization and the work you do. But this requires some explanation." He posted a photo of the DHS press release naming LAHC as one of the CVE grant recipients for all to see.

Ayoub's post caused a stir locally, galvanizing activists from Michigan and beyond to join in on the criticism of LAHC. LAHC had applied for the grant in secrecy, hoping that nobody would learn about its involvement with CVE policing, a program lay Muslim Americans, particularly in working-class and immigrant communities, are hardly aware of. The grassroots and social media efforts of activists, Muslim and otherwise, brought knowledge of LAHC's collaboration with CVE policing out of the shadows.

Pressured by social media shaming, op-eds, and behind-the-scenes phone calls, LAHC declined its CVE grant nine days later. It was a major victory against CVE policing in Detroit, but a slew of other organizations, in "locations across the country such as Boston, Minneapolis, Los Angeles"—cities with already established hardline CVE policing programs—as well as other locations tapped for similar programs, accepted the funding.[31] MPAC kept the reported $400,000 it received and still collaborates with DHS in carrying forward CVE policing within and beyond Los Angeles, where a hardline CVE policing program has existed since 2014. Even universities cashed in on CVE funding—the University of North Carolina Chapel Hill was the biggest recipient.

Divide and conquer is a stated objective of American foreign policy in the Arab world, and with CVE policing, it is an evolving counterterror strategy. This is evidenced by the exploitation of the tense and divided sectarian landscape in the metropolitan Detroit area, the leveraging of ethnocentric and class-based paternalism that drives groups like MPAC to advance CVE policing in places like Los Angeles, and the economic vulnerability of recent immigrant communities like the Somali population in Minneapolis, where, as Asha Noor shares, "CVE and surveillance of the Somali community has created a rift and a sense of mistrust. Individuals who were once friends are no longer on talking terms because of the choices they made: to accept grants that meant framing your community as inherently violent or to not."[32]

Turning Muslim Americans against one another, as native informants or community informants, watchdogs-for-hire or sectarian rivals, is a vital cog in the war-on-terror machine, and as exhibited by CVE policing, an evolving dimension of structural Islamophobia. While foreign policy tactics in the Middle East have long capitalized on intensifying sectarianism as a strategy for intensifying tumult, division, and conquest, DHS has wielded this very strategy at home, in the heart of Muslim American communities, to bring about the same end.

The war-on-terror playbook is complex and fluidly developing, in line with the changing face of Muslim Americans. CVE policing is a testament to this complexity, as vividly illustrated by the distinct ways DHS employs this program in cities like Detroit, where sectarianism is rife, and Minneapolis, the Somali Muslim hub. Muslims, particularly youth and young adults, are either viewed as presumptive radicals or tapped by DHS as cogs in its machine. They are seldom, if ever, treated as young people whose futures and talents deserve investment.

"We need to wake up and say, 'You know what? Enough is enough,'" stated Hibaaq Osman, whose family owns a small café in a Somali shopping mall in Minneapolis. "We are citizens, we are taxpayers, we own businesses, we need people to understand that we also are part of this country just the way anybody else is."[33] While Muslims are asleep, DHS and local law enforcement are pushing CVE policing, planting informants, and paying collaborators to be part of this new war-on-terror witch hunt—a persecution against which citizenship, sadly, offers little protection.

CHAPTER SIX

Between Anti-Black Racism and Islamophobia

Sure, I know I got it made while the masses of black
people are catchin' hell, but as long as they ain't free,
I ain't free.

  Muhammad Ali, 1975

The guy from immigration ... asked me, "What is
your religion?"... And I said, "I'm a Muslim."

  Muhammad Ali, Jr., 2017

The greatest Muslim American was black. In fact, the man many
will remember as the most iconic American in history was both
Muslim and black. His reign in the hearts of Americans of every
shade and in the hearts of billions more across the world lasted
far longer than his championship runs in the 1960s and 1970s.
Few people were as loved and revered as Muhammad Ali, a man
with a quintessential Muslim name and a defiant, unapologetic
love for his blackness. This was evident in his unparalleled life,
and indeed, when he left the world on June 3, 2016.

  Foreign and domestic dignitaries, Muslim religious and political leaders, and adoring fans traveled from every corner of the

world to attend his funeral in his hometown of Louisville, Kentucky, on June 10, 2016. The death of Ali, a black Muslim giant who symbolized so much to so many, manifested that even the transcendence of this beloved figure did not deliver the empowerment of the very people he represented, gave voice to, and fought for. Too often, the harmonized identity that inspired his commitment to racial justice was vilified, obfuscated, and dismembered. People took what they wanted from Ali, not the entirety of the man, appropriating his image or a quote, his blackness or his Muslim identity, without championing the whole of who he was: a black Muslim committed to radical structural reform.

His passing came at a very turbulent time in American history, when the rising tide of Islamophobia intersected with a Black Lives Matter movement that was already in full swing. This movement condemned the institutional racism and systemic violence inflicted on black bodies with the same ferocity and fight as the champion buried before thousands in Louisville and billions more watching at home. Ali, up until his final day, was unapologetically black and unrepentantly Muslim and spoke out against the bigotry directed at both halves of his identity. Ali embodied, in loud and living color, that black Muslim was a coexistent and harmonized identity, not a divorced and dissonant one; that these were not, as implied by the law rooted in the antebellum era, contradictory racial classifications that could not be reconciled. Ali fought these legal strictures by condemning the structures that crafted them and by speaking up in the ways that only he could—challenging racism, anti-Muslim animus, and the demonization of black Muslims as ferociously as he fought Joe Frazier and George Foreman in the ring.

Everybody listened to him, but very few heard the intersectional message he delivered. Islamophobia and anti-black racism were not unfolding on separate tracks, or inflicted on distinct populations; they were, and are, entwined by a kindred source and common targets. Despite the heights Ali reached in sport, and the throne he claimed in the hearts and minds of everyone, the very black Muslim experience and people he represented are still, today, marginalized and ignored. Allegations of Ali's funeral being "whitewashed" were widespread,[1] and many of the black figures who brought Ali into Islam were excluded from the fallen champion's funeral. Ironically, the funeral of the most famous Muslim American in history, a black man equally remembered for his fierce and unrelenting assault on racism and his in-ring feats, replicated the erasure that has loomed over black Muslims since the earliest stages of this country's history. This erasure, inflicted by the state, society at large, and most notably, by non-black Muslim Americans, is explored in this chapter.

Before going any further, I want to address the proposition that Muslim Americans are the "new blacks." Scholars, politicians, and pundits, beyond and within the Muslim American population, made this very declaration after 9/11 and continue to claim today that Muslim identity is marred and maligned in the same fashion that black identity has been and continues to be. Muslims have always been, and still remain, black. The claim that "Muslims are the new blacks" ignores the extensive history of black Muslims in the United States, and ignores the very existence of black Muslim communities, indigenous and immigrant, today. Demographics, history, and modern narratives testify to the inextricable relationship between blackness and Muslim American identity. To treat black and Muslim as distinct and divided identities is to make this community even less visible and more vulnerable, at a time when anti-black racism and Islamophobia are not only proliferating, but converging, with vile and violent consequences.

Despite constant and conspiring efforts to erase their existence, black Muslims do exist, and they occupy the intersection where mounting anti-black racism and Islamophobia collide. Too often, non-black Muslim Americans only acknowledge the existence of black Muslims when celebrating their excellence, which, ironically, is often done in terms that entirely eclipse their blackness with their Muslimness. In other words, when black Muslim Americans shine at the Olympic Games, or when a luminary like Ali passes, there is celebration in the Muslim community, but a celebration that focuses on a shared Muslim identity and ignores blackness. In short, non-black Muslim Americans want to celebrate black Muslims only when they make Muslims at large look good. And we do so in a fashion that sets aside and ignores their blackness and narrowly uplifts their Muslimness. Over and over, we pat ourselves on the back while simultaneously propagating the erasure of blackness from the Muslim American experience.

After providing a snapshot of the Movement for Black Lives, this chapter examines the specific intersection African American Muslims occupy and the perils that intersection poses. I discuss the ways non-black Muslim individuals and institutions participate in the anti-black erasure of African American Muslims, and finally, illustrate how anti-black racism and Islamophobia converged during the Muslim ban.

THE MOVEMENT FOR BLACK LIVES

On August 9, 2014, Mike Brown was no longer the name of an eighteen-year old teenager few people knew, but a rallying cry. In an instant, a young man with so much to live for was reduced to a corpse spread on the street. Mere hours later, he had become everything from a social media hashtag to an adolescent vilified postmortem to a martyr. Brown was killed by Darren Wilson, a Ferguson police officer, who shot him six times as Brown walked home from a store. Two of those bullets lodged in Brown's head. Brown, whose name and face the whole world would come to know, was left for dead, face-first on the hot summer pavement in Ferguson, Missouri.

His murder inspired a movement that would unfold on that same pavement in the months to come. This movement would transform a generation and reawaken the world to the injustices the state and its agents inflict on African American communities, as evidenced by a string of murders by police officers that claimed the lives of unarmed black men and women around the country. Videos of these murders would be captured and viewed by billions, the names of the victims uplifted and immortalized by way of social media hashtags and protest signs. The Movement for Black Lives evolved into a transformative movement, emblazoned on shirts and in the minds of an entire generation that would no longer wait for structural reforms to deliver racial justice, but sought to claim that racial justice now.

The name that inspired a movement, however, had been formally created roughly a year and a half before the murder of Mike Brown in Ferguson, Missouri. Three black women, Alicia Garza, Patrisse Cullors, and Opal Tometi, coined Black Lives Matter, "as a call to action for black people after 17-year-old Trayvon Martin was posthumously placed on trial for his own murder and the killer, George Zimmerman, was not held accountable for the crime he committed."[2] Like Brown, young Trayvon Martin was unarmed, brandishing nothing but a skin complexion and racial identity tied to crime. On February 26, 2012, Zimmerman fatally shot Martin while Martin was walking home in his Sanford, Florida, neighborhood. The story quickly became national news and mobilized activists in Florida, nationally, and on the internet. "The murder of Trayvon Martin in Sanford, Florida, in the winter of 2012 was a turning point. Like the murder of Emmett Till nearly fifty-seven years earlier, Martin's death pierced the delusion that the United States was postracial," writes Keeanga-Yamahtta Taylor.[3]

The election of President Obama in 2008 signaled for millions that the United States was approaching, or had reached, a new era where racism was a relic of the past. Advocates of this mythic worldview, and the attendant ideology of color-blindness, resisted the salience of race and opposed the need for affirmative action to rehabilitate past and present inequity, arguing that any assertions of race or racism were moot. The murder of Trayvon Martin, and the string of deaths of unarmed black men and women killed in the months and years after Martin's death, vanquished the fiction that the United States was postracial.

Black voices led the claim that Martin's murder was no isolated incident but emblematic of an institutionalized racism internalized by perpetrators like Zimmerman who were spurred to fatal action by the very sight of a young black man in a hoodie. As observed by Su'ad Abdul-Khabeer, "The debate over Martin's hoodie highlights the problem of the criminalization of black people in the United States. Criminalization binds race to crime by advancing the false idea that black people commit more crime than do other racial and ethnic groups."[4] A hoodie is stereotypically associated with criminality, particularly when worn by black youth, men, and women, and as illustrated by the murder of Martin, invites racist violence that can lead to death at the hands of vigilante killers or the police.

The three words "Black Lives Matter" encompassed this and other salient critiques of structural racism and its disproportionate effect on black communities. Garza, Cullors, and Tometi furnished a burgeoning movement with a banner to gather around, a rallying cry that spoke volumes about structural racism, white supremacy, and the conspiring forces that decimate black communities and gun down innocent black men and women. Many more names followed—Eric Garner, Jordan Crawford, Rekia Boyd, Tanisha Anderson, Akai Gurley, Tamir Rice, Aura Rosser, Walter Scott, Freddie Gray, Sandra Bland— testifying that the call that black lives matter was more urgent than ever. To uplift and say their names, in and of itself, was an act of protest.

In her timely book *From #BlackLivesMatter to Black Liberation,* Princeton University professor Keeanga-Yamahtta Taylor writes, "The killing of Mike Brown, along with an ever-growing list of other unarmed black people, drove holes in the logic that black people simply doing the "right things,' whatever those things might be, could overcome the perennial crises within Black America. After all, Mike Brown was only walking down the street. Eric Garner was standing on the corner. Rekia Boyd was in a park with friends. Trayvon Martin was walking with a bag of Skittles and a can of iced tea."[5] Black men, women, and youth were vulnerable when engaged in the most benign acts, which illustrated that any and every black person in America could be similarly targeted. Being an exemplary citizen offered no safeguard from the prospect of police violence. Respectability, and the politics that sang its praises, offered no protection.

In a piece titled "Respectable Genocide," black Muslim poet and Baltimore native Tariq Touré, who took part in the Black Lives Matter (BLM) protests in his home city, echoes this very point, rebutting the respectability politics coming from within and beyond the black community:

> They tell us pull up our pants and it'll be ok.
>
> I can't help
> But notice
> The black men lynched
> In 3 piece suits
>
> From back in the day ... [6]

Whether dressed to the nines in three-piece suits or walking home with candy in hand and a hoodie atop their head, black men, women, and youth are suspected by police officers and vigilante offenders alike, and are being killed in droves.

While committed to mobilizing around the unjust killings of unarmed black women and men and exposing the structural racism that triggered those killings, the Movement for Black Lives was also wed to the "tactic to (re)build the Black liberation movement." Centering black leadership, voices, and struggles was vital to that mission, particularly at a national moment when police violence was reaching a frightening pitch and some politicians were accusing those in the movement of being "rioters," "thugs," and even members of "a terrorist movement,"[7] a claim that stirred the fear of black Muslims, who observe a faith routinely conflated with terrorism.

Efforts to delegitimize the movement sprang from every direction, and most sharply from an opposing movement that dovetailed with the Trump campaign. Critics attempted to derail the call that Black Lives Matter with the rebuttal that "All Lives Matter," claiming that the mere mention of blackness made the movement a racist one. These attempts to stifle a grassroots movement that was inspiring millions, and to suppress core liberties extended by the First Amendment, took me back to similarly spirited movements on the other side of the hemisphere, in a region long branded as violent, inferior, and undemocratic.

The protests that proliferated on the streets of Ferguson, Baltimore, and everywhere the BLM movement inspired activists reminded me of the Arab Spring revolution in Egypt several years earlier. As an Egyptian American with family members and friends who put their lives on the line during that nation's historic 2011 revolution, I heard in the demands made by BLM protestors an echo of those that rang out in Tahrir Square in Cairo. In an article that appeared in *Ebony* days after the killing of Freddy Gray in Baltimore, Loyola Law School professor Priscilla Ocen and I wrote, "Poverty and the police state prevailed in Ferguson and Cairo, Baltimore and Benghazi. Soldiers and patrol cars closely monitored city blocks—where unemployed youth roamed with little purpose and even shallower prospects for the future. Emaciated communities, rich in only nihilism and hopelessness, kept their residents trapped."[8] Many of the symptoms that gave rise to the Arab Spring were similar to those that ignited the Movement for Black Lives. Understanding these parallels helped mobilize non-black Muslim Americans to stand in solidarity and be active participants with the Movement for Black Lives. These precedents primed many Arab and Muslim American youth to stand alongside their black allies as the Movement for Black Lives emerged and pushed forward.

The 2017 "Muslim Survey Poll" published by the Institute for Social Policy and Understanding found that "Muslims [were] the most likely faith group to support the Black Lives Matter Movement."[9] Muslim Americans supported the movement at a clip of 66 percent, compared to 57 percent for Jewish, 39 percent for Catholic, and 55 percent for non-religiously-affiliated Americans. The general public only supported BLM at 45 percent.[10] Without question, the size of the black Muslim population contributed heavily to the high rate for Muslim Americans. But broad and emphatic Muslim American support may also be attributed to a generational shift in which younger people are openly challenging anti-black racism within their households, communities, and mosques—an indirect but very real consequence of the Arab Spring revolutions, and an indelible effect of the Movement for Black Lives on the scores of non-black Muslim Americans who marched and protested alongside their black brothers and sisters of faith. Dalia Mogahed, one of the authors of the survey and a Muslim American community leader, adds, "Non-black Muslims, especially young Muslims, are as likely as black Muslims to support BLM. I think today they find common cause with other marginalized communities because they've experienced institutionalized racism first hand, especially at the hands of law enforcement."[11]

These figures and developments signal some progress. It is perhaps incremental or isolated progress, but these are shifts that are needed to confront the anti-black racism thriving in the country today. Layla Abdullah-Poulos, a black Muslim scholar and author of a popular blog committed to addressing racism within the Muslim American community, rebuts that far more has to be done: "Muslims need to decolonize their minds, engage in active anti-racism to purge our communities of toxic anti-Blackness."[12] Her call resounds as the intersection of being black and Muslim in the United States becomes more dangerous by the day. This intersection is seldom addressed within the convening halls of Muslim American power.

AT THE INTERSECTION OF RACISM, ISLAMOPHOBIA, AND ERASURE

African American Muslims are simultaneously celebrated, demonized, and perhaps most potently, delegitimized as authentic Muslims. These processes seem conflicting; what ties them together is the way in which institutions and individuals readily exploit black American Muslims. This tradition began with the historical erasure of the enslaved African Muslim population, examined in chapter 2. Erasure gave way to demonization and delegitimization in the 1930s, and garnered national attention in the 1950s with the rise of the Nation of Islam. Led by Elijah Muhammad and the charismatic Malcolm X, the Nation of Islam's membership swelled in the late 1950s. Its message of black nationalism, empowerment, and self-sustaining community resonated deeply with a population ravaged by poverty, Jim Crow, and the residual effects of slavery.

"The fiery speeches of its charismatic and articulate spokesperson attracted thousands of new members to the Nation of Islam," writes Kambiz GhaneaBassiri, speaking of Malcolm X, "and tens of thousands more sympathizers, who were not ready to convert to the Nation of Islam but certainly agreed with its assessment of race relations in the United States."[13] The Nation of Islam's mission of empowering black people and lifting them from the social and psychological bondage of slavery transcended religion, attracting black Americans of all faiths—though always through the framework and language of Islam. Black radicalism, coupled with Islam, frightened the state like few grassroots movements had ever done.

The Nation of Islam's reclamation of black dignity by way of emphasizing the importance of family, racial pride, and community empowerment threatened the state. Yet the state, latching on to the narrow view that Muslims were an immigrant bloc from the Middle East, largely viewed the Nation of Islam and its leaders as religious charlatans. Thus, attacks on the Nation of Islam were largely racial and political; when it was attacked on religious grounds, it was attacked more as a cult than as Islam.

Still branded as a "criminal occult" and "Black supremacist" outfit by the state,[14] the Nation of Islam grew in influence in the 1960s—and, along with the growth, it attracted greater opposition. Immigrant Muslims and their leaders often delegitimized the Nation of Islam as "non-Muslim" and even "anti-Muslim."[15] In an ironic twist of fate—or more factually, in an act of political tokenism—the very people American courts deemed unfit for naturalized citizenship were used by the state to delegitimize the religious bona fides of the Nation of Islam and its leadership.

In "Islamism and Its African American Muslim Critics," historian Edward E. Curtis reflects on this critical impasse, when immigration quotas were dissolved and immigrant Muslims came to the United States in large numbers: "As negative portrayals in the mainstream press and criticism from black leaders increased, more and more Muslims in the United States joined to condemn, dispute, and reject the teachings of Elijah Muhammad and the NOI. Their criticism of the NOI was a public performance of Muslim identity that expressed the growing cultural power of foreign and immigrant Muslims."[16] With the lifting of quotas limiting the entry of Muslims from the Arab world and the South Asian subcontinent, a rising number of international students came to the United States from Iran, Turkey, Syria, Pakistan, and other Muslim-majority countries. They "had a major impact on the development of national

Muslim institutions in the United States by founding the Muslim Students Association,"[17] and these immigrant Muslim students led the charge in delegitimizing the Nation of Islam and its leadership. Although the Nation of Islam played a key role in fighting for legislation dissolving restrictive immigration quotas, thereby enabling non-black Muslims to come to the United States, immigrant Muslims swiftly turned their back on black Muslims in favor of placating the state that had restricted their entry for nearly two centuries.

Anti-black racism is still robust and recurring within the Muslim American community today. Non-black Muslim Americans, who tend to be the gatekeepers in prominent Muslim advocacy, political, and religious institutions, are largely wed to community models bound to Arab or South Asian ethnocentrism and model minority status, and to an aspirational whiteness that too often is expressed in racism toward African Americans, including African American Muslims. Emulating and becoming more proximate to whiteness mandates expression of one of whiteness's cornerstone traits, anti-black racism, which non-black Muslims have actively performed in order to claim, or attempt to claim, the coveted privileges of whiteness.

International students often bring racism with them from their native lands, and combine it with the distinctly American racism they adopt on their new college campuses and beyond. This dynamic plays out vividly within Muslim student associations on American campuses, as well as at national conventions held by mainstream Muslim American organizations, including the Islamic Society of North America and the Islamic Circle of North America, and at the Reviving the Islamic Spirit gathering held annually in Toronto.

In his landmark book *Islam and the Blackamerican: Looking toward the Third Resurrection,* prominent African American Muslim scholar Sherman Jackson argues that "the central preoccupation of Black Religion is the desire to annihilate or at least subvert white supremacy and anti-Black racism,"[18] which African American Muslims today find within their religious communities as often as they do beyond them. An incident involving one of the most prominent non-black Muslim American imams, Sheikh Hamza Yusuf, at the 2017 Reviving the Islamic Spirit conference, illustrates how the dialectic Jackson speaks of unfolded on one of Muslim America's greatest stages..

Only months after eulogizing Muhammad Ali at his funeral in Louisville, Yusuf illustrated that anti-black racism existed at the very top of the mainstream Muslim American establishment. In response to a question about whether Muslim Americans should get more involved in the Black Lives Matter movement, Yusuf shrugged and gave a response laden with appeals to color blindness and victim blaming, claiming, "The United States is, in terms of its laws, one of the least racist societies in the world. We have some of the best anti-discriminatory laws on the planet.... We have ... 15–18,000 homicides a year, 50 percent are black on black crime."[19] His response, a tacit condemnation of Black Lives Matter and downplaying of structural racism in the United States, sent shock waves through the Muslim American community and deepened the wounds of black Muslims. This was not just any Muslim making these painful assertions, but one of the most influential and beloved Muslim leaders in the country.

A day later, instead of properly apologizing, Yusuf—a white Christian convert to Islam—doubled down: "[My point is that] the biggest crisis facing the African-American communities in the United States is not racism; it is the breakdown of the Black family."[20] Instead of heeding the voices of black Muslim men and women who spoke up after his first statement and trying to understand their experiences for what they were, Yusuf dug an even deeper hole by continuing the same rhetoric. He viewed the breakdown of the black family as a phenomenon entirely separate from (institutional) racism, and he manifested the blindness of white male privilege by rejecting the claim that racism ranks as a major impediment for black Muslims. For Yusuf, the decimation of the black family was a phenomenon not linked to the contemporary perils of disproportionate policing and incarceration of black men and women, the school-to-prison pipeline, and other manifestations of structural racism. Nor was it linked to the residual and lasting effects of slavery, Jim Crow laws, and state-sanctioned segregation. His view, both ahistoric and myopic, illustrated an ignorance of black struggle at the very top of the mainstream Muslim American community, an ignorance that trickles down into the organizations, institutions, and communities that closely follow Yusuf.

The events in Toronto, which spurred a firestorm of criticism and debate within the Muslim American community, were foreshadowed by another instance of black Muslim erasure at the 2016 Islamic Society of North America conference in Chicago, an annual gathering of approximately 50,000 Muslim Americans featuring panels on culture, faith, politics, and advocacy. After speaking on a panel addressing poverty, racism, and surveillance within the Muslim American community, a prominent Egyptian American Muslim activist told me about "a secret meeting for Muslim American leaders" to be held in the hotel that Saturday evening. Unsure who would be attending and uncertain about the meaning of "Muslim American leader," I asked him about the roster of invitees. He reeled off a series of names; I was familiar with some and did not recognize others. I did realize, however, that none of the African American Muslim individuals I knew and routinely worked with were on the list of invitees. I made some phone calls and sent some texts; ultimately it was revealed that none of the African American Muslim activists and leaders I knew were invited to this secret meeting of "Muslim American leaders" at one of the most important Muslim American gatherings of the year. I was hardly surprised, and I resolved to leverage my status as a recognized community "leader" to mount a small protest.

I conspired with two of my closest colleagues, Margari Hill and Asha Noor, both black Muslim women, to storm the meeting. I was unclear why they, a head of an important racial justice education organization and an emergent community leader, among other black Muslims attending the conference, were not invited to the meeting. Hill and Noor agreed, and we brought two young African American Muslims along with us to the secret convening in a nondescript hotel banquet room. I looked around and found that the attendees included government employees, aspiring politicians, known Muslim American organizers, activists, and social media figures—all of them Arab, South Asian, or white. The organizers looked at us with obvious discomfort, reflecting either disapproval or an admission that their exclusion of African American Muslims had been exposed.

The presence of my four African American Muslim friends was in and of itself an act of protest against the ongoing and incessant erasure of black Muslim bodies from high-stakes conversations, institutions of power, and very simply, demonstrations of existence. After the meeting, Asha Noor asked one of the organizers of the event, "Why were no black Muslims, who make up one-fourth of the Muslim population, included in this event?" Her question was met with a blank stare and promises to do better in the future. This is a promise heard before, one made more vain by the rush to appropriate and instrumentalize black Muslim struggle, images, and icons for personal gain while rarely including actual African American Muslims.

In her book *Muslim Cool,* Su'ad Abdul Khabeer poignantly asks, "What would U.S. American Muslim communities be like if they loved Black people as much as they love Black culture?"[21] Indeed, blackness has been selectively co-opted by Muslim Americans when it suits situational existential or political interests, but the broader struggles, concerns, and bodies of black Muslim Americans are routinely sidelined, excluded, and, for non-black Muslim Americans striving for whiteness or coveting the "moderate Muslim" label, wholly rejected as being an impediment toward these ends. Non-black Muslim Americans largely regard the radical political voices and traditions of black Muslims, whether the BLM of today or the Nation of Islam of yesterday, as obstacles toward the normalization and assimilation that offers greater proximity to (white-dominated) state power and societal acceptance. This tension fuels the exclusion of black Muslims from mainstream Muslim American spaces, only leaving room for black Muslims who explicitly or tacitly agree to the project of being politically moderate—or, far more frequently, and without their attendance, appropriating or championing black Muslim bodies or ideas when it suits mainstream Muslim American ends or discrete political interests.

Muhammad Ali, whom American presidents and statesmen, non-black Muslim American clergy and leaders rushed to eulogize and honor on June 3, 2016, was one of the most visible faces of the Nation of Islam in the 1960s. Ali and Malcolm X remain the two most beloved and widely known Muslim Americans, so why is the specific demographic they represent, African American Muslims, still pushed to the fringe? And why, given that African American Muslims are the biggest plurality of the Muslim American population today, are discussions of Islamophobia divorced from assessments of anti-black racism? The state and mainstream Muslim American circles and institutions are quick to invoke the names of Muhammad Ali and Malcolm X when it furthers their interests, but remain silent when examining the intersectional dangers and injuries experienced by African American Muslims today—a time of rapidly intensifying anti-black racism and Islamophobia.

Racism from within the Muslim American community, combined with the broader dis-identification of African American Muslims as bona fide Muslims, is a reality black Muslims in the United States continually grapple with. They remain largely excluded from the Muslim American civil rights and advocacy organizations responsible for fighting racism and Islamophobia within Muslim American communities and the country at large.[22] Donna Auston of Rutgers University, one of the most trenchant voices examining the intersection of Islamophobia and anti-black racism, characterizes the weaponized anti-black racism unfolding on the streets, and the Islamophobia proliferating privately and structurally, as "intimate bedfellows."[23] In "Mapping the Intersections of Islamophobia and #BlackLives-Matter," Auston argues, "Dominant narratives ... in both media and scholarly literature tend to doubly efface the existence and voices of black American Muslims—even in this moment when black bodies are at the very center of the unrest. Black Muslims do not come to this issue as bystanders or allies—even well meaning ones. Yet we are often erased—even from the narrative of our own struggle." She goes on to say, "That erasure renders our communities more vulnerable"—to Islamophobia and anti-black racism separately, and most dangerously, to their convergence in predominantly African American Muslim spaces.[24]

Scholars and activists like Auston, who are rising to the fore of pressing Muslim American discourses today, consistently remind us that anti-black racism and Islamophobia are hardly operating on separate tracks. They are intimately fused, which intensifies the policing and punishment of black Muslim communities during the war on terror and the war on drugs, a similarly amorphous and unconventional campaign that, like the Islamophobic baseline linking Muslim identity to terrorism, conflates blackness with criminality. Black Muslims are vulnerable to both of these wars and the many dangers the hate fueling the wars prompts. They are susceptible to the police violence that targets the communities they call home. They are also targets of surveillance and religious profiling, counter-radicalization policing, and, as illustrated in the immediate wake of Trump's Muslim ban, structural Islamophobia thought to only affect Arab and South Asian Muslims—the caricature of Muslims embedded by Orientalism and propagated by (private) Islamophobia.

THE (BLACK) MUSLIM BAN

Three out of the seven Muslim-majority states listed in the (first) Muslim ban are in Africa. Two of them—Somalia and Sudan—are home to black Muslims. In the same way that Islamophobia intersects with anti-black racism to intensify the targeting of black Muslims living in the United States, the convergence of these two forms of animus was experienced by Somali and

Sudanese immigrants impacted by the Muslim ban. For black Muslims from these two nations, and black Muslims from beyond these two nations who were profiled and detained, the Muslim ban is more than merely structural Islamophobia; it is anti-black racism and Islamophobia fused together.

The experience of Nisrin Elamin, a Sudanese woman traveling back to the United States on a student visa the day after the Muslim ban was enacted, painfully illustrates this fusion. Elamin, a thirty-nine-year-old graduate student at Stanford University, was detained at New York's JFK Airport while in transit to San Francisco.[25] In addition to being detained, Elamin was handcuffed, a step that not only held her out as an immigrant outsider, but also as some sort of criminal. It was as if she were a black woman protesting on the streets of Ferguson, or more routinely, a black woman driving through a white neighborhood. Elamin was denied entry to the United States and subsequently arrested, handcuffs and all, on account of being a Muslim and a black woman.

"For the brief moment I was handcuffed, I couldn't control myself and I just started crying," Elamin said as she reflected on the reality that non-black Muslims from the restricted states were not handcuffed. Her religious identity as a Muslim led to her detainment, while her racial status as a black woman spurred the decision of Customs and Border Control to handcuff her, and treat her like a criminal. She stood at the dangerous crossroads of anti-black racism, Islamophobia, and xenophobia, which prompted a more violent brand of treatment from immigration officers.

A day after her detainment, Elamin stated, "I think this order is a reflection of a larger trend in this country to criminalize black people, to criminalize immigrants, to criminalize Muslims. And as a black Muslim immigrant, I'm really concerned about that. And I do think that the Somalis and Sudanese, people of African descent who are going to be affected by this, you know, I think they're going to be treated differently, frankly."[26] Story after story confirmed Elamin's point that black Muslims were in fact treated differently in the wake of the ban. Her detainment and arrest illustrated the very experiences of several other black Muslim men and women.

The erasure of black Muslims was again on full display in the media coverage in the wake of the Muslim ban. Elamin's story and those of other black Muslims were perpetually eclipsed by coverage of Arab and Iranian Muslims. Even the media's well-intentioned and spirited efforts to bring to light Muslim victimhood perpetuated the private Islamophobic tenet that conflates Muslim identity with Arab or South Asian identity, evidencing just how entrenched and pervasive this tenet is. As we have seen, this erasure is rooted in American law, starting with enslaved African Muslims who worshipped while in bondage and continuing with the ignored and overlooked experiences of black Muslims detained and handcuffed. It is exemplified when Trump vilifies communities with large Sudanese and Somali populations, as he did on the campaign trail in November 2016 in Minnesota, when he spoke to an audience of largely white attendees, claiming that Somalis are somehow associated with radicalism, and that President Obama's policies, which would be extended by Hillary Clinton, would facilitate the entry of "generations of terrorism, extremism and radicalism into your schools and throughout your communities."[27]

The impact of the Muslim ban on black Muslims begs discussion of another grossly neglected concern at the intersection of immigration and race. While popular concern about and advocacy for the 11.3 million undocumented individuals in the

United States centers almost exclusively on Latinx communities, the Center for American Progress reported that in 2012, there were approximately 400,000 undocumented black immigrants without legal status.[28] A sizable portion of this population is Muslim, coming from Ethiopia, Kenya, Somalia, Sudan, and other African countries. Immediately upon entry into the United States, they become subject to the converging animus of anti-black racism and xenophobia, and the perpetual threat of arrest and deportation. However, this neglected segment of the undocumented population receives little to no attention from mainstream media or advocacy groups, making their plight and vulnerability exponentially more acute. This was on full display, although largely unseen, in late January of 2017 in the immediate wake of the Muslim ban, and in the months after it.

Of course the ban did not impact undocumented or immigrant black Muslims alone. As demonstrated by the detainment of Muhammad Ali, Jr., in the immediate aftermath of the ban, black Muslims indigenous to the United States, with fathers who just five months earlier were being remembered by American presidents and honored by the state, were also vulnerable to the Muslim ban—and vulnerable to the many policing and profiling tentacles of structural Islamophobia. While being black in America today is challenging, being black and Muslim in a nation where anti-black racism and Islamophobia converge is even more daunting.

CHAPTER SEVEN

The Fire Next Time

you broke the ocean in
half to be here.
only to meet nothing that wants you.
    Nayyirah Waheed, "Immigrant"

"When will my son come home?" asked the stranger on the other end of the phone, in a language and voice that were intimately familiar. "When will my son come home," she repeated, desperately seeking to be consoled by a stranger who could only offer tenuous guidance during a moment of absolute madness.

It was Saturday, January 28, 2017, the morning after President Trump passed the first rendition of his Muslim ban, and a Yemeni mother somewhere in Michigan was reaching out to anybody and everybody she could to inquire about when and whether her son, who had left for their native country to bring back his new bride, could come home. She was only one of a countless number of Muslim mothers who, at the time of the departure of their daughters or sons, could not imagine that the casual farewell they bid might very well be their last.

Roughly forty-eight hours earlier, on the morning of Thursday, January 26, my own mother dropped me off at the Detroit

Metropolitan Airport. I was en route to Washington, D.C., to speak at the George Washington University School of Law, ready to share my new research on Islamophobia and the heightened civil liberties challenges the newly inaugurated administration posed for Muslim Americans.

"Be careful," my mother told me, as she always did, before we arrived at the terminal.

"Don't worry," I replied, as I always did, and I embraced her and bid her goodbye.

"When will you come back home?" she asked, a routine question, fully expecting me to return safely from yet another work-related trip. I walked away from the curbside and into the terminal, pausing before walking inside to wave goodbye one final time. She remained parked, as she always did, watching me depart with the hope, and that distinctly motherly concern, that I would come home safely several days later. It was a routine scene for us; my mother always dropped me off at the airport for my many work-related trips, expecting that I would come back home with an exciting story of some kind, or a memento from an event I spoke at.

"When will my son come back home?" the woman on the phone again pled, this time with tears that highlighted her rising fear and desperation. Despite my legal education, years of practice, and background teaching immigration and constitutional law, I had no answer. I was stumped. Particularly for Muslim immigrants from the seven restricted nations listed on President Trump's Muslim ban, the world had turned entirely on its head. The law did not matter now, it seemed.

On the morning of Friday, January 27, I arrived at the GWU School of Law, where I was to lecture about the structural Islamophobia the new administration was poised to expand. I had no idea that the first step would be taken so soon. Just hours later, the

Muslim ban was no longer a campaign proposal, a hashtag, or a slogan shouted at rallies; it was a *real policy*. My friend, West Virginia University law professor Atiba Ellis, leaned over during a presentation to show me the update on his phone: "President Trump signs travel ban." This pushed my good friend, American Arab Anti-Discrimination Committee legal director Abed Ayoub, to call me and demand, "We need you at the office, as soon as possible."[1] I rushed out of George Washington University Law School and raced from Foggy Bottom to the committee's headquarters on foot, at the intersection of 20th and L, fearful of the destination the country was heading toward and even more fearful of the intersection at which we—Muslims inside and outside the country—found ourselves.

The Muslim ban passed by Trump on Friday, January 27, 2017, impacted scores of Muslim immigrants and their family members. But it was more than just a stand-alone policy that wrought mayhem in American airports, broke up families, and formally ushered in a heightened form of structural Islamophobia. It also foreshadowed what was to come with this new administration—a form of Islamophobia that would be common and continuous, enforced in new laws and policies. The ban was part and parcel of a broader, stark Islamophobic vision that tied Muslim identity directly to terror suspicion.

The fights against the first Muslim ban and the one that followed on March 16, 2017, were in and of themselves daunting. But they foreshadowed more, and perhaps even more ominous, challenges ahead. The fights unfolding at airports, within communities, and in courtrooms witnessed unprecedented coalitions—grassroots unions spanning racial and religious lines—coalitions needed to meet the challenge of today's Islamophobia, and even more importantly, to meet the "the fire next time."

In *The Fire Next Time,* James Baldwin writes, "I know what the world has done to my brother and how narrowly he has survived it. This is the crime of which I accuse my country and my countrymen, and for which neither I nor time nor history will ever forgive them. They have destroyed and are destroying hundreds of thousands of lives and do not know it. And do not want to know it."[2] The book that Baldwin wrote in the midst of the civil rights movement has remained tattooed on my brain since I read it for the first time as an undergraduate at the University of Michigan, and it rose to the fore of my mind in the immediate wake of the Muslim ban. Baldwin became my greatest companion, again, in the midst of the hateful tide that emerged during the 2016 presidential campaign season and ultimately came to define it.

Nobody spoke as trenchantly as Baldwin did about the racial injustice and dignity stripped from blacks in the United States. But apart from his unmatched ability to give complex analysis a humanity that made you *feel* his writing, Baldwin's prescience while surrounded by immediate and imminent peril was unmatched. He looked beyond the challenges in front of him, and during a moment of mass hysteria and fear, I looked to Baldwin as my guide. The words he wrote nearly half a century ago provided clarity that public intellectuals of today were unable to muster up, and the guidance even the law could not provide. So, I listened closely to Baldwin, and turned to him more than I did anybody else, trusting that he would shepherd me to the answers the law or the living could not identify.

"When will my son come home?" Her voice haunted me days later as I embraced my mother at the same airport terminal where she left me days ago. It haunted me weeks afterward, when Trump ordered drone attacks in Yemen, the country of the woman's birth and the one to which her son had traveled to meet his new bride.

It haunted me months later when Trump passed his second Muslim ban, after the Ninth Circuit Court of Appeals affirmed a temporary restraining order on the first ban. In a bizarre twist of fate, or a reversal of God's plan, the woman on the other end of the phone could have been my mother, and I could have been her son, detained at the airport where she left me—bidding farewell as she looked in my direction, with a mother's look of concern and care, fully expecting me to return home. *That could've been me,* I thought as I spoke to the Yemeni mother the morning after the Muslim ban, *and she could have been my mother.*

The crimes the state dealt on that day, detaining thousands and leaving thousands more deserted in distant lands, far from their mothers, was only the most recent blow dealt by structural Islamophobia. Islamophobia had been fully institutionalized, and the Trump administration expanded it with lightning speed. More crimes against innocents, and more injury, were on the horizon. The fires of today, as Baldwin wrote, often foreshadow greater ones ahead. Preparing for the fires in the distance enhances one's ability to fight them and protects those most in danger.

There are lessons to be learned by examining the new politics of Islamophobia formally ushered in by the Trump administration, and the blueprint it provides for a new wave of politicians, pundits, and institutions sure to follow in Trump's footsteps. How can we best sustain the new fronts, coalitions, and movements that are galvanized to resist Islamophobia on the ground in America? And how do we face the fear looming in the minds of Muslim Americans everywhere, the elephant in the room: another terror attack, and how such an attack might cause the state to unleash even more harmful policies against Muslim citizens and immigrants? These questions, juxtaposed with the recurring question of that Yemeni mother, still scroll through my mind.

NEW COALITIONS, OLD CHALLENGES

November 9, or 11/9—the date Donald Trump was elected president—felt like 9/11 all over again. While the two dates were separated by a generation, the election of Trump restored the fears Muslim Americans had after 9/11.[3] Muslim Americans faced scapegoating, rising hostility, and hate crimes, and most strikingly, an executive branch that subscribed to the worldview that the United States was at war with Islam. Some argued that "the profound changes in America's political culture and values in response to 9/11 created a crack that Trump, the entrepreneur and political opportunist, was able to open wide enough so as to slip into the White House."[4] The war on terror and the Islamophobia it proliferated sowed the seeds of hate that lingered long after 9/11, and Trump identified, marshaled, and molded them into a winning campaign strategy.

Roughly a month after 9/11, I attended a coalition-building meeting with a range of activists from organizations in the metropolitan Los Angeles area. The meeting, attended by students, organizers, nonprofit employees, and others, was diverse along racial and religious lines. But the meeting became tense minutes after it began. A Chicano organizer commented, "Where were Arabs and Muslims when profiling was a black and Mexican issue?" The poignant statement spurred head nods across the room, and an affirmation by a young black woman who shared, "I get that Muslims are experiencing a lot of discrimination right now, but you weren't at this table until your community became targeted." These statements were not aberrational, but widely held. As Kimberlé Crenshaw claims with regard to race and gender, men of color want women of color to "ride or die for them, but [they] won't ride or die for us."[5] These words were true with regard to Muslim Americans and communities of color in the immediate wake of 9/11, and I heard them over and again at meetings, in discussions with friends, and at organizing sessions in California, Michigan, and places in between.

These words were very painful, but they were indisputable. Like the old saying goes, nothing hurts more than the truth. The broader Muslim American population, with the exception of the black Muslim community and other discrete groups, was not part of the progressive movement until it was targeted. But a sea change began within Muslim America, particularly among the generation that endured the rampant Islamophobia that arose after 9/11. Many Muslim individuals in Arab and South Asian American communities became more visible, involved, and integral in progressive circles and causes for racial justice. In addition to the aftermath of 9/11 and the pain and injury it inflicted, the Movement for Black Lives pushed the successive generation even further to the left and led them to embrace a more universal racial justice message. Muslim Americans, along with the black and brown, LGBTQ, and progressive elements they worked with absorbed that the mission for racial and social justice was a collective one, and not transactional. The framing of activism was shifting for the better, and the culture moved along with it.

In addition to mobilizing action and solidarity, the BLM movement was fiercely educational. It inculcated Muslim Americans with the language of racial justice, and words that were once confined to sociology, anthropology, or law school classes, like "intersectional feminism," "structural racism," and "white privilege," became routine terms for non-black Muslim American teens, college students, and organizers, who began to speak in terms of collective liberation instead of discrete community interest. Racial and social justice was less about *just us* and centered more on collective liberation.

This dynamic was made vivid in the immediate aftermath of the Muslim ban and the weeks that preceded and followed it. Critical race theory and its language were now mainstream and were translated into praxis and protest by organizers of every shade. For critical race theorists like myself, it was fascinating to see this blossom, in real time, on the street, at protests, on social media, and in other spaces unconfined by the four walls of a classroom. Young Muslim American activists were increasingly identifying themselves as "intersectional feminists," and teens at mosque gatherings spoke fluently about the "school-to-prison pipeline" during protest actions. The politics of coalition were clearly evident, and the language of protest on full display.

The very airports that, overnight, became holding cells for Muslim immigrants from the seven restricted countries underwent another radical transformation. On Saturday evening, January 28, 2017, only twenty-four hours after President Trump signed the Muslim ban, airport terminals became sites of mass protest. Corporate and nonprofit lawyers marched into JKF and LAX airports to provide pro bono guidance to detained immigrants; activists of all races and faiths gathered outside and inside, chanting, "No ban, no wall!"; and the unprecedented coalitions that had already been forged on the streets of Ferguson, Chicago, and other cities where the BLM Movement was formed now reconvened, signaling to the Trump administration—and all those who supported it—that the resistance was strong, diverse, and fully intent on resisting every step of the way.

The fight against Islamophobia, the swift resistance signaled, was no longer narrowly placed on the shoulders of Muslim Americans, but was carried by a broadening coalition that was beginning to understand this rising form of animus as a central civil rights issue. This was on full display during the historic women's march staged in Washington, D.C., on January 21, 2017, strategically slated to take place the day after President Trump's inauguration. Hundreds of satellite marches took place around the world and across the country, including in Chicago, where I attended the march alongside my younger brother Mohammed and his fiancée, Fairouz. We joined the protest on Wabash Avenue, where signs demanding "Impeach Trump" and "Down With Islamophobia, Xenophobia and Racism" were juxtaposed with the gaudy Trump name showcased on the Trump International Hotel and Tower, where the protest convened. The crowd seemed infinite, and the diverse faces, shades, and voices that comprised it reflected a microcosm of the American people, vividly proclaiming that the Islamophobia unleashed by the newly inaugurated president would be staunchly opposed. We marched alongside individuals of every age, creed, and color for miles, and stopped to take photos near a diverse group of young protestors.

"We have your back, sister," a young white woman who identified as queer and held up Frank Shepard Fairey's portrait of a young Muslim woman in an American flag headscarf, said to Fairouz. Fairouz, like the woman in the portrait, wore a headscarf.

"Thank you, we got your back too," Fairouz responded, followed by a warm embrace that signaled far more than a moment of political solidarity.

Reducing that moment, and the millions more like it that took place on that day and in the turbulent days that followed, to mere "politics" would diminish its importance and the momentous shifts sweeping across the country. It was a moment of human recognition by one white woman who represented millions more who felt precisely the same way she did, who recognized that Islamophobia was real, and that the menace it posed to Muslim Americans like my sister-in-law Fairouz was even more real.

That encounter reminded me of another intersection in my past. While living in Orlando, I would frequently drive by the Pulse nightclub on Orange Avenue en route to a café where I liked to read and write. The club was on my right on my way to the café, on the left when I drove back home. I thought nothing of it at the time. But only weeks after moving for a job back home in Detroit, the club I had routinely passed became the focus of the entire world. On the night of June 12, 2016, ten days after I left Orlando, Omar Mateen walked into the Pulse nightclub and indiscriminately opened fire, killing forty-nine people and injuring fifty-three more. Suddenly, the nondescript club I had driven past over and over was the site of another horrific terror attack.

Terrorism struck a city I made my home for two years, less than two miles from where I lived. The majority of the victims were LGBTQ, and they were predominantly Latinx, and the culprit had been born to a Muslim American family. The familiar conjectures of "Islamic extremism" and "ISIS radicalization" were immediate, and as expected the media and politicians pounced on them. But the victims, the families of the victims, and the leadership of LGBTQ groups did not bite. Instead, they rejected the scare-mongering and scapegoating that pervaded the mainstream media and that politicians clamored for and capitalized on for votes, while Muslim American groups, by and large, fell short of reciprocating in terms of solidarity with LGBTQ groups.

Without question, leadership within the LGBTQ community could have very easily pushed the Muslim extremism and terror narrative following the Orlando shooting, considering the mainstream media's fixation on the trope that Islam is inherently homophobic. But for the most part, LGBTQ leadership, at both the national and local levels, did not take the bait, perhaps because the leaders were cognizant of a specific group that tied their victimized community to the one being vilified. The LGBTQ community showed great solidarity with Muslim Americans during a time of unspeakable tragedy, but there was more at play than one marginalized community standing alongside another.

"Solidarity" is a term infused with much power and possibility. But it is also a term that implies boundaries and divides, and neglects that individual identities—standing alone—can oftentimes be the most powerful expressions of solidarity. The aftermath of the Orlando shooting sounded a signal about the existence of LGBTQ Muslims and the coexistence of these two identities. LGBTQ Muslims demand equality on two fronts, despite the Islamophobia unleashed from one direction and rejection coming from the other; in the aftermath of the Orlando shooting, but also well before that, they were a group at the crossroads of complex emotions and even more complex existential challenges.

"Gay and Muslim American," for far too many people, reads like an oxymoron. Yet, is a coexistent yet largely hidden identity that characterizes the experience of many Muslim American men and women. Muslim America has long been caricatured along monolithic racial, spiritual, and political lines—misrepresentations that distort its multilayered and rich diversity. Muslim America is not only caricatured as being patriarchal, misogynistic, and sexist, but also stridently homophobic. These are stereotypes, but it is true that the wounding words of homophobes have drowned out the far-too-scarce declarations of support and solidarity within the Muslim American community and, at their extreme, have intimidated supporters into silence.

Few struggles are as daunting as those faced by LGBTQ Muslim Americans, who are stigmatized beyond and from within their spiritual communities. Indeed, a sizable segment of the Muslim American population feels that coming out must be accompanied by renouncing one's adherence to Islam. This is not unique to Islam, of course, and is echoed by segments of Christian, Jewish, and other faith communities. Evangelical Christians, including Vice President Mike Pence, are active proponents of conversion therapy—a pseudo-science that seeks to convert one's sexual orientation.

As with much of evangelical Christianity, there is sentiment within the Muslim community that homosexuality and adherence to Islam are clashing lifestyles that cannot be integrated. The accusation that Islam is homophobic is more frequent and fierce, and is intensified by assigning to the whole of Islam the crimes of fringe groups like ISIS, which infamously threw a gay man off a roof in Mosul. Yet, despite the vapid and simplistic indictments coming from beyond the bounds of the Muslim American community, or the disavowals and denial issued from within, LGBTQ Muslims can only be who they are, observing the faith they know and love while pursuing lives and love like everybody else does.

I returned to Orlando on July 14, 2017, and visited the Pulse nightclub, which had been converted into a memorial honoring those killed roughly a year earlier. Pictures of the victims and notes from family, loved ones, and complete strangers adorned the makeshift shrine built around the fence and driveway of the club. The victims were predominantly brown men who resembled my family members and could have very easily been mistaken as Arab or Muslim, and very likely, targeted by Islamophobic violence.

Hate, whether along lines of religious, racial, or sexual orientation, usually has a common source.

As I marched alongside my brother and his fiancée in Chicago, I thought about the struggle of Muslim Americans who identify as LGBTQ, those yet to come out, and others who live by dividing their lives in two. Some of these people are friends I have known since childhood; others I met later in life through political organizing. I reflected on how the Orlando shooting hit close to home on two very intimate, and existentially perplexing, fronts for them. Many of them were devout Muslims, possessing a spirituality and faith that inspires me, but burdened with the fear that coming out may alienate them from family, friends, and the communities they have grown up in and loved since youth.

After the Orlando shooting, I listened to them closely as they sought to harmonize both halves of their identity, at a time when they were enduring attack from all angles. "You can't be Muslim and gay," they often heard while among Muslim family and friends; while in the company of their non-Muslim friends and acquaintances, they were subject to the rhetoric and hate of Islamophobia. *Where was their safe haven?* I reflected. Would the unprecedented coalitions being forged today, along lines of inclusion, acceptance, and solidarity, offer a better tomorrow for LGBTQ Muslims? Some vocal elements within the Muslim American community gave reason for hope, while the familiar silence and scorn of others countered it with concern. I was unsure where this wing of the broader Muslim American march would veer, but in the spirit of consistency and collective liberation, I promised myself that I would be a part of helping it march forward.

"Can you take a picture of us?" the young woman asked me at the women's march, waking me from my walk down memory lane.

"Sure," I responded, snapping several shots—and after they disapproved of my first photos—more pictures of the queer white women and my headscarved sister-in-law, who had far more in common after 11/9 than they would have had following 9/11. We bid farewell, and marched onward.

LEAD, SISTERS

"I stand here before you unapologetically Muslim American!" shouted Linda Sarsour, one of the national co-chairs of the women's march in Washington and an undeniable voice for an emergent movement of progressive Muslim American activists, advocates, and thinkers led and dominated by women. "Unapologetically Palestinian American. Unapologetically from Brooklyn, New York. Sisters and brothers, you are what democracy looks like," she continued, addressing the estimated half million people attending the march in Washington and the millions more watching from home and afar. Loud and proud, donning a black puffy Patagonia jacket and a white headscarf, with her signature Brooklyn slang and swag, Sarsour claimed her position as not only a visible leader of the Muslim American community, but of the broader movement against the new administration.

Sarsour was already a fixture, widely known to black and brown, straight and LGBTQ, Muslim and non-Muslim activists, occupying a platform that few Muslim Americans, let alone women, held before her. She was hardly a new commodity in social justice circles, but an activist who had earned her stripes in her native New York City and later emerged as one of the most forthright voices against sexism, racism, and anti-blackness within the broader Muslim American community. She symbolizes the new face and voice of Muslim America—the coalitional spirit that her generation, and the generations following, are championing.

In an article written in the immediate wake of Trayvon Martin's murder, Sarsour and I, two Arab American Muslims, stated, "Institutional and structural racism is still robust in the US. This is evidenced by the disparate incarceration rates of brown and Black Americans, the decimation of affirmative action and race-conscious legislation in the US, and the crumbling public education systems in minority-populated communities with the all too common cold blooded murders of people of color."[6] The killing of Martin, we wrote, was not an aberrational or unexpected act, but a vile emanation from a deeply institutionalized racism, as Sarsour powerfully asserted, both in print and in person. Sarsour had arrived, and her cross-racial literacy and coalition-building genius would blaze new trails for young Muslim American leaders to follow.

Sarsour's rallying words have resonated beyond the walls of Muslim American spaces and penetrated deep within the hearts and minds of a broad milieu of Trump resisters. Her ascent, in great part, symbolizes the arrival of Islamophobia as a mainstream civil rights issue mentioned in the same breath as racism, sexism, homophobia, and xenophobia. Sarsour has risen along with other Muslim American grassroots political and legal leaders who helped forge vital coalitions before the ascent of Trump—women like black Muslim activist Donna Auston and Somali American Asha Noor, who come from communities at the very intersection of racism, Islamophobia, and xenophobia and speak about the perils posed by Islamophobia in ways that reach broader audiences. This broadening of leadership and audience, and a growing legion of allies, has been absolutely vital in the short term to confront the structural Islamophobia the Trump administration has been poised to expand. It is even more important in addressing the blueprint of political Islamophobia that will be followed by politicians waiting in the wings, and the private Islamophobia it will embolden.

Islamophobia is no longer a term uttered exclusively by academics in ivory towers, or a word that only comes out the mouths of Muslim American activists and advocates. It has been featured on the Twitter timelines of Jewish and Christian college students, discussed by young politicians rising in response to the hate coming from Trump and those following in his footsteps, and the frequent topic of news headlines and opinion pieces featured in the *Washington Post* and the *New York Times*. Islamophobia has fully arrived, as has the consciousness around it and the will to combat it, marshaled on street corners, social media platforms, college and university campuses, in airports, and in public and private spaces in between and beyond. A new crop of Muslim American leaders, the majority of them women, is taking charge of the broader campaign to counter Islamophobia.

Dynamic organizers and activists like Margari Hill in Los Angeles and Namira Islam in Detroit, Drost Kokoye in Nashville and Darakshan Raja in Washington, D.C., have crushed the Islamophobic myths that Muslim women are appendages of men, silent, subordinate, and powerless. In fact, they often lead and direct men, and have stood at the fore of institutions that have brought about the kind of progressive reform that exposed the fumbling and futility of male gatekeepers. The dominance of Muslim American women on the ground is mirrored within academia, where the most potent voices are those of Muslim women, including Sahar Aziz of the Rutgers School of Law, Zareena Grewal at Yale, Su'ad Adul Khabeer at the University of Michigan, Intisar Rabb at Harvard Law School, Shirin Sinnar at Stanford Law School, and Amna Akbar of the Ohio State Law School. Muslim American women have also become giants in the media world, with moguls like Amani Al-Khatahtbeh debunking stereotypes with her MuslimGirl movement, Dena Takruri changing the narrative with her widely viewed AJ+ reporting, and Malika Bilal leading the digital media wave with her program *The Stream*. Muslim American women have been outshining Muslim American men, and this is better for the movement against Islamophobia.

Unlike the post-9/11 moment, when (non-black) Muslim Americans were largely absent from radical and progressive spaces, cross-racial coalitions, and efforts pushing for racial justice, Muslim Americans are now integral participants, collaborators, and leaders. They issue marching orders and mobilize the swelling legions of allies needed to fight the fires ahead, and to navigate the new politics of Islamophobia that loom beyond the current administration. The rise of this leadership, on national and local levels, highlights that Muslim Americans are not only leading the charge against Islamophobia, but are also visible and vocal on the front lines of social justice matters that impact targeted communities of all types. Today's politics of coalition building and sustained solidarity are retrenching the transactional and self-interested politics of previous generations, which gives reason for optimism—albeit an optimism that, if not converted into sustained action reaching beyond Trump and the Islamophobia of today, will mean little.

THE NEW POLITICS OF ISLAMOPHOBIA

While the core structural Islamophobic baseline, which assigns the presumption of terror suspicion to Muslims, guided the two previous presidential administrations, Trump peddled and mainstreamed an outwardly explicit Islamophobia to match it. The success of his campaign, which most pundits and experts doubted up until his "historic and stunning upset" over Hillary Clinton on November 9, 2016,[7] proved that explicit and unhinged Islamophobia was an effective campaign tactic. It resonated with a sizable segment of the American electorate, which registered its approval in the voting booth. Despite the fact that the United States had seemed, on the surface, to become a more progressive and inclusive society in recent years, hate still proved to be a winning message.

Trump's campaign rallies, where Islamophobia, xenophobia, and racism openly thrived, and which were dubbed by some as "racism summits,"[8] offered a glimpse of the country the candidate promised to deliver. The Muslim ban became far more than a central policy proposal; it was a core component of the grand vision for the America that Trump intended to preside over and of the broader structural Islamophobic policies he was poised to enact when elected. The words "Muslim ban" became a common chant at his rallies; Islamophobic slurs and slogans were emblazoned on paraphernalia worn by his supporters; and Muslims were ejected—for no other reason than *being* Muslim—at several of his campaign pit stops.[9] The bulk of the "heaping doses of anti-Muslim rhetoric" that saturated the 2016 presidential campaign was contributed by the Trump campaign,[10] which strategically employed "political Islamophobia as a campaign strategy" to mobilize and galvanize voters.[11]

Trump's deployment of political Islamophobia proved resonant and effective. Raising boisterous cheers at rallies and debates when he conflated Syrian refugees with ISIS, and doubling up on the Muslim ban by calling for "extreme vetting" of all Muslim immigrants coming into the country, his message obtained wide Republican voter support in national polls. Only days after he introduced the proposal for a Muslim ban, a December 9, 2015, Bloomberg poll found that over two-thirds of likely Republican voters supported the idea.[12] Over half of likely Republican voters said they "strongly support[ed]" the ban, with 14 percent expressing "not so strong favor" for the measure.[13] On the other side, 25 percent of likely Democratic voters either supported the ban or were unsure, illustrating that Trump's explicit Islamophobic appeals resonated not only with a large majority of Republican voters, but with a sizable segment of Democratic voters as well. These figures again illustrate that Islamophobia is not exclusive to the right and the swelling segment of new-wave conservative hatemongers dubbed the "alt right," but, as examined in chapter 1, is also a rising form of animus on the left.

The Trump campaign and administration highlight that the deployment of explicit Islamophobia is a tried, true, and proven political strategy. The rhetoric Trump used on the campaign trail appealed to sizable segments of the American electorate, providing national and local politicians with a blueprint to follow. "Trumpism," and the politics of hate on which it capitalized, evolved into a political strategy for both upstart and established politicians. Incoming and incumbent candidates at all levels of politics, seeking to win in jurisdictions where the rhetoric of explicit Islamophobia finds fertile ground, will certainly look to Trump as a guide.

The "Trump effect," or Trumpism, may very well prove to be more destructive and lasting than the polarizing president it is named after.[14] And yet, the effect and the movement represented by Trump are not entirely new. They have roots "as far back as

Pat Buchanan and Ross Perot's third-insurgencies in the 1990s"[15] and, as this book highlights, far beyond. Given these deep roots, Islamophobia will remain a fixture in the rhetoric of politicians and a staple of political discourse in the United States for a long time to come—a situation that will become even more violent and intense if the country experiences another terror attack committed by a Muslim actor. This leaves Muslim Americans perpetually one attack away from an explosive rise in private and structural Islamophobia, a fear that all Muslim Americans carry with them and can never fully evade.

Donald Trump was not the first American demagogue to mobilize hate and division in order to claim political office, and he certainly will not be the last. Particularly in a nation where minorities will soon outnumber whites, Islam is the fastest grow-ing religion, and the wealth gap grows wider and wider, explicit racial and religious populism will likely be a routine (and robust) dimension of the American political landscape. And this land-scape will be most profuse, and violent, in the aftermath of a ter-ror attack.

However, this new era of Islamophobia requires no terror attack to incite hate and backlash. The murder of Nabra Has-sanen, a seventeen-year-old Egyptian American girl in Sterling, Virginia, in the early morning of June 18, 2017, illustrates that very point. After completing her Ramadan prayers at 3:00 a.m., Nabra and her friends walked from the All Dulles Area Muslim Society Mosque to a nearby McDonald's, eating one final meal before the day's fast began. On their way back to the mosque, Nabra and her friends crossed paths with Darwin Martinez Torrez, who chased the teens with a baseball bat. All of them except Nabra escaped. Martinez struck Nabra in the head with the baseball bat, threw her into his car, and drove off. She was later found dead at a pond miles away from her mosque.

Police swiftly ruled that Nabra's murder was no hate crime, but the result of road rage, implying that the two cannot coexist. I attended Nabra's vigil in Reston, Virginia, on June 21, 2017, alongside my close friends Abed Ayoub and Mohammed Maraqa and thousands who came together only blocks away from her home. Her friends were there, as were her parents. Her father echoed what he told investigators and police immediately after he learned about his daughter's murder: "He killed my daughter because she is Muslim. That's what I believe."[16] Every Muslim American at the vigil that day agreed with Nabra's father, as did millions more who followed her story and mourned her death from afar.

One attack away—a phrase that has double meaning for Muslims. The first meaning, as illustrated by Nabra's murder, is that Muslim Americans are perpetually in danger of an attack that may end their lives, an attack that is more likely to come during the holiest times, like Ramadan, when Muslim Americans are worshiping, congregating, and celebrating. The second meaning, discussed below, is the perpetual fear Muslim Americans have of the next terror attack, which, depending on the identity of the culprits and the scale of the attack, spells enhanced structural Islamophobia and, if imaginable, even more intense private hate and backlash.

ONE ATTACK AWAY

"You think your pain and your heartbreak are unprecedented in the history of the world, but then you read," wrote James Baldwin. So I read, and read more, until I was moved to write and pursue a career in teaching. The study of American legal history is, perhaps more than anything, an examination of how law was molded and maneuvered to accumulate power for the elite few, and to justify and inflict horror on the remaining masses. Laws were made to enforce the displacement and extermination of one people (Native Americans) and the enslavement of another (African Americans), and to mark an entire faith group (Islam) as unassimilable and violent. The tragedy of Islamophobia unfolding in America today rises from seeds sowed centuries ago, and it stands alongside other tragedies, similar and distinct, experienced by a host of other groups.

As a constitutional law professor, I teach the infamous *Korematsu v. United States,* popularly known as the "Japanese internment case," several times every year.[17] In it, the Supreme Court, in 1944, upheld President Franklin Delano Roosevelt's Executive Order 9066, which compelled the rounding up and internment of 110,000 to 120,000 Japanese American citizens and residents several months after the Pearl Harbor attacks. Locked in an intensifying battle with the empire of Japan in World War II, the United States military designated the Japanese a monolithic "enemy race" that encompassed anybody and everybody of Japanese descent—including longtime U.S. residents and Japanese American citizens born in the United States.

Ruling on behalf of the court, Justice Hugo Black wrote, "We uphold the exclusion order.... In doing so, we are not unmindful of the hardships imposed by it upon a large group of American citizens. But hardships are part of war, and war is an aggregation of hardships. All citizens alike, both in and out of uniform, feel the impact of war in greater or lesser measure."[18] By upholding Roosevelt's executive order mandating internment, the Supreme Court justified the discriminatory, strident, and racist policy.

National security, the court opined, was the most "compelling state interest," even if the fear that Japanese Americans would commit espionage or acts of subversion was not the product of real evidence, but of stereotypes and demonization.

The *Korematsu* ruling has not been overturned by the Supreme Court. And the opinion issued by Justice Black advanced an even more dangerous precedent than the ruling itself. His appeal to the "hardships of war" mirrored the standards applied today to Muslim Americans in the war on terror, standards that assign suspicion and guilt to anybody tied to an "enemy race." The national security interests and fears of the state, real or imagined, enabled the en masse internment of individuals who had nothing to do with the Pearl Harbor attack. Due process of law and the constitutional safeguards that should have been extended to these Japanese Americans, as to all immigrants and citizens, was stripped and supplanted by the "hardships of war," levied squarely on their backs. Citizenship did not protect them, and the guarantees tied to it did not save them from internment.

The war on terror, and the eras before it, have familiarized Muslim Americans with the "burdens of war" logic and the collective guilt Justice Black justified in *Korematsu*. The expansion of structural Islamophobia, by way of the creation of the Department of Homeland Security, the enactment of the USA PATRIOT Act, CVE policing, NSEERS, Muslim bans one, two and three and a range of other policies and programs enacted before and during the war on terror, are driven by the suspicion and presumption of collective guilt assigned to Muslim Americans and immigrants. And what comes next in the case of another attack? What additional or expanded policing programs targeting Muslim Americans will be enacted following a large-scale terror attack?

What if something the size and scale of the Paris attacks of November 13, 2015, which claimed the lives of 130 people and galvanized a heightened state of Islamophobia in France, unfolded in a major American city?[19] What degree of structural Islamophobia would be unleashed by President Trump (or his successor) if something like the Orlando shooting of June 12, 2016, were to take place under his watch?[20] How might an executive already infamous for his unhinged Islamophobia respond if given the opportunity to take it even further?

Depending on the scale of the attack, might he levy unimaginable "burdens of war" onto eight million Muslim Americans and the many millions more who call the United States home? Is internment possible?[21] If Muslim Americans are not already interned within the walls of their homes, mosques, or community centers, could another large-scale attack bring about en masse Muslim-American internment? Although it seems a remote possibility, the sum of pernicious legislation, still-rising Islamophobia, and the precedent of Japanese internment place that possibility firmly at the center of the collective Muslim American psyche.

This is the existential burden Islamophobia, in all of its forms, places on Muslim Americans. Citizenship, and the rights extended by it, is a tightrope that Muslim Americans must carefully walk during the protracted war on terror. Cautiously stepping forward and surviving, quietly dreading the next terror attack, and when and if it does come, praying, "Please don't let it be a Muslim."[22] For Muslim Americans, the psychological weight of Islamophobia, which scholar Nadine Naber called the "internment of psyche,"[23] is without question just as heavy as the vitriol unleashed by hatemongers and the policies enacted by the state. Muslim Americans remain confined by the fear of the next terror attack. After every horrific episode, whether in Charleston, Oklahoma City, Manchester, Orlando, or Las Vegas, Muslim Americans will stand united in prayer, echoing, "Please don't be a Muslim," and brace for the structural and private Islamophobia that is sure to come whether the culprit is proven to be a Muslim or a non-Muslim white "lone wolf."

Epilogue

Homecomings and Goings

I have learned and dismantled all the words in order
to draw from them a single word: *Home.*

    Mahmoud Darwish, "I Belong There"

You returned home just before my own return to
Allah. From him we come and to him we return.

    My father, Ali Amine Beydoun

I buried my father in a metro Detroit graveyard on October 3,
2016. It was only four months after I had accepted a tenure-track
teaching position with the University of Detroit Mercy School
of Law, which presented me with the opportunity to continue
my legal academic career at home—near the friends, family,
and city that I loved. The timing of my homecoming was bitter-
sweet, but was perhaps arranged according to some divine
design to provide me with one final opportunity to mend
wounds with the man I had been estranged from nearly all of my
life. During the next four months, my father and I forged a surreal semblance of a father-and-son relationship—within the

bleak and gray contexts of hospital intensive care units—before his final departure, which would come only months after I set foot back home.

I vividly remember helping wash my father, in line with the Islamic custom, on the day of his burial, reflecting on his absence for much of my childhood, and on how the country that lured him far from his native Lebanon gradually broke him and sent our family into a tailspin. My father spent much of his adult life, and my entire life, living between Michigan and the Middle East, a rolling stone blown by the winds and his whims far from my mother, older sister, younger brother, and myself. His void left us without a father at home for long stints, and it compelled my mother to work odd job after odd job, supplementing her modest wages with welfare and the money my siblings and I could muster up.

I never understood why my father made the choices he made, but learning about the earliest phases of his life, on the streets of Beirut, as a child from a poor Shiite Muslim family from southern Lebanon, provided some answers. He spent his whole life running toward something and away from something else, whether it was the family he was born to or the one he spawned and continuously spurned. Poverty, war, and the quest to make something of himself molded him, and at the same time, pulled him far from his loved ones. He was always gone, but this time, gone for good.

"Been waiting on you all my life / All my life, you've been missing all my life," sang Frank Ocean. I must have played that song, "Nights," off of his album *Blond* a hundred times the day of my father's burial. Ocean's words looped over and over in my head, with images from the distant and not so distant past springing up alongside them. That song today, and I am sure for many years to come, will remain a looming reminder of my father's passing. The day of his funeral felt endless, and the weight of the finality of it all—the running to and from, the soul-piercing cries and sea of black, the turbulence of our relationship—sank my mind deep into the past. Memories of his sudden arrivals and departures, the financial and personal troubles his void created for my family, and the endless burdens my mother carried as a result—reflecting and remembering as my mind raced and my legs stood still.

En route to the graveyard, I reflected on the good times, and on his last days of life, plugged to a ventilator and an unsightly host of other medical devices, their numbers, graphs, and graphics spelling out that death was near. I thought about the dreams he voiced out loud for himself as I sat on his lap as a toddler, and the dreams he envisioned for me. Those days felt like ages ago, and his big voice and even bigger presence were whittled down to an emaciated body in a hospital bed.

"You are the man I always wanted to be," my father whispered to me on a rainy April day in Detroit, the last time I heard his voice, weeks before he lost it permanently. His small, nondescript room, with a window looking onto Jefferson Avenue, was less than five miles from my new office and roughly thirty-four years from the day he took a snapshot of me smiling widely, in my lambskin jacket, in front of Detroit's Renaissance Center on that same road.

"Perhaps he was summoning me home," I often thought as I sat at his bedside during his final days, when, after years of rebuffing his attempts to start anew, I finally heeded his call. Only moments before it was too late.

My homecoming converged with his final departure, and the choreography of daily hospital visits, one-directional bedside chats, and an exchange of tears that communicated regret and fear danced away from the Reaper looming nearby. But the Reaper was unrelenting, always creeping forward despite my father's best efforts to hold him off, and to hold on. Death's advances were always unmistakable—at times stripping him of his voice, leaving his body with incorrigible sores, and causing streams of tears when he sensed that its sickle was nearing. If life begins with the promise of everything, then it ends with the emptiness of nothing.

My father and I always had a turbulent relationship, beginning even before my parents' divorce in 1994. Our views often clashed and our paths diverged. But we pieced together a bond while he lay still, scared, and silent in a myriad of metropolitan Detroit hospitals that he cycled in and out of for nearly two years. Most importantly, I learned how a Muslim man who dropped out of school in the fifth grade in his native Lebanon and hustled on the streets of Beirut to provide for his family ultimately achieved his dreams through me. He fell short, as a husband, and for me, as a father. But before he took his final breath, I promised to carry him and his dreams to the finish. Or at the very least, to try my best to do so.

We said goodbye to my father for the final time that cool autumn day in Michigan. I remember his cold body rolling into the dirt and seeing his face one last time, pale but poised for the afterlife, and hearing the prayers of friends and family converging with the piercing cries of my sister, Khalida, who tended to him most closely during his final years. From God we come and to him we return. My father departed for his final homecoming shortly after I made my own.

Today, he lies buried only a few miles from the cafés he frequented, the friends he made, the streets and corners that perpetually remind me of him, where his long-estranged son returned and made a home. My father, a man who was a shadow for much of my life became real, present, and finally, a *father,* in his last days. Since his death, his shadow is ubiquitous in the city he brought us to in 1982, a city that would become the most concentrated, celebrated, and scrutinized Muslim American community in the country. I see him more today than I ever did before, and I listen closely to the vision he had for me and the pride that would beam from him when he read about my work.

His burial site is full of names like Mohammed, Hassan, Zeinab, Kareem, Marwa, and Fawzia, old and young Muslim Americans, who, like my father, migrated to, lived, and believed in the dream America offered. Like mine did on that day, their families congregated atop a patch of dirt—American dirt—to bid farewell and permanently lay loved ones to rest. Those same families continued to pursue dreams on behalf of the departed, and to give birth to new dreams by forming families and having children, building businesses and institutions, achieving professional and academic success. Muslim Americans of all ages, ethnicities, and generations are buried here, alongside my father, joined by millions of other Muslims buried elsewhere in the United States, who helped construct the very backbone of this nation, made immeasurable and irreplaceable contributions to it, and traveled from long distances and ravaged lands to enrich it—and despite what Islamophobia and its predecessor systems propagate by popular view and law, made this country what it is today.

My Detroit homecoming was met with immense difficulty, mourning, and heartbreak. I had been lured by an ailing father who lived long enough to see me on a consistent basis. My new office was a short drive from his hospital bed, and after his departure, a short drive to his final resting place. But in the coming months, my summoning back to Detroit would make even more sense. Roughly a month after my father's passing, Donald Trump was elected to office, and the unhinged Islamophobia his presidency formally inaugurated would be acutely felt in metropolitan Detroit, the symbolic seat of Muslim America and the city I called home once again.

I watched the election returns alongside hundreds of Muslim American students and activists, mothers and fathers, on November 9, 2016, at the Arab American Museum Annex in Dearborn, Michigan. The crowd that came together that night overwhelmingly believed that Hillary Clinton would claim victory, as the political pundits and experts had forecast, and by doing so would put an end to the brazen Islamophobia unleashed by Donald Trump. Well, they and we were wrong, and Trump claimed Florida, North Carolina, Ohio, Wisconsin, and one battleground state after another to win the presidency. The unexpected result of the 2016 presidential election, and the Islamophobia it endorsed, would usher in a different kind of mourning.

The room in the museum annex in Dearborn was gutted after the collective realization that Trump would become the country's forty-fifth president, and fear crept onto the faces of Muslim Americans young and old. One young college student I had known since she was child, Nora, was visibly shaken. Like thousands upon thousands of women in metropolitan Detroit, Nora wore a headscarf. For the twenty-one-year-old, the article of cloth she diligently wrapped around her head every morning, as had the late Yusor and Razan Abu-Salha, was central to her identity. It was an expression of religious devotion and a symbol of solidarity with Muslim women who wear the *hijab*, a disproportionately maligned segment of the Muslim American community. Yet, that night, Nora revealed that she was considering removing her headscarf, fearing that it would attract the hateful backlash she read about in newspapers during the presidential race—a palpable fear shared by many young Muslim women in her social media feed on election night.

"I don't know what to do," she revealed to a circle of family and friends. Being Muslim in America has always been wrought with scrutiny and suspicion. But the entrance of Trump spelled emboldened Islamophobia, and for conspicuous Muslims like Nora, a far higher likelihood of harm.

"Acting Muslim" today in the United States invites suspicion from the state and maximizes the prospect of backlash from hatemongers. For Muslim Americans who confirm their religious identity by wearing headscarves or Islamic dress, fasting on Ramadan and regularly attending the mosque, merely practicing their First Amendment rights is perilous. Muslim Americans like Nora, driven by fear to conform, cover, or conceal their Muslim identity, may diminish the prospect of suspicion from the state or backlash from bigots, but in doing so they are complicit in supporting the very mission Islamophobia aims to advance—eroding and eliminating every manifestation of Islam, until it is gone from America altogether. Like the naturalization era discussed in chapter 2, when Muslims were legally prohibited from becoming citizens, Islam today is still effectively viewed as unassimilable and irreconcilable with American identity. Much has changed, but so much more has not.

As I have written elsewhere, "The decision to act as non-Muslim as possible is an emergent phenomenon in Trump's America."[1] And as this book illustrates, it is a contemporary consequence of Islamophobia, an effect of the centuries-old systems that spawned it. Nora is not somebody I read about in a newspaper; she is someone I have known since she was a child. She grew up just blocks away from my mother's home, in one of the most densely populated Muslim communities in the country. Nora is only a handful of years older than my two eldest nieces, Du'aa and Kawkab, who attended the same university she did and who also wore the *hijab*.

On the night of the election, fear was robust within my hometown and within my family. Given the challenges that lay ahead with Trump and the escalating Islamophobia he ushered in, I was precisely where I needed to be. After years spent living far from home, I was back in Detroit. The city my father brought us to after fleeing civil war in Lebanon. The city where poverty and single parenthood forced my mother to raise us in eleven different houses, until she was finally able to purchase and make a home for us on the west side. The city where the streets taught me as much as any textbook or teacher did, taught me through rough instruction to confront each fight with a willingness to punch back, and punch back harder than the foe standing in front of me. Standing alongside familiar faces and family members, I had no choice but to fight. And I was ready to do just that.

The city that taught me how to fight also gives me great reason to continue fighting. The familiar sight of mosque minarets, Arabic script adorning restaurant and grocery shop awnings, and headscarved and bearded elders strolling up and down Warren Avenue are once again my routine panorama. This is neither foreign nor frightening, but home—in the heart of America. Memories of my father, and his ever-looming shadow, remind me that he is nearby. I have much to fight for, within this town and beyond it. Muslim America is bigger than any one city, larger than one community, far more heterogeneous than caricatures old and new, and the threat of American Islamophobia lives everywhere.

No longer a young activist but a seasoned advocate and professor, I find that young faces look to me for leadership in the throes of disaster. At the university where I work, blocks away from where I grew up and currently reside, I feel obligated to try to channel their anxiety and fear toward resistance and activism. Islamophobia, in its most explicit and apparent form, now lives in the White House. Large segments of this country rushed to the polls to elect a candidate who campaigned on hate, one who made Islamophobia a hallmark of his message and a cornerstone of his vision for the country. His message and vision resonated strongly, revealing that Islamophobia was once again swelling in minds, households, and halls of power in the United States.

But this was not the first time Muslim Americans had faced this brand of hate from the state and fellow citizens, as I reminded an audience of nearly 2,500 people at an emergency community town hall in Dearborn in February 2017. I spoke alongside activists Abed Ayoub, Asha Noor, and Noel Saleh only days after Trump's Muslim ban caused mass hysteria and fear among the town's large Arab and Muslim American population.[2] Nor was it uncharted territory for Muslim Americans to fight, resist, and rebel against Islamophobia and the systems that mothered it. The roots of Islamophobia are deep, but the might of the Muslim American narrative and rightly guided tradition of resistance is even deeper. Our history chronicles systems devised to dehumanize Muslim Americans as anti-American and terrorists, but it also chronicles valiant stories of resisting, enduring, and overcoming.

Enslaved Muslims resisted the slave code and rebelled against slave masters before the United States was a sovereign nation. They built roads and railroads, cities and state buildings, without compensation. "After two hundred fifty years of slavery. Ninety years of Jim Crow. Sixty years of separate but equal," they are still denied reparations.[3]

This country is where Muslim immigrants were pushed and pulled to a new land to piece together better lives for their children, lured by dreams that were deferred by discrimination—and still realized despite that discrimination. This nation is where racism overlaps with xenophobia, crossed by and compounded with an Islamophobia that strips or diminishes the citizenship of Muslim Americans. By voting, marching, and struggling to exercise a religion demonized by law and policy, these same Muslim Americans bring to life the civil liberties that although enshrined in the Constitution, have been systematically denied them.

This is the land where we buried our sisters and brothers, mothers and fathers, and where, *insha'Allah*—God willing—we will one day bury Islamophobia deep in the very soil that spawned it.

Notes

INTRODUCTION

1. I have altered the name of the driver to protect his identity.

2. For a vignette of a young Latino Muslim voter in central Florida, and a snapshot of this growing demographic of Muslims in the state at large, see Khaled A. Beydoun, "Muslim-Americans Can Impact Elections," *Orlando Sentinel,* March 15, 2016.

3. Khaled A. Beydoun, "Between Indigence, Islamophobia, and Erasure: Poor and Muslim in 'War on Terror' America," *California Law Review* 104 (2016).

4. Matt Welch, "Trump May Have Bad Intentions, But Obama Was a Deporter-in-Chief," *Los Angeles Times,* February 17, 2017.

5. I refer to the community of Muslim citizens in the United States as Muslim Americans, over the "American Muslim" descriptor others prefer.

6. Khaled A. Beydoun, "Please Don't Be Arabs or Muslims," Al Jazeera English, April 16, 2013.

7. Executive Order No. 13,769, Protecting the Nation from Foreign Terrorist Entry into the United States, *Daily Compilation of Presidential Documents* no. 00076 (January 27, 2017).

8. Khaled A. Beydoun, "Donald Trump: The Islamophobia President," Al Jazeera English, November 9, 2015.

9. Khaled A. Beydoun, "'Muslim Bans' and the (Re)Making of Political Islamophobia," *University of Illinois Law Review* 2017, no. 5 (2017).

10. On the ways politicians deploy coded messaging against non-whites to further their objectives or campaigns, see Ian Haney López, *Dog Whistle Politics: How Coded Racial Appeals Have Reinvented Racism and Wrecked the Middle Class* (New York: Oxford University Press, 2014).

11. Daniel Funke and Tina Susman, "From Ferguson to Baton Rouge: Deaths of Black Men and Women at the Hands of Police," *Los Angeles Times*, July 12, 2016.

12. "According to an August 2008 report by the U.S. Census Bureau, those groups currently categorized as racial minorities—blacks and Hispanics, East Asians and South Asians—will account for a majority of the U.S. population by the year 2042." Hua Hsu, "The End of White America," *Atlantic*, January/February 2009, p. 3.

13. U.S. Census Bureau, "New Census Bureau Report Analyzes U.S. Population Projections," March 3, 2015.

14. D'vera Cohn, "It's Official: Minority Babies Are the Majority among the Nation's Infants, but Only Just," Pew Research Center, June 23, 2016.

15. A national security program formally implemented by President Barack Obama in 2011, whereby DHS works closely with local law enforcement and elements within the Muslim American community to identify prospective radicals and prevent terror attacks. Countering Violent Extremism programs were piloted in three cities in 2014: Boston, Los Angeles, and Minneapolis.

16. Victims of Immigration Crime Enforcement, U.S. Immigration and Customs Enforcement (ICE). Although the explicit mission of the program is to "support victims of crimes committed by criminal aliens through access to information and resources," the hotline also enables individuals to call in and report the whereabouts and identity of an undocumented individual.

17. Khaled A. Beydoun, "America Banned Muslims Long before Donald Trump," *Washington Post*, August 18, 2016.

18. Poor or working-class whites are commonly caricatured to be the primary proponents of Islamophobia, a population effectively examined and humanized in J.D. Vance's *Hillbilly Elegy: A Memoir of a Family and Culture in Crisis* (New York: HarperCollins, 2016).

19. Edward Said, *Orientalism* (New York: Vintage, 1979).

20. Erik Love, *Islamophobia and Racism in America* (New York: New York University Press, 2015).

21. Cindy Carcamo, "Like an Invisibility Cloak, Latina Muslims Find the Hijab Hides Their Ethnicity—from Latinos," *Los Angeles Times*, March 24, 2017.

22. Abdullahi Ahmed An-Na'im, *What Is an American Muslim? Embracing Faith and Citizenship* (New York: Oxford University Press, 2013), p. 3.

23. Ashley Moore, "American Muslim Minorities: The New Human Rights Struggle," *Human Rights and Human Welfare* 91 (2010): 1.

24. Toni Johnson, "Muslims in the United States," Council on Foreign Relations, 2011.

25. The term "intersectionality" was coined by Kimberlé W. Crenshaw in her landmark law review article, "Mapping the Margins: Intersectionality, Identity Politics, and Violence against Women of Color," *Stanford Law Review* 43 (1993): 1241, 1244. Crenshaw defines intersectionality as the various ways in which multiple social categories shape the complexity, and determine the vulnerability, of lived experiences.

26. Kimberlé Crenshaw, "Why Intersectionality Can't Wait," *Washington Post*, September 24, 2015.

1. WHAT IS ISLAMOPHOBIA?

Epigraphs: Muneer I. Ahmad, "A Rage Shared by Law: Post–September 11 Racial Violence as Crimes of Passion," *California Law Review* 92 (2004): 1318. Yusor Abu-Salha quoted by her father in Margaret Talbot, "The Story of a Hate Crime," *New Yorker*, June 22, 2015.

1. Margaret Talbot, "The Story of a Hate Crime," *New Yorker*, June 22, 2015.

2. "'We're All One': Chapel Hill Victim Talks Diversity in America," Al Jazeera America, February 13, 2015.

3. Omar Alnatour, "10 Things We Can Learn from Our Three Winners," Huffington Post blog, February 10, 2017.

4. Jorge Valencia, "Razan and Yusor Abu-Salha Were All-American Sisters Who Loved Their Family, Service and the Beach," North Carolina Public Radio, February 9, 2016.

5. Saeed Ahmed and Catherine E. Shoichet, "3 Students Shot to Death in Apartment near UNC Chapel Hill," CNN, February 11, 2015.

6. Talbot, "The Story of a Hate Crime."

7. Dalia Mogahed and Youssef Chouhoud, "American Muslim Poll 2017: Muslims at the Crossroads," Institute for Social Policy and Understanding, March 21, 2017, p. 9.

8. "Dislike of or prejudice against Islam or Muslims, especially as a political force," *Oxford Dictionary* online.

9. Khaled A. Beydoun, "Islamophobia: Toward a Legal Definition and Framework," Columbia Law Review Online 116 (2016).

10. Hamid Dabashi, "The Liberal Roots of Islamophobia," Al Jazeera English, March 3, 2017.

11. Khaled A. Beydoun, "Muslims between Hillary Clinton and a Hard Place," Al Jazeera English, July 25, 2016.

12. Khaled A. Beydoun, "Why Can't Muslims Talk about the Muslim Ban on US TV?" Al Jazeera English, February 17, 2017.

13. Julie Alderman and Nina Mast, "When Discussing Trump's Muslim Ban, Cable News Excluded Muslims," Media Matters for America, February 9, 2017.

14. Nathan Lean, *The Islamophobia Industry: How the Right Manufactures Fear of Muslims* (London: Pluto Press, 2012), p. 66.

15. Kalia Abade, "Anti-Muslim Protests—Some Armed—Planned for at Least 20 Sites across the Country," Imagine 2050, September 29, 2015.

16. Sara Rathod, "2015 Saw a Record Number of Attacks on US Mosques," *Mother Jones,* June 20, 2016.

17. Scott Malone, "U.S. Anti-Muslim Bias Incidents Increased in 2016, Group Says," Reuters, May 9, 2017.

18. Southern Poverty Law Center, "Hate Groups Increase for Second Consecutive Year as Trump Electrifies Radical Right," February 15, 2017.

19. Nancy Coleman, "On Average, 9 Mosques Have Been Targeted Every Month This Year," CNN, August 7, 2017.

20. Christopher Mathias, "2016 Election Coincided with Horrifying Increase in Anti-Muslim Hate Crimes, Report Finds," Huffington Post, May 9, 2017.

21. Erik Love, *Islamophobia and Racism in America* (New York: New York University Press, 2015).

22. Emma Green, "Americans Still Confuse Sikhs with Muslims," *Atlantic,* January 27, 2015.

23. Tamar Lewin, "Sikh Owner of Gas Station Is Fatally Shot in Rampage," *New York Times,* September 17, 2001.

24. Victoria Kim and Joseph Serna, "For Sikhs, Often Mistaken As Muslims, It's 'A Hostile and Scary Time,'" *Los Angeles Times,* December 29, 2015.

25. Interview with Arjun S. Sethi, May 14, 2017.

26. Beydoun, "Islamophobia," 115.

27. Leti Volpp, "The Citizen and the Terrorist," *UCLA Law Review* 49: 1586.

28. Evelyn Alsultany, *Arabs and Muslims in the Media: Race and Representation after 9/11* (New York: New York University Press, 2012).

29. See Marie A. Failinger, "Islam in the Mind of American Courts: 1800 to 1960," *Boston College Journal of Law and Social Justice* 32 (2012): 1.

30. Khaled A. Beydoun, "Between Indigence, Islamophobia, and Erasure: Poor and Muslim in 'War on Terror' America," *California Law Review* 104 (2016): 1471.

31. "Obama's Speech in Cairo" (text of speech), *New York Times,* June 9, 2009. The historic address, dubbed the "speech to the Muslim World," was delivered at Al-Azhar University, one of the leading institutions of Islamic thought and *the* flagship center of Sunni Islamic thought.

32. Kaveh Waddell, "America Already Had a Muslim Registry," *Atlantic,* December 20, 2016.

33. Ryan Ahari, "Policy Brief: Designating the Muslim Brotherhood as a Foreign Terrorist Organization," Muslim Public Affairs Council, 2017.

34. John Eligon and Michael Cooper, "Blasts at Boston Marathon Kill 3 and Injure More than 100," *New York Times,* April 15, 2013.

35. Sarah Kendzior, "The Wrong Kind of Caucasian," Al Jazeera English, April 21, 2013.

36. Alex Dobuzinskis, "Two Men Stabbed to Death on Oregon Train Trying to Stop Anti-Muslim Rant," Reuters, May 29, 2017.

37. See www.buzzfeed.com/talalansari/columbus-ohio-brawl?utm_term=.ftKaN4k4O#.uxGQlAPAY.

38. Kelly James Clark, "Why Don't Moderate Muslims Denounce Terrorism?" Huffington Post, December 4, 2015.

39. Shirin Sinnar, "Preparing American Muslim Daughters for What Awaits," Opinion, *Mercury News,* November 25, 2015.

40. Amanda Sakuma, "Muslim Women Wearing Hijabs Assaulted Just Hours after Trump Win," NBC News, November 10, 2017.

41. Theodore Schleifer, "Donald Trump: 'I Think Islam Hates Us,'" CNN, March 10, 2016.

42. Ahmad, "A Rage Shared by Law," 1319.

43. Michael S. Schmidt and Richard Pérez-Peña, "F.B.I Treating San Bernardino Attack as Terrorism Case," *New York Times,* December 4, 2015.

44. Victoria Shannon, "Brussels Attacks: What We Know and Don't Know," *New York Times,* March 22, 2016.

45. Julie Ann Taylor, Sanaa Ayoub, and Fatima Moussa, "The Hijab in Public Schools," *Religion in Education* 41 (2013): 8.

46. Khaled A. Beydoun, "Islamophobia Has a Long History in the US," Viewpoint, *BBC Magazine,* September 29, 2015.

2. THE ROOTS OF MODERN ISLAMOPHOBIA

Epigraphs: Theodore Schleifer, "Donald Trump: 'I Think Islam Hates Us,'" CNN, March 10, 2016. Judge Stephen Field in Ross v. McIntyre, 140

U.S. 453, 454 (1891); this case addressed the applicability of American law to foreign sailors on U.S. ships while in the territory of another country.

1. Richard Brent Turner, *Islam in the African-American Experience* (Bloomington: Indiana University Press, 1997), pp. 39–40.

2. *Fajr* is "break of dawn" or "sunrise" in Arabic. Sunrise marks the time for the first of the five daily prayers.

3. Khaled A. Beydoun, "Antebellum Islam," *Howard Law Journal* 58 (2015): 143–144.

4. Khaled A. Beydoun, "America Banned Muslims Long before Donald Trump," *Washington Post,* August 18, 2016.

5. Mike Gonzalez, "Multiculturalism and the Fight for America's National Identity," Heritage Foundation, November 23, 2016.

6. Harper Neidig, "Trump Warns against Syrian Refugees: 'A Lot of Those People Are ISIS,'" The Hill, June 29, 2016.

7. Ian Haney López, *White by Law: The Legal Construction of Race* (New York: New York University Press, 1996).

8. Sylviane A. Diouf, *Servants of Allah: African Muslims Enslaved in the Americas* (New York: New York University Press, 1998), p. 47.

9. Beydoun, "Antebellum Islam," pp. 147–148.

10. Daniel Martin Varisco, *Reading Orientalism: Said and the Unsaid* (Seattle: University of Washington Press, 2007), p. 4.

11. Edward Said, *Orientalism* (New York: Vintage, 1979), pp. 1–2.

12. Varisco, *Reading Orientalism,* p. 47.

13. Said, *Orientalism,* p. 2.

14. Ibid., p. 9.

15. Michael Omi and Howard Winant, *Racial Formation in the United States: From the 1960s to the 1990s* (New York: Routledge, 1994), p. 55. Omi and Winant describe race as "an unstable and 'decentered' complex of social meanings constantly being transformed by political struggle," and they describe racialization as the use of race as a basis for distinguishing among human groups.

16. López, *White by Law,* p. xiii. López continues, "Race exists alongside a multitude of social identities that shape and are themselves shaped by the way in which race is given meaning."

17. Erik Love, *Islamophobia and Racism in America* (New York: New York University Press, 2015), p. 10.

18. The Levant is the westernmost region of the Asian continent and includes modern-day Lebanon, Syria, Israel, Palestine, and sometimes Jordan.

19. "The term Middle East likely emerged in the 1850s from Britain's India Office. It did not enjoy widespread usage in policy circles, however, until the early twentieth century, when it was used in the work of American naval strategist Admiral Alfred Thayer Mahan. In an article first published in September 1902, Mahan used the term Middle East to refer to a region of growing strategic importance in the emerging conflict pitting Britain and the United States against Germany and Russia." John Tehranian, *Whitewashed: America's Invisible Middle Eastern Minority* (New York: New York University Press, 2009), p. 65.

20. Denise Spellberg, *Thomas Jefferson's Qur'an: Islam and the Founders* (New York: Vintage, 2014), p. 6.

21. Robert Allison, *The Crescent Obscured: The United States and the Muslim World, 1776–1815* (Chicago: University of Chicago Press, 1995), pp. 45–46.

22. Ibid.

23. Ibid.

24. Precious Rasheeda Muhammad, "Muslims and the Making of America: 1600s to the Present," Muslim Public Affairs Commission, 2013, p. 23.

25. Beydoun, "Antebellum Islam," p. 145.

26. Cheryl I. Harris, "Whiteness as Property," *Harvard Law Review* 106 (1993): 1716.

27. Frederick Douglass, *The Frederick Douglass Papers,* Series 2, *Autobiographical Writing,* vol. 3, *Life and Times of Frederick Douglass,* ed. John R. McKivigan (New Haven, CT: Yale University Press, 2012), p. 118.

28. Muslim-led rebellions were common in the New World. Wolof and Fulani Muslims spearheaded the first slave revolt in the history of the Americas in Hispaniola in 1522, with subsequent insurrections in present-day Puerto Rico, Panama, and Colombia from 1533 to 1580. These insurrections illustrated the distinct brand of insubordination that emanated from Islamic belief. Since many of the slave codes in the antebellum South were specifically concerned with preempting insur-

rections, rebellions in the United States were comparatively fewer than in Latin America. However, Muslim slaves did play key roles in the insurrections that took place, including Florida's "Seminole Slave Rebellions" in 1835–1838. See Beydoun, "Antebellum Islam," p. 191.

29. Diouf, *Servants of Allah*, p. 3.

30. Khaled A. Beydoun, "Ramadan: A Centuries-Old American Tradition," Al Jazeera English, June 24, 2014.

31. Five central responsibilities are required of each Muslim. These "five pillars" include five daily prayers, abstinence from food or drink during the holy month of Ramadan, pilgrimage to the holy sites in Mecca, almsgiving to the poor, and the declaration that there is "only one God, and the Prophet Mohammed is his messenger." "Pillars of Islam," Oxford Islamic Studies Online, 2014.

32. Joseph R. Haiek, "Department of Justice Affirms Arab Race in 1909," in *The Arab American Almanac*, 6th ed. (Glendale, CA: News Circle, 2010).

33. Khaled A. Beydoun, "Between Muslim and White: The Legal Construction of Arab American Identity," *NYU Annual Survey of American Law* 69 (2013): 31–33.

34. Sarah Gualtieri, "Syrian Immigrants and Debates on Racial Belonging in Los Angeles, 1875–1945," *Syrian Studies Association Bulletin* 15 (2009).

35. López, *White by Law*, p. 2.

36. James Baldwin, "On Being White ... and Other Lies," *Essence*, April 1984, http://engl101-rothman.wikispaces.umb.edu/file/view/On+Being+White+and+Other+Lies.pdf.

37. Tehranian, *Whitewashed*, p. 15.

38. Ex parte Shahid, 205 F. 812, 813 (Eastern District Court of South Carolina, 1913).

39. Ibid., 816.

40. Beydoun, "Between Muslim and White," p. 223.

41. Dow v. United States, 226 F. 145, 146 (4th Circuit Court, 1915). See generally Sarah M. A. Gualtieri, *Between Arab and White: Race and Ethnicity in the Early American Diaspora* (Berkeley: University of California Press, 2009), for a history of the experience of the early waves of Syrian immigrants.

42. Kambiz GhaneaBassiri, *A History of Islam in America* (Cambridge: Cambridge University Press, 2010), p. 141. "Many Syrian Muslims sought to pass as Christian in order to be more easily accepted into the United States and to circumvent Ottoman regulations which forbade the emigration of Muslims." Ibid.

43. Samir Khalaf, "The Background and Causes of Lebanese/Syrian Immigration to the United States before World War I," in *Crossing the Waters: Arabic-Speaking Immigrants to the United States before 1940*, ed. Eric J. Hooglund (Washington, DC: Smithsonian Institution Press, 1987), p. 23.

44. *In re* Ahmed Hassan, 48 F. Supp. 843, 845 (Eastern District of Michigan, 1942).

45. Ibid., p. 845.

46. Gualtieri, *Between Arab and White*, p. 158.

47. BBC News, "US Republican Hopeful Ben Carson: No Muslims as President," September 29, 2015.

48. Jeremy Diamond, "Jindal: Some Muslims Trying to 'Colonize' West," CNN Politics, January 21, 2015.

49. A case involving a Muslim petitioner from Saudi Arabia, Mohamed Mohriez (Ex Parte Mohriez, 54 F. Supp. 941), argued within the District Court of Massachusetts, ended the longstanding Muslim naturalization ban in 1944.

50. Christopher Mathias and Carol Carovilla, "Women's March Organizer Targeted by Vicious Islamophobic Attacks Online," Huffington Post, January 24, 2017.

51. See Derrick Bell, "Brown v. Board of Education and the Interest-Convergence Dilemma," *Harvard Law Review* 93 (1980): 518, 525, for a famous law review article that frames "interest convergence theory," which contends that civil rights progress is generally had when it aligns with, and advances, majoritarian (white) interests.

52. Gualtieri, *Between Arab and White*, p. 161.

53. "Unlike many other racial minorities in our country, Middle Eastern Americans have faced a rising, rather than diminishing, degree of discrimination over time—a fact highlighted by recent targeted immigration policies, racial profiling, a war on terrorism with a decided racial bent, and growing rates of job discrimination and hate crime." Tehranian, *Whitewashed*, p. 3.

54. "For example, in 1993, the Arab American Institute and the American-Arab Anti-Discrimination Committee lobbied Congress to create a separate 'Middle Eastern' or 'Arab American' category, arguing that by moving Arabs from the 'Caucasian' category, they would obtain eligibility for certain remedial programs and better protection under antidiscrimination laws." Ibid., p. 168. These efforts were renewed starting in 2014, when a broader group of ethnic groups and organizations, representing Arabs, Turks, Iranians, Coptics, and Chaldeans, showed support for the MENA classification being considered for the 2020 U.S. Census.

55. See Khaled A. Beydoun, "Boxed In: Reclassification of Arab Americans on the U.S. Census as Progress or Peril?" *Loyola University of Chicago Law Journal* 47 (2016).

56. "From 1948 to 1965, the number of students from Muslim-majority countries in the United States increased more than five-fold from 2,708 to 13,664. The Muslim-majority country that sent the most students to the United States was Iran [then a staunch ally of the United States], followed by Egypt, Pakistan, and Turkey. A sizable number of students also came from Lebanon, Syria, Jordan, Saudi Arabia, and Indonesia." GhaneaBassiri, *A History of Islam,* p. 264.

57. "Under these quotas, only 100 immigrants from most Muslim-majority countries were allowed entry into the United States. The quotas did not apply to visitors, foreign students, immediate family members of U.S. citizens, and members of certain professions, such as professors and religious workers." Ibid., p. 292.

58. Ibid., p. 273.

3. A REORIENTED "CLASH OF CIVILIZATIONS"

1. W. Joseph Campbell, *1995: The Year the Future Began* (Berkeley: University of California Press, 2015).

2. Jim Naureckas, "The Oklahoma City Bombing: The Jihad That Wasn't," Fairness and Accuracy in Reporting (FAIR), July 1, 1995, p. 2.

3. Ibid., p. 5.

4. Larry B. Stammer and Carla Hill, "Terror in Oklahoma City: American Muslims Feel Sting of Accusations in Bombing's Wake," *Los Angeles Times,* April 22, 1995.

5. "Certain groups may now enjoy nominal citizenship status, but their members are, in fact, afforded less in the way of substantive citizenship than others in society." Linda Bosniak, *The Citizen and the Alien: Dilemmas of Contemporary Membership* (Princeton, NJ: Princeton University Press, 2006), p. 30.

6. Naureckas, "The Oklahoma City Bombing," p. 8.

7. Ibid., p. 4.

8. See Jack G. Shaheen, *The TV Arab* (Bowling Green, OH: Bowling Green State University Press, 1984), for an analysis of damaging representations of Arabs, Muslims, and Middle Easterners on television and film through 1984. For a more recent study by Shaheen, see *Reel Bad Arabs: How Hollywood Vilifies a People* (Northampton, MA: Olive Branch Press, 2014).

9. Ayatollah Ruhollah Khomeini, "American Plots against Iran" (speech), Emam Archive, November 5, 1979.

10. Kambiz GhaneaBassiri, *A History of Islam in America* (Cambridge: Cambridge University Press, 2010), p. 329.

11. Samuel P. Huntington, "The Clash of Civilizations?" *Foreign Affairs* 72, no. 3 (Summer 1993): 22–49.

12. Ibid.

13. Eugene Volokh, "State Rep. John Bennett Stands by Anti-Islam Comments, 'Islam Is Not Even a Religion,'" Huffington Post, September 22, 2014.

14. Bernard Lewis, *The Crisis of Islam: Holy War and Unholy Terror* (London: Phoenix, 2003), p. xv.

15. Hamid Dabashi, *Brown Skin, White Masks* (London: Pluto, 2011), p. 11.

16. Ibid., p. 12.

17. Bosniak, *The Citizen and the Alien,* p. 30.

18. Khaled Beydoun and Abed Ayoub, "Hollywood Shoots Arabs: The Movie," Al Jazeera English, January 25, 2015.

19. Ibid.

20. Pamela McClintock, "Box Office Milestone: 'American Sniper' Hits $500 Million Globally, Becomes Top 2014 Title in the U.S.," *Hollywood Reporter,* March 8, 2015.

21. Evelyn Alsultany, *Arabs and Muslims in the Media: Race and Representation after 9/11* (New York: New York University Press, 2012), pp. 8–9.

22. For an excellent and concise read about the Islamic Revolution, see Hamid Algar, *Roots of the Islamic Revolution in Iran* (Oneonta, NY: Islamic Publications International, 2001).

23. Carol K. Winkler, *In the Name of Terrorism: Presidents on Political Violence in the Post–World War II Era* (Albany: SUNY Press, 2006), p. 41.

24. GhaneaBassiri, *A History of Islam,* p. 274.

25. Ibid., p. 329.

26. Ibid., p. 332.

27. Ibid.

28. Wolf Blitzer, "The Whole World Was Watching," CNN, May 29, 2015.

29. Edward Said, *Covering Islam: How the Media and the Experts Determine How We See the Rest of the World* (New York: Vintage, 1981), p. 34.

30. See www.revealnews.org/article/home-is-where-the-hate-is/.

4. WAR ON TERROR, WAR ON MUSLIMS

1. "The First 9/11 Backlash Fatality: The Murder of Balbir Singh Sodhi," Sikh American Legal Defense and Education Fund (SALDEF), August 30, 2011.

2. Ibid., p. 1.

3. Kambiz GhaneaBassiri, *A History of Islam in America* (Cambridge: Cambridge University Press, 2010), p. 328.

4. Ed Pilkington, "Donald Trump: Ban All Muslims Entering US," *Guardian,* December 7, 2015.

5. "President Bush Addresses the Nation" (text of speech), *Washington Post,* September 20, 2001.

6. Donald W. Garner and Robert L. McFarland, "Suing Islam: Tort, Terrorism and the House of Saud," *Oklahoma Law Review* 60 (2007): 228.

7. Rebecca Copeland, "War on Terrorism or War on Constitutional Rights? Blurring the Lines of Intelligence Gathering in Post–September 11 America," *Texas Tech Law Review* 35 (2004): 21.

8. Evelyn Alsultany, *Arabs and Muslims in the Media: Race and Representation after 9/11* (New York: New York University Press, 2012), p. 3.

9. "President Bush Addresses the Nation," op. cit.

10. Alsultany, *Arabs and Muslims in the Media*, p. 5.

11. Jack Shaheen, *Reel Bad Arabs: How Hollywood Vilifies a People* (Northampton, MA: Olive Branch Press, 2014), p. 11.

12. John Tehranian, "The Last Minstrel Show? Racial Profiling, the War on Terrorism and the Mass Media," *Connecticut Law Review* 41 (2009): 4.

13. Ibid.

14. Ashley Moore, "American Muslim Minorities: The New Human Rights Struggle," *Human Rights & Human Welfare* 91 (2010): 92–93.

15. Leti Volpp, "The Citizen and the Terrorist," *UCLA Law Review* 49: 1586.

16. "How Americans Feel about Religious Groups: Jews, Catholics and Evangelicals Rated Warmly, Atheists and Muslims More Coldly," Pew Research Group, July 16, 2014.

17. Asifa Quraishi Landes, "5 Myths about Sharia Law Debunked by a Law Professor," *Dallas Morning News,* July 19, 2015.

18. Andrea Elliot, "The Man behind the Anti-Shariah Movement," *New York Times,* July 31, 2011.

19. Asma T. Uddin and David Pantzer, "A First Amendment Analysis of Anti-Sharia Initiatives," *First Amendment Law Review* 10 (2012): 371.

20. Interview with Kameelah Mu'min Rashad, May 15, 2017.

21. Ibid.

22. "Obama's Speech in Cairo" (text of speech), *New York Times,* June 4, 2009.

23. Hamid Dabashi, *Brown Skin, White Masks* (London: Pluto, 2011), p. 123.

24. Lauren Gambino, "Hillary Clinton Outlines Plan to Fight Homegrown Terrorism and ISIS," *Guardian,* December 15, 2015.

25. Michelle Boorstein and Juliet Eilperin, "Obama to Make First Visit of His Presidency to a U.S. Mosque Next Week," *Washington Post,* January 30, 2016.

26. Jack Jenkins, "Obama on Rise of Islamophobia: 'An Attack on One Faith Is an Attack on All Our Faiths,'" ThinkProgress, February 3, 2016.

27. "Remarks by the President at the Islamic Society of Baltimore," February 3, 2016, https://obamawhitehouse.archives.gov/the-press-office/2016/02/03/remarks-president-islamic-society-baltimore.

28. Zachary Tarrant, "Zaki Barzinji Named White House Liaison to American Muslims," Arab America, May 28, 2016.

29. Interview with Kameelah Mu'min Rashad.

30. Albert Camus, *The Stranger* (New York: Knopf, 1988), p. 84.

31. Edward Said, *Out of Place: A Memoir* (New York: Knopf, 1999).

32. Gloria E. Anzaldúa, *Borderlands / La Frontera: The New Mestiza* (San Francisco: Aunt Lute, 1997).

33. "Remarks by the President at the Islamic Society of Baltimore," op. cit.

34. Kenneth L. Karst, "Paths to Belonging: The Constitution and Cultural Identity," *North Carolina Law Review* 64 (1986): 305.

35. Peter Morey and Amina Yaqin, *Framing Muslims: Stereotyping and Representation after 9/11* (Cambridge, MA: Harvard University Press, 2011), p. 208.

36. Leti Volpp, "Impossible Subjects: Illegal Aliens and Alien Citizens," *Michigan Law Review* 103 (2004): 1595.

37. Natsu Saito, "Symbolism under Siege: Japanese American Redress and the Racing of Arab Americans as Terrorists," *Asian American Law Journal* 8 (2001): 12.

38. Devon W. Carbado and Mitu Gulati, *Acting White? Rethinking Race in "Post-Racial" America* (Oxford: Oxford University Press, 2013), p. 168.

39. Karen Engle, "Constructing Good Aliens and Good Citizens: Legitimizing the War on Terror(ism)," *University of Colorado Law Review* 75 (2004): 62–63. Principal among "good Muslim" expressions are "denouncing terrorism, supporting the war on terror, and waving the

American flag." See also Mahmood Mamdani, *Good Muslim, Bad Muslim: America, the Cold War, and the Roots of Terror* (New York: Harmony, 2004), for an anthropological examination of the genesis of the good versus bad Muslim binary and its global application.

40. Khaled A. Beydoun, "Acting Muslim," *Harvard Civil Rights and Civil Liberties Law Review* 53 (2018).

41. Khaled A. Beydoun, "The Myth of the 'Moderate' Muslim," Al Jazeera English, May 20, 2017.

42. Nesrine Malik, "I Am Not Your Muslim," NPR, May 6, 2017.

43. Declan Walsh, "American Muslims and the Politics of Division," *New York Times,* August 11, 2016.

5. A "RADICAL" OR IMAGINED THREAT?

1. This person's real name and some facts about his story have been altered to protect his, and his family's, anonymity.

2. Fawaz A. Gerges, *ISIS: A History* (Princeton, NJ: Princeton University Press, 2016), p. 221.

3. David Ignatius, "How ISIS Spread in the Middle East: And How to Stop It," *Atlantic,* October 29, 2015, p. 2.

4. Ibid.

5. Janet Reitman, "The Children of ISIS," *Rolling Stone,* March 25, 2015.

6. Richard Engel, Ben Plesser, Tracy Connor, and John Schuppe, "The Americans: 15 Who Left the United States to Join ISIS," NBC News, May 16, 2016.

7. Ignatius, "How ISIS Spread," p. 23.

8. Khaled A. Beydoun, "America, Islam, and Constitutionalism: Muslim American Poverty and the Mounting Police State," *Journal of Law and Religion* 31, no. 3 (2016): 279–292.

9. Samuel J. Rascoff, "Establishing Official Islam? The Law and Strategy of Counter-Radicalization," *Stanford Law Review* 64 (2012): 137.

10. Sahar Aziz, "Policing Terrorists in the Community," *Harvard National Security Law Journal* 5 (2014): 164.

11. Amna Akbar, "Policing 'Radicalization,'" *University of California Irvine Law Review* 3 (2014): 811.

12. Ibid., 814.

13. FBI Counterterrorism Division, *The Radicalization Process: From Conversion to Jihad*, FBI (2006), p. 2.

14. Akbar, "Policing 'Radicalization,'" 817.

15. Ibid., 815.

16. Olivier Roy, "What Is the Driving Force behind Jihadist Terrorism? A Scientific Perspective on the Causes/Circumstances of Joining the Scene," speech at the Bundeskriminalamt (BKA) Autumn Conference, November 18, 2015.

17. W. E. B. Dubois, *The Souls of Black Folk* (Chicago: A. C. McClurg, 1903), p. 8.

18. Pew Research Center, "Muslim Americans: No Signs of Growth in Alienation or Support for Extremism," August 30, 2011. The federal poverty level for 2011 was $29,990 for a family of six, $22,350 for a family of four (https://aspe.hhs.gov/2011-poverty-guidelines-federal-register-notice).

19. Dalia Mogahed and Youssef Chouhoud, "American Muslim Poll 2017: Muslims at the Crossroads," Institute for Social Policy and Understanding, March 21, 2017, p. 9.

20. Ibid.

21. Khaled A. Beydoun, "Between Indigence, Islamophobia, and Erasure: Poor and Muslim in 'War on Terror' America," *California Law Review* 104 (2016): 1477.

22. Amanda Sperber, "Somalis in Minnesota Question Counter-Extremism Program Targeted at Muslims," *Guardian*, September 14, 2015.

23. Beydoun, "Muslim American Poverty and the Mounting Police State."

24. Pew Research Center, "Muslim Americans"; Maryam Asi and Daniel Beaulieu, "Arab Households in the United States: 2006–2010," U.S. Census Bureau, May 2013.

25. Ibid.

26. Hamid Dabashi, *Brown Skin, White Masks* (London: Pluto, 2011), p. 36.

27. M. Zuhdi Jasser, "September 11 Terrorist Attacks Awakened Us to a 'Battle for the Soul of Islam,'" *Washington Post,* September 18, 2012, p. 2.

28. Niraj Warikoo, "Dearborn Group Gets $500,000 Grant from DHS to Counter Extremism," *Detroit Free Press,* January 19, 2017.

29. Ibid., p. 1.

30. Ibid.

31. Department of Homeland Security, "Statement by Secretary Jeh Johnson Announcing First Round of DHS's Countering Violent Extremism Grants," January 13, 2017.

32. Interview with Asha Noor, May 17, 2017.

33. Sperber, "Somalis in Minnesota Question Counter-Extremism Program."

6. BETWEEN ANTI-BLACK RACISM
AND ISLAMOPHOBIA

Epigraphs: Muhammad Ali, from a 1975 *Playboy* interview republished upon his death in 2016, http://www.playboy.com/articles/muhammad-ali-playboy-interview-1975. Muhammad Ali, Jr., from a February 2017 interview on MSNBC, after being detained at a Florida airport in the wake of the Muslim travel ban, www.colorlines.com/articles/muhammad-alis-son-airport-profiling-im-not-american.

1. "And while the boxing champion should be celebrated, some have questioned the authenticity of those tributes owing to the rise of Islamophobia and racism that still takes place throughout the world today." Mehdi Hassan, "Let's Not Whitewash Muhammad Ali's Legacy," Al Jazeera English, June 10, 2016.

2. Alicia Garza, "A Herstory of the #BlackLivesMatter Movement," http://blacklivesmatter.com/herstory/.

3. Keeanga-Yamahtta Taylor, *From #BlackLivesMatter to Black Liberation* (Chicago: Haymarket, 2016), p. 147.

4. Su'ad Abdul Khabeer, *Muslim Cool* (New York: New York University Press, 2017), p. 222.

5. Taylor, *From #BlackLivesMatter to Black Liberation*, p. 13.

6. Tariq Touré, *Black Seeds: The Poetry and Reflections of Tariq Touré* ([North Charleston, SC]: CreateSpace, 2016), p. 78.

7. John Bowden, "Trump Considers Sheriff Who Called Black Lives Matter 'Terrorists' for DHS Post," The Hill, April 28, 2017.

8. Priscilla Ocen and Khaled A. Beydoun, "Are We Witnessing the Emergence of a Black Spring?" *Ebony*, May 5, 2015.

9. Dalia Mogahed and Youssef Chouhoud, "American Muslim Poll 2017: Muslims at the Crossroads," Institute for Social Policy and Understanding, March 21, 2017, p. 8.

10. Ibid.

11. Interview with Dalia Mogahed, May 11, 2017.

12. NBA Muslims, "Muslims, Say No to Events Erasing Black Muslims," Patheos, April 23, 2017.

13. Kambiz GhaneaBassiri, *A History of Islam in America* (Cambridge: Cambridge University Press, 2010), p. 243.

14. Richard Brent Turner, *Islam in the African-American Experience* (Bloomington: Indiana University Press, 1997), p. 101.

15. Khaled A. Beydoun, "Islam Incarcerated," *University of Cincinnati Law Review* 84 (2016): 119.

16. Edward Curtis, "Islamism and Its African American Muslim Critics: Black Muslims in the Era of the Arab Cold War," *American Quarterly* 59 (2007).

17. GhaneaBassiri, *A History of Islam*, p. 265.

18. Sherman A. Jackson, *Islam and the Blackamerican: Looking toward the Third Resurrection* (Oxford: Oxford University Press, 2005), p. 29.

19. 5Pillars, "Hamza Yusuf Stokes Controversy with Comments about Black Lives Matter and Political Islam," December 25, 2016, http://5pillarsuk.com/2016/12/25/hamza-yusuf-stokes-controversy-with-comments-about-black-lives-matter-and-political-islam/.

20. Emma Green, "Muslim Americans Are Divided by Trump—and Divided by Race," *Atlantic*, March 11, 2017.

21. Khabeer, *Muslim Cool,* p. 226.

22. Khaled A. Beydoun, "Why Ferguson Is Our Issue: A Letter to Muslim America," *Harvard Journal on Racial and Ethnic Justice* 31 (2015): 4.

23. Donna Auston, "Mapping the Intersections of Islamophobia and #BlackLivesMatter: Unearthing Black Muslim Life and Activism in the Policing Crisis," Sapelo Square, May 19, 2015.

24. Ibid., p. 6.

25. Queenie Wong, "Sudanese Student at Stanford Detained, Handcuffed at JFK Airport," *Mercury News,* January 28, 2017.

26. "Sudanese Stanford Ph.D. Student Speaks Out after Being Detained at JFK under Trump Muslim Ban," Democracy Now, January 30, 2017.

27. Tessa Berenson, "Donald Trump: Minnesota Has 'Suffered Enough' Accepting Refugees," *Time,* November 6, 2016.

28. Helina Faris, "5 Fast Facts about Black Immigrants in the United States," Center for American Progress, December 20, 2012.

7. THE FIRE NEXT TIME

1. Abed Ayoub and Khaled A. Beydoun, "Executive Disorder: The Muslim Ban, Emergency Advocacy, and the Fires Next Time," *Michigan Journal of Race and Law* 23 (2017).

2. James Baldwin, *The Fire Next Time* (New York: Dial, 1963), p. 5.

3. Khaled A. Beydoun, "9/11 and 11/9: The Law, Lives and Lies That Bind," *City of New York University Law School Law Review* 20 (2017): 501.

4. Chauncey Devega, "From 9/11 to 11/9: Is Donald Trump's Election Collateral Damage from the 'War on Terror'?" Salon, November 16, 2016.

5. Speaking at the 20th Anniversary Gala Celebration of the African American Policy Forum, "Say Her Name: 20 Years of Intersectionality in Action," June 10, 2017.

6. Khaled A. Beydoun and Linda Sarsour, "Trayvon Martin: The Myth of US Post-Racialism," Al Jazeera English, March 22, 2012.

7. Meghan Keneally, "Donald Trump Captures Presidency in Historic and Stunning Upset of Hillary Clinton," ABC News, November 9, 2016.

8. See "As Trump's Rallies Become 'Racism Summits,' Linda Sarsour and Mohamed Elibiary Debate Islamophobia," Democracy Now! March 11, 2016.

9. Jeremy Diamond, "Silently Protesting Muslim Woman Ejected from Trump Rally," CNN, January 11, 2016.

10. Bridge Initiative Team, "Islamophobia in the 2016 Elections," Bridge, April 15, 2015.

11. Khaled A. Beydoun, "'Muslim Bans' and the (Re)Making of Political Islamophobia," *University of Illinois Law Review* 2017, no. 5 (2017): 1237.

12. "Bloomberg Politics Poll: Nearly Two-Thirds of Likely GOP Primary Voters Back Trump's Muslim Ban," Bloomberg, December 9, 2015.

13. Ibid.

14. Marc Fisher, "What Is the Long-Term Effect of Donald Trump," *Washington Post,* October 22, 2016.

15. Ibid.

16. David Smith, "Virginia Muslim Teenager's Death Being Investigated as Road Rage, Police Say," *Guardian,* June 19, 2017.

17. Korematsu v. United States, 323 U.S. 214 (1944).

18. Ibid., p. 219.

19. Khaled A. Beydoun, "Beyond the Paris Attacks: Unveiling the War within French Counterterror Policy," *American University Law Review* 65 (2016): 1275.

20. Jack Healy and John Eligon, "Orlando Survivors Recall Night of Terror: 'Then He Shoots Me Again,'" *New York Times,* June 17, 2016.

21. Khaled A. Beydoun, "Fred Korematsu: An Unsung 'Muslim-American' Civil Rights Hero," Islamic Monthly, February 2, 2015.

22. Wajahat Ali, "Please Don't Let It Be a Muslim," Salon, April 17, 2013.

23. Nadine Naber, "The Rules of Forced Engagement: Race, Gender, and the Culture of Fear among Arab Immigrants in San Francisco Post-9/11," *Cultural Dynamics* 18, no. 3 (November 1, 2006).

EPILOGUE

1. Khaled A. Beydoun, "Being a Muslim under Trump Is Risky. That's Why Many Are Hiding Their Identity," *Guardian,* March 30, 2017.

2. Dana Afana, "'Emergency Townhall' Scheduled over Trump Immigration Orders," MLive, February 1, 2017.

3. Ta-Nehisi Coates, "The Case for Reparations," *Atlantic,* June 2014.

Index

Harris, Cheryl, 7; *Whiteness as Property*, 56
Hassan, Ahmed, *65 table*, 66
Hassanen, Nabra, 193–94
hate crimes, 25, 29, 33–34, 103–4, 193–94
Havana, Cuba, 130–31
headscarves. *See hijabs*
Hicks, Craig, Chapel Hill murderer, 25–28, 33, 41–42, 53–54
hijabs, 23–26, 72, 204–5
Hill, Margari, 167–68
Hirsi Ali, Ayaan, 145
History of Islam in America, A (GhaneaBassiri), 69
"homegrown radicals," 14–18, 38, 129–30, 135–38, 146, 147–48
Homeland Security, Department of: counter-radicalization program of, 13–14; divide and conquer strategy of, 144–51; in imagined threats, 128–30, 135–38, 141; in structural Islamophobia, 37; in war on terror/Muslims, 97. *See also* national security
homogenization of the Muslim World, 79–80
homophobia, 184–85
hoodies in murders of black men, 157–58
Huntington, Samuel P., 70, 75, 78–83; *The Clash of Civilizations*, 80–81, 84
Hussein, Saddam, 88–90, 99
Hutton, George H., 59–61

ideology: of color-blindness, 157; of Islam as a rival, 18, 107–8; Islamophobia as, 13; in Orientalism, 81
Ignatius, David, 132
"illegality" and "terrorism," 13–18

immigrants/immigration: anti-black racism of, 163–65; black, in the Muslim ban, 170–73; in campaign rhetoric, 191–92; and civil liberties, 208; in the "clash of civilizations," 91; policies on, 38–39, 41, 43, 46–48, 57–58, 68–69, 219n57; policing of in Los Angeles, 4, 14; registries of, 9, 100–101; Sikh, 92–96; undocumented, 172–73; in war on terror/Muslims, 105. *See also* bans of Muslim immigrants
Immigration Act of 1924, 68–69
Immigration and Nationality Act of 1965, 69
imposter syndrome, 117
inclusion, 59–60, 186
informants, 104, 112–13, 122, 129, 137–38, 143–51. *See also* collaborators/collaboration
Institute for Social Policy and Understanding, 140
Institute for Social Policy and Understanding: "Muslim Survey Poll," 160–61
interlocutors, 113, 122, 143–44
"internment of psyche," 196–98
intersectionality, 21–22, 153–54, 161, 162–70, 180–81, 211n25
intruder syndrome, 117
Iran hostage crisis, 1979–1981, 86–88
Iranian Muslims, 88, 172
Iraq, 86, 88–90, 99, 132, 133–34
Iraqis, 83–84, 143–44
Iraq War, 83–85, 105
ISIS terrorists (Islamic State of Iraq and Syria), 99, 129–35, 130–35, 191–92
Islam: antebellum, 55–59; as civilizational foil, 36, 50, 54; in the "clash of civilizations," 78,

"clash of civilizations," 90; CVE policing in, 137; in defining Islamophobia, 29–30, 32–36, 39, 40–44; in war on terror, 29–30, 103–4, 111–12

profiling, religious and racial: and anti-black racism, 170; in dialectical Islamophobia, 41, 43; in imagined threats, 125–30, 135, 137; in war on terror/Muslims, 103, 119

propaganda, 79–80, 86–90, 132–33, 138

protest and protest movements, 12–13, 33, 155–61, 167–68, 176–77, 181

Pulse nightclub, Orlando, FL, 183–84, 185–86

quotas on immigration, 68–69, 219n57

race: criminalization of, 156–57, 170, 171–72; defined, 215n15; in good Muslim/bad Muslim binary, 116–17, 120–21; legal construction of, 55–59, 61; and poverty, 140, 141–42; in xenophobia, 4–5

racialization: of blackness, 48–49; definition of, 215n15; of Muslim identity, 20–21, 52–53; in private Islamophobia, 34–36

racial justice, 153, 156, 180–81, 190

racism: anti-black, 153–61, 162–73; in fear mongering, 12–13; institutional, 10–11, 39, 153, 157–58, 188; in Muslim bans, 63, 170–73; in the Trump campaign, 191–92

radicalism: black, 162–63, 168; "homegrown," 14–18, 129–30, 135–38, 146, 147–48; poverty in,

139–43; and the rise of Isis, 130–35; and Shari'a law, 107; as a social fad, 117–18; Somalis associated with, 172; suspected of recent converts, 14–18

radicalization: divide and conquer in countering, 144–51; homegrown, 135–38; ISIS terrorists in, 129–35; in Obama's rhetoric, 113–14; presumed, of Muslim youth, 125–30; prevention of, 135–36, 137–38

radicalization theory, 135–38

Rascoff, Samuel, 135

Rashad, Kameelah Mu'min, 109–10, 115–16

Reagan, Ronald, 77

Real Time with Bill Maher, 30–31

recruitment: of informants, 113, 144; by terror groups, 131, 133, 141

Reel Bad Arabs (Shaheen), 102

registry of Muslim immigration, 9, 38–39, 100–101

religion: of the 9/11 terrorists, 98; freedom of, 108–9, 120–21, 124, 129, 137, 159–60, 205; in imagined threats, 135, 141–42; in the roots of Islamophobia, 57, 61; in xenophobia, 4–5. *See also* Christianity/Christians; Islam

religious identity, 2, 56–57, 148–49. *See also* Muslim identity

representations of Muslims, 37, 103. *See also* caricatures of Muslims; stereotypes

Republicans, 54–55, 114, 192

resistance to Islamophobia, 181–82, 187–90, 207

revenge. *See* vengeance, American

Reviving the Islamic Spirit gathering, 164, 165–66

administration, 112–16; in war on terror/Muslims, 101–2, 103, 104–9, 114, 121; women's activism against, 188–89
student associations, 14, 101–2, 138
students, 69, 163–64, 171–72, 180–81, 219n46
subversion, 15, 37, 121–22, 137, 141–42, 165, 196
Sudanese Muslims, 170–72
Sunni Muslims: identity of, 116, 118; as informants, 143, 144; in the media, 89; tensions of with Shiites, 148; and terror networks, 142; vulnerability of, to recruitment, 133; in war on terror/Muslims, 98
Supreme Court, 195–96
surveillance programs: and anti-black racism, 170; in dialectical Islamophobia, 41; in good Muslim, bad Muslim binary, 119; poverty in vulnerability to, 140–43; in war on terror/Muslims, 99–100, 101–2, 105. *See also* Countering Islamic Violence program; Countering Violent Extremism (CVE) program
suspicion: "acting Muslim" in, 205; in the "clash of civilizations," 91; in dialectical Islamophobia, 41–42; legal justification of, 195–97; of radicalism, 126–35; recent converts under, 14–18; in war on terror/Muslims, 97, 101–2
Syria, 63, 65, 133–34
Syrian Christians, 68

Takruri, Dena, 190
Taliban, 99
Taylor, Keeanga-Yamahtta, 157

Tehranian, John, 68, 103
television media, 87–88, 102. *See also* media
terminology: in Orientalism, 81, 82–83; in structural Islamophobia, 106–7
terror groups/networks: in good Muslim, bad Muslim binary, 119, 122; Islam conflated with, 30, 102; and radicalization, 135–36; recruitment by, 131, 133, 141; Sunni communities targeted by, 142
terrorism: backlash from, 6, 41, 71–73; in campaign strategy, 179–80; by Christians, 70–75; in the "clash of civilizations," 70–75, 87, 90–91, 122; in creating Islamophobia, 19; in dialectical Islamophobia, 40–41, 43; in fear of rising Islamophobia, 194–98; and "illegality," 13–18; and political identity, 15; poverty in suspicion of, 142; September 11, 2001, 5–7, 9–10, 120, 179–80
terrorists: Black Lives Matter activists as, 159; demographics of, 91; "Middle Eastern" as proxy for, 85–87, 101–2; Muslim identity conflated with, 13, 43, 74–75, 101–2, 114–15, 176; portrayals of, 84, 85–86
threats, imagined: counter-radicalization strategies for, 144–51; homegrown radicals as, 135–38; ISIS terrorists in, 129–35; Muslim youth as, 125–30; poverty in, 139–43
Tometi, Opal, 156–57
Touré, Tariq: "Respectable Genocide," 158–59
traditions, Muslim, 58, 141, 144, 168, 207

About the Author

Khaled A. Beydoun is Associate Professor of Law at the University of Detroit Mercy School of Law and Senior Affiliated Faculty at the University of California–Berkeley Islamophobia Research and Documentation Project. A critical race theorist, he examines Islamophobia, the war on terror, and the salience of race and racism in American law. His scholarship has appeared in top law journals, including the *California Law Review, Columbia Law Review,* and *Harvard Civil Rights– Civil Liberties Law Review.* In addition, he is an active public intellectual and advocate whose commentary has been featured in the *New York Times* and *Washington Post* as well as on the BBC, Al Jazeera English, ESPN, and more. He is a native of Detroit and has been named the 2017 American-Arab Anti-Discrimination Committee Advocate of the Year as well as the Arab American Association of New York's 2017 Community Champion of the Year.